Yes, I Can Read!

By Linda Klein Weisman

Order this book online at www.trafford.com
or email orders@trafford.com

Most Trafford titles are also available at major online book retailers.

Formatting and layout design: Jeri Hebert
                                Katharine Roberts
Cover Design: Susan Christensen, Studio 4, www.susanchristensenart.com

Yes, I Can Read! is available at special discounts when purchased in bulk for library and educational use. For details, contact the publisher or send an e-mail to llweisman@gmail.com.

www.yesicanread.org

Printed in the United States of America.

ISBN: 978-1-4669-8073-0 (sc)
ISBN: 978-1-4669-8074-7 (e)

Library of Congress Control Number: 2013905489

Trafford rev. 05/08/2013

 www.trafford.com
North America & international
toll-free: 1 888 232 4444 (USA & Canada)
phone: 250 383 6864 ♦ fax: 812 355 4082

This book is dedicated to Charlie, E.K., and Margo, who have offered their support and interest in this project from the beginning. They have been so generous with advice, books, and encouragement. They make me proud.

Most of all, this book is dedicated to Luther, who has been a pillar of support, always willing to help think through dilemmas with his common sense and objectivity. Although he won't believe it, he does matter more than the book.

This workbook was written for and is dedicated to all those who may use it, and at some point, say with pride, "Yes, I can read!"

Acknowledgments

I am so grateful to Jeri Hebert for her exacting eye and meticulous work. She was neither deterred by erratic technology nor time constraints. Jeri found and placed a great number of images and polished each page to her exacting standards. Furthermore, without her layout design, proofreading, editing, and technical expertise, *Yes, I Can Read!* would not be a finished product. She is a pleasure to know and work with.

Thanks go to Katharine Roberts who did a tremendous amount of work, formatting each page and finding and placing over 1800 illustrations. I am still amazed at the sheer amount of work she did and the fine quality of her work. Most of all, I am so glad I came to know Katharine: she is an extraordinary person.

As busy as she is, Ruth Colvin, founder of Literacy Volunteers, spent hours scrutinizing the book and offering detailed suggestions, all of which were extremely helpful.

I appreciate Blanche Podhajski, President of the Stern Center for Language and Learning, who took time from her busy schedule to offer incisive comments, valuable suggestions, and encouragement.

In particular, Mary Huckeba has been especially helpful, not to mention kind, with her careful reading, expert technical support, and ongoing help.

I am truly grateful to Marcia Gottschall, Mary Jo Mann, Norma Menard, Maggie Talford, Jean Arthur, and Bridgette Arthur for taking time with *Yes, I Can Read!* and sharing their thoughts honestly and openly. Their feedback has been invaluable.

Thanks also go to Elle Berger, Jan Stanley, Bonnie Shimko, and Amy Guglielmo for unselfishly and patiently sharing their writing and publishing experiences, advice, and for offering their heartfelt encouragement.

I am grateful to my family and friends who have been so supportive; it means so much.

Contents

Introduction

Yes, I Can Read! was written for fourth graders through adults who are nonreaders, beginning readers, or struggling readers, those who speak English as well as ESL learners. The workbook was designed for learners who may be working with minimal assistance in a one-on-one, small group, or classroom setting, and its reading levels range from 0 to 5.9.

I had two goals in mind when I wrote *Yes, I Can Read!* First, my purpose was to simplify the reading process, and second, to provide learners with a technique, a method by which they could decode unfamiliar words within an age-appropriate format. The workbook focuses on the syllable and six syllable types (Peterson, 1998) combined in an Orton-Gillingham-based approach and page format. If the learner knows that the words he or she encounters can be divided into syllables, and that nearly all those syllables fit into only six groups, the reading process is simplified. As a result, using Yes, *I Can Read!*, the learner can acquire a significant sight vocabulary of over 2,000 words and a method he or she can utilize to decode unfamiliar words and become an independent reader.

The Three Approaches Explained
First, students are instructed to underline vowel sounds in featured words, as the number of vowel sounds equals the number of syllables. They are then able to divide a word based on its number of syllables. Second, learning the six syllable types enables them to look for syllable patterns, sound out syllables, and thus the word. Third, learning is maximized using the Orton-Gillingham-based multi-sensory approach, as students/learners see, say, hear, trace, and write the words. Specifically, the learner's knowledge of consonant and vowel sounds, syllables, and sight vocabulary, as well as his/her spelling and handwriting skills are solidified, all of which in turn promotes his/her automaticity and fluency (Lyon,1998).

Sequence
With some modifications, *Yes, I Can Read!* is based on the "Stern Center Sequence of Phonological Awareness, Word Analysis and Spelling Skills" which follows a traditional, structured sequence found in most reading programs that graduate from beginning reading instruction through the end of the fifth grade.

The Remedial Student
Research shows that many students who have had trouble learning to read lack phonemic awareness, or the concept of a sound-letter connection (Lyon, 1998). As a result, explicit, sequential phonics as well as the multi-sensory approach (VAKT technique) are two research-based, effective methods of instruction that are central to *Yes, I Can Read!* In the same way, running through the entire workbook is the decoding method students learn and use so they can become independent readers. Although there is no one approach or material that holds the key to teaching someone to read, this workbook offers the above-mentioned approaches combined with extensive lessons, repetition, practice, and words in context.

In addition to effective materials, encouragement is an essential component of a reading program. All students need encouragement, but none do more than the remedial student, who has experienced frustration and failure. Offer support, praise, and congratulatory comments such as *good, yes, good job, okay!*, etc. whenever possible. Stickers, trinkets, certificates, or other rewards are also effective. Furthermore, offer encouragement during assessments using nonverbal and facial cues that he or she is doing well: It helps calm a learner's nerves.

Flexibility

First, *YICR** can be used as a decoding program wherein the student starts on his or her reading level and progresses through the book. Second, one can teach the six syllable types by using the six units in the workbook devoted to those syllables. Third, *YICR* can be used as a supplement in conjunction with other materials to reinforce learning in particular areas. *Yes, I Can Read!* is an essential component of a balanced literacy program.

Diagnosis and Prescription

Administer a standardized reading test or informal reading inventory, phonics checklist, or other assessments to determine the student's reading level and diagnose strengths and weaknesses. Keeping a folder on each student in which ongoing assessment, interviews, interest surveys, and informal notes (anecdotal records) on the student documenting reading errors, such as *bog* for *dog*, *guess* for *guests*, etc. is invaluable in keeping track of strengths, weaknesses, progress or lack of progress, assigned materials and how they work with your student. Even if your student is not beginning with the unit that corresponds to his reading level, your diagnosis will help determine the particular lessons you assign in the workbook. This practice also helps establish a rapport with your learner, which is important if he or she is to have a positive attitude about working with you.

Where to Start

Unit 1 is the best place to start for nonreaders, and they should proceed in order through the units.

Unit 2 provides practice with the 21 consonants in initial position (beginning consonants). If your student knows the alphabet, knows the consonants and vowels, and can discriminate among beginning consonants in words, start here.

Unit 3 focuses on ending consonants and rhyming words, or word families. If your student has difficulty with ending consonants, start here.

Unit 4 If the student does not know the short vowel sounds, but he knows the skills practiced in the first three units, begin with Unit 4. If he is to make progress, the student must know the short vowel sounds. Unit 4 is also the first of the six units which focus on the six syllables. Once the learner reaches Unit 4, teaching the six-syllable concept can begin.

The six syllable types are taught in Units 4, 5, 6, 7, 10, and 11. For any students using this workbook, the author recommends teaching the six-syllable concept (See Lesson Plan). The remaining units can be used in order, or unit pages can be used as needed. For students who are at the fourth grade level and need syllabication, teach the six-syllable concept; then learners can complete Units 12 and 13.

The author recommends a three- or four-pronged approach wherein as soon as students are able, a primer, or basal reader on their instructional reading level is added to the workbook in order to have students reading in context. Also, as soon as possible, they should be reading a book they enjoy on their independent reading level. Assign other materials such as one that targets comprehension, and a high-frequency word list such as the Dolch sight words. As students progress and your ongoing assessment dictates, change and modify assignments, keeping in mind that three to four of these types of materials are recommended as part of a balanced literacy program. With their growing skills, students will gain fluency and confidence by practicing reading.

---

* *Yes, I Can Read!*

Units and their corresponding grade levels are listed below.

Where to Start	
Units	**Grade Levels**
1 – 4*	Beginning – 1.9
5 – 7	2.0 – 2.9
8 & 9	3.0 – 4.8
10 – 13	4.9 – 5.9

Success

The six-syllable concept is featured in *Yes, I Can Read!* because it is successful and doable, especially for "older" students who are struggling readers. The author introduced the concept by pointing to an unabridged dictionary in her classroom of adults, whose reading levels ranged from 0 to 5.0, and asked them what they would think if she told them that nearly all of the words in the English language, words in that dictionary, could be divided into syllables, and that those syllables could be placed into just six categories or groups: They were immediately on board with the idea. The author taught the concept to the class as a whole, teaching one syllable type at a time, in the same order they are taught in the workbook. After all six syllables were taught, reviewed, and practiced, students used the same procedure individually, in writing, on the GED spelling list. Most students scored over 90% on the list, and, on the TABE test (Test of Adult Basic Education), most motivated students progressed one year per month.

Daily Lesson Plan (20-30 minutes)

- Overview

  At the board, teach the concept to the class as a whole, teaching one syllable at a time. Have several copies of Appendix D, the six-syllable worksheet, to hand out so students can record syllables in the proper category during lessons. In *Yes I Can Read!*, start with Unit 4 and go in order, using the opening pages of units 4,5,6,7,10, and 11. These pages provide instructional content and examples. Following your classroom lessons, you can assign *YICR* pages in the appropriate unit for students to complete.

- Instruction

  If students have their own copies of *YICR*, work with them using the material at the beginning of Units 4, 5, 6, 7, 10, and 11 to teach the six syllables. In any case, they will have the six-syllable worksheet. Teach the defining characteristics of each syllable type. For example, beginning with Unit 4, the first syllable is a closed syllable which ends with a consonant and has a short vowel. List and call for examples, directing students to record them in the square on their worksheet. Write a word on the board, like *hat*. At students' direction, underline and count the number of vowel sounds. If they have difficulty hearing the vowel sounds, have them tap out sounds with thumb and finger or on the edge of their desks. Exaggerate the short *a* sound if necessary, and encourage them to say the word out loud. This is an interactive lesson which calls for participation. The number of vowel sounds equals the number of syllables. "How many vowel sounds?" (response: 1) "How many syllables?" (response: 1) The numbers must be the same. Write the number on the board to the right of the word.

---

* Students working in Units 1-4 require one-on-one attention.

With multisyllabic words, follow the same procedure. Then divide the word, sound out each syllable, and play with the accent, prompted by students, and sound out the word together. They most likely know the words even if they have not read them before; exceptions may be ESL students. Direct them to record syllables in their categories on the worksheet. Discuss the word meaning(s) and use them in sentences. Also, encourage students to generate their own sentences.

Begin each 20- to 30-minute session with a review of material taught during the previous class. After students know the syllable types, practice aloud together with numerous multisyllabic words on the board, words of their choice as well as yours. Direct them to record the syllables in the appropriate categories on their worksheets. Encourage them to play with the division and stress until the word sounds familiar. Once they demonstrate competency decoding words, they no longer need to categorize the syllables on their worksheets. For practice and vocabulary acquisition, they can complete assigned pages and/or units in *YICR*.

Features and Recommendations in *Yes, I Can Read!*
- VAKT technique(visual-auditory-kinesthetic-tactile)
  The VAKT technique is an Orton-Gillingham-based approach that uses the senses to input information into the learner's long-term memory bank. This approach involves several senses, so when students say, hear, read, trace, and write a word, they are using the VAKT technique, and, they are using the senses with which they learn best. To add movement (kinesthetic) and promote visualization, students can spell words with their finger in the air, on their arm, or in a tray filled with salt, sand, or sugar. In addition, tracing, which is both tactile and kinesthetic, is particularly effective for struggling students (Helson, 1971).

- Subvocalizing
  Subvocalizing is part of the VAKT technique. Students are directed to say and read (aloud) throughout *YICR*. Because learners are often hesitant to say words aloud as they work, teach them to subvocalize. Direct them to put a finger on their Adam's apple and make a sound. If they feel a vibration, they are subvocalizing even if they are speaking quietly or whispering. Explain that this practice facilitates learning words easier and faster than many other methods. Encourage them to say and read aloud as often as possible throughout the book, as it is part of this proven technique.

- Syllabication
  The three-step decoding approach is as follows:
  1. Underline the vowel sounds: the number of vowel sounds equals the number of syllables;
  2. Divide the word;
  3. Sound it out.
  Because the goal is to provide the reader with a method he/she can use to decode unfamiliar words, he should divide the word and play with the stress and pronunciation of its syllables until it sounds like a word he knows. Having learned many word patterns, the six syllable types, and syllabication rules in the workbook contribute to his ability to syllabicate. With the decoding goal in mind, it is not essential that he divide words according to the dictionary (Helson, 1971). However, in writing for submission, it is necessary to divide words correctly; therefore, stress the value of dictionary usage.

- The Schwa Sound
  In a word of two or more syllables, the schwa is the vowel sound(s) in the unaccented syllable(s). It sounds like *uh* and is represented in the dictionary and other sources by ə. Because it sounds like ŭ, the schwa

sound is represented in lessons' "Sounds like" columns as ŭ. The schwa sound is explained with the introduction of two-syllable words in Units 7 and 12.

- Symbols Pages
  The "Symbols" pages contain a word such as *end* or *ending*, the symbol name, such as *caboose*, and an illustration of a caboose. The "Symbols" pages help make *YICR* user friendly for the learner. Directions used throughout the book, verb tenses, and pronouns are among the symbols with which he can familiarize himself and to which he can refer.

- Pronunciation Key
  The pronunciation key provides a guide to the "Sounds like" column in *YICR* lessons. It also provides variant spellings for phonetic pronunciations. Students may use it if they are unsure of a pronunciation of a syllable or word within a lesson. You may find it useful as a reference or as a springboard to introduce additional spellings of the same sound, such as the *oi* sound spelled *oy* as in *boy*, and *oi* as in *point*.

- Teacher's Guide
  A "Teacher's Guide" precedes each unit providing an overview of the unit, objectives, strategies, and techniques designed to help the teacher implement the unit successfully. In later units, if the student can read this information, he may be able to proceed independently.

- Review directions and page layout in lessons to ensure students can proceed. At first you may want to assign one lesson and practice exercises at a time to gauge the student's comprehension and mastery. The author recommends assigning no more than a few (fewer than ten) pages at a time; correct completed pages and work with your student on any material that has not been mastered.

- Beginning in Unit 3, words are arranged in word families wherever possible to maximize vocabulary development. They are arranged throughout the book and graduate in difficulty.

- Beginning with Unit 4, the first page of each unit explains the unit's featured rule(s). Review those pages with students to teach or reinforce the rule(s), syllable type, sounds, explanations, etc.

- Repetition of words throughout the book is intentional. Focus on the skill noted in the page heading, and focus your student's attention on the same. For example, in Unit 2, *box* is used to teach beginning consonant *b*; in Unit 3, it is used to teach ending consonant *x*; and in Unit 4, it is used to teach the short ŏ sound.

- An answer key is provided for Unit 12. It is located at the end of the book for easy removal.

Lessons and Exercises
- The page format in Units 2 and 3 follows the same pattern; furthermore, the format in Units 4 through 10 follows the same pattern. Practice exercises include word finds (searches), matching, sentence fill-ins, tracing, and reading aloud. This repetitive layout reduces unpredictability that might detract from decoding. For the teacher, answers to the exercises are obvious. For example, words in the word finds are horizontal and vertical; they are easy to spot.

- Page headings indicate the skill practiced on that page whether it is the beginning consonant *m*, in Unit 2, or as in Unit 6 "Vowel Teams: ew, /o͞o/". Calling students' attention to the spelling-sound heading helps focus their attention on the lesson's content as well as various spellings and their phonetic pronunciations (within slanted lines). For example, a word such as *new* spelled with the vowel team *ew* that sounds like $\overline{oo}$ as in *spoon* will help students generalize as they sound out written words.

- Directions in Units 4-11: In the three columns on the left side of the page, students use the featured word, an illustration, and the phonetic pronunciation in the "Sounds like" column to help them decode words. Moving from left to right, there are two columns in which students work. They say and trace the word in the fourth column. In the last column, they write the word and underline the vowel sound.

- Completed examples comprise the first row of lessons and exercises throughout the book. Picture clues, phonetic pronunciations, and symbols also help students complete their work successfully. Illustrations and symbols are included through Unit 10. In say, trace, circle, fill-in, and read exercises, encourage learners to say, and/or read aloud before, during, and after completion of each sentence. In this way, students are using the VAKT technique which reinforces learning, they are reading words in context, practicing proper usage, and they are improving their fluency.

- Within lessons and exercises, sentences, and charts, directions to "trace" refer to the light gray, 18-point type words.

  Example: In Unit 2, "The book is on the bus." Students should read the sentence, trace the word *book*, saying it out loud as they trace it; then they should reread the entire sentence aloud.

- Students learn "star" words, or sight words, beginning in Unit 2. Star words are difficult to sound out, illustrate, and are often high-frequency words that should be learned; they can be memorized. Examples include *the*, *is*, and *has*. Review each word, its meaning, use it in a sentence, and direct the student to repeat it. Make a flash card for her to study.

Assessment for Mastery

After they complete an assignment in *Yes, I Can Read!*, students should be able to read the words in the lessons and the sentences that follow the lessons. By assigning a few pages at a time, correcting those pages, and having students read from a particular lesson, the teacher can assess their level of mastery, including strengths and weaknesses. A spelling test or dictation would also indicate mastery. Spend time on any areas, including sounds, that need work. If students make any errors, review the material with them, making flash cards for them to study. They can also record problem words in their notebook for further study.

Strategies, Activities, and Materials

The following strategies serve as ongoing, effective practices which help students grasp word meaning and acquire vocabulary. Relevant strategies and examples are also listed under Vocabulary Acquisition Strategies in each unit. To facilitate instruction, have a dictionary and *Word by Word Picture Dictionary* by Steven Molinsky and Bill Bliss at your desk.

Strategies for Vocabulary Acquisition
- Word Families
  Beginning with Unit 3, "Ending Consonants and Rhyming Words," words are arranged according to word families wherever possible and are prevalent throughout the book.

Word families sound and are spelled the same from the vowel to the end of the word. Examples include *at*, *bat*, *cat*, *hat*, *rat*, and *that*, etc. Make students aware of word families and their same -sound characteristics as they are learning new vocabulary words by learning the word families, or word chunks.

As they encounter word families in lessons, challenge students to think of additional words, and to write sentences using the words, ensuring that they understand each word's meaning. Direct them to add those words to their vocabulary lists in their notebooks. If they find a word pattern difficult to learn, make flash cards with the word on one side and a picture on the other, its definition, or a sentence which uses the word. Particularly in Units 1-4, you can also use letter cards, one consonant or vowel letter per card, to build word families with your student. (See Instructional Activities.) Make the word pattern such as *en*, and have the students add a consonant letter to the beginning of the word, such as *p-en*, *t-en*, and *m-en*. Substituting beginning or ending consonants and/or middle vowels, such as *pan*, *tan*, *pat*, *pot*, *set*, *sit*, *sun* etc. to make new word families increases their vocabulary and increases their awareness of word patterns in larger words.

- Multiple Meaning Words: Multiple meaning words are those words that have more than one meaning. Many common words are in this category, such as *can*, *check*, *face*, *fair*, *ring*, etc.

    Fire is one example:
    1. *Fire* burned down Sam's house. (to light; ignite)
    2. Ray *fired* his clay pot in the kiln. (to bake in a kiln)
    3. Lee *fired* her rifle. (to discharge a firearm)
    4. Bob was *fired* from his job. (to dismiss or discharge from a position)
    5. Nat is all *fired* up about his new job.(to become excited or ardent)

Select a multiple meaning word from a *YICR* lesson, discuss its meaning, and elicit additional meanings from your student. Direct him to use each word's meaning in a sentence to illustrate comprehension. If he experiences difficulty, define the word and use it in a sentence.

- Synonyms
  Synonyms are words which have the same or similar meaning as another word. Examples of synonyms are *pail-bucket*, *car-automobile*, *close-shut*, etc.; however, many words convey shades of meaning and cannot be exchanged for their counterparts. An example is *rain: drizzle, mist, shower*, and *downpour*. Encourage students to use the dictionary rather than a thesaurus to be assured of exact, entire meanings.

- Antonyms
  An antonym is a word that means the opposite of another word such as *cold-hot*, *light-dark*, *clean-dirty*, *war-peace*, *tall-short*, etc. Trust yourself to think of synonyms or antonyms to help your student understand word meaning. It also helps to have the dictionary or a word-list book at your desk. *

- Homonyms (Homophones)
  In later units, particularly in Units 9 and 10, students encounter some words which sound the same but are spelled differently and whose meanings differ, such as *pair, pear; stair, stare; bear, bare; they're, their, there; its, it's*, and *hear* and *here*. Discuss how the words are used differently in sentences, their respective

---

* *The New Reading Teacher's Book of Lists, Vocabulary Teacher's Book of Lists* by Edward B. Fry Ph. D. and *ESL/ELL Teacher's Book of Lists* (2008) by Jacqueline Kress are also valuable resources.

meanings, and connotations. Encourage them to think of additional words, create their own sentences, make flash cards, and add them to the vocabulary lists in their notebooks.

- Heteronyms
  These are words which are spelled the same but are either pronounced differently or have their stress on different syllables depending on their part of speech and meaning. Examples are *bass*/bās/, a deep sound or tone, and *bass*/băs/, European perch. Other examples include *compact, progress, entrance, perfect*, and *contest*. Unit 13's "Teacher's Guide" offers additional examples and teaching suggestions for heteronyms within the unit.

- Dictionary Usage
  Teaching your students to use the dictionary is essential. It offers pronunciation, the many meanings and shades of meaning of words, their parts of speech, word usage, etymology, (word origin), all of which adds to the depth of vocabulary acquisition. They should be encouraged to use the dictionary to look up unfamiliar words, and in doing so, explore the entire entry for full understanding of the word. This is one more method learners can use to decode unfamiliar words.

- Prefixes and Suffixes
  The study of prefixes, suffixes, and roots is referred to as structural analysis. If the learner knows the meaning of a prefix or suffix, and has an idea of the base word or root, it helps him decode unfamiliar words. Learning prefixes and suffixes can greatly improve a learner's vocabulary. In *Yes, I Can Read!*, several affixes are explicitly taught beginning with Unit 7.

  Prefixes are syllables added to the beginning of a base word or root to add to or change the word's meaning. The prefix *re-* means to do over or do again. Examples include *redo, replace, reheat, retool, reverse, and rewrite*.

  Suffixes are syllable added to the end of a base word or root to indicate the word's part of speech and often add meaning. The suffix *-less* means without. Examples include *sleepless, helpless, hopeless, fearless, careless, restless, and useless*.

Reading Activities
- Reading One-on-one with Students
  As part of your ongoing assessment, diagnosis of your student's strengths and weaknesses, and establishing rapport with your learner, have him read to you from a book on his instructional reading level, such as a basal reader. Take notes, correct him selectively, and ask questions to check on comprehension. Share your notes on his progress, prescription, and praise him as often as possible.

- Reading Aloud to Students
  Everyone loves being read to, whatever their age. You will find that when you read material that is too difficult for learners to read themselves, they will relax, comprehend, and enjoy your reading to them. Poetry, lyrics, fiction, nonfiction, etc. are all good. This is a nice way to end a session.

Instructional Activities

- Flash Cards
  Students should have note cards and lists they keep in their notebooks of words they need to learn. Print the word on one side and its synonym, definition, or illustration on the flip side. They should practice them daily in class and after class until the words are learned. In class, they can read the words aloud to you to check for mastery. Flash cards are convenient because troublesome words can be separated from the "mastered" cards. Frequent review ensures that these words become part of your student's vocabulary.

- Letter Cards
  Letter cards are manipulatives used to form words and word families using "substitution, deletion, insertion, and transposition" (Stern Center, 1998, "Stern Center Sequence..."). They are available commercially, but you may prefer to make your own. Make a few cards of each vowel and consonant to use for beginning and ending consonants. Make one card for each vowel team (ea), consonant blend (pr), r-controlled vowel (ar), and consonant combination (digraph ch). Refer to *YICR* units as a guide.

- Writing
  Students can: write their own stories or "books", creating sentences with featured words from the lessons, dictate original stories to the teacher, take a spelling test or take dictation below practice exercises or on a separate page in *Yes, I Can Read!*

Symbols

Word	Symbol Name	Illustration
1. **Begin, beginning**	a train engine	
2. **Circle**	a circle	
3. **End, ending**	a caboose	
4. **Find**	a detective with a magnifying glass	
5. **Future (tense)**	a futuristic car	
6. **Hear, listen, sound**	a person holding his hand to his ear	
7. **He**	an arrow pointing to a male	
8. **I**	a person pointing to him/herself	
9. **It**	a person pointing to an animal or tree	
10. **Long vowels**	a dachshund	
11. **Look**	a pair of glasses	
12. **Match, matching**	a word and its illustration	chair
13. **Middle**	middle car of a train	
14. **Past (tense)**	an old or antique car	

Word	Symbol Name	Illustration
15. **Present (tense)**	a current car	
16. **Quiet**	shh	
17. **Read**	people holding an open book	
18. **Remember**	a bow tied around a finger	
19. **Rhyme, rhyming**	a cat and a hat	
20. **Say**	megaphone	
21. **She**	an arrow pointing to a female	
22. **Short vowels**	a pug	
23. **They**	people pointing to another group of people	
24. **Trace**	dotted letter 'A' next to a solid letter 'A'	
25. **You**	a person pointing to another person	
26. **Vowels**	A,E,I,O,U	A a, E e, I i, O o, U u
27. **We**	2 or more people	
28. **Write**	a pencil in a hand writing	

Yes, I Can Read!

Pronunciation Key

The first word listed is a common spelling. Additional words
are variant spellings of words with the same sound.

Sound	Word	Illustration
1. ă	hat	
2. ā	ape, rain, day, gauge, eight, they, steak	
3. air	air, pair, bear, care, there, they're, their	
4. âr	car, heart, guard	
5. aw	saw, talk, sauce, all, cough	
6. b	bat	
7. ch	chop, itch, picture	
8. d	dad	
9. ě	pen, head	
10. ē	read, peel, either, yield, baby, eve, key, studio	
11. f	fan, phone, cough	
12. g	go, ghost	

24

Yes, I Can Read!

Sound	Word	Illustration
13. h	hot, who	
14. ĭ	sit, gym, build	
15. ī	I, bite, sky, eye, buy, right, pie, guide	
16. îr	ear, cheer, pier, severe, irrelevant	
17. j	jam, gym, edge	
18. k	kiss, cat, deck, chemistry, unique	
19. l	lip	
20. m	man, lamb, hymn	
21. n	no, knob, gnat, pneumonia	
22. ng	ring	
23. nk	sink, uncle	
24. ŏ	hot, father	
25. ō	go, mow, road, toe, though	

Sound	Word	Illustration
26. oi	boy, point	
27. o͝o	book, pull	
28. o͞o	boot, suit, sue, stew, soup, flu, crude, move, neuter	
29. ôr	corn, warm, source	
30. ou	cow, house	
31. p	pig	
32. qu	queen, Kwanza	
33. r	run, write, rhyme	
34. s	sit, cent, scent, psyche	
35. sh	shell, special, nation, mission, chef, sugar, ocean	
36. t	top, mopped, debt, ptomaine	
37. th	thick, thin	
38. *th*	*th*is, *th*at	

Sound	Word	Illustration
39. ŭ	cut, son, rough	
40. ŭ (ə)	soda, mitten, engine, button, circus, able, rhythm, teacher	
41. ū	unit, cube, you, few, cue, feud, beauty	
42. ûr	fur, bird, her, word, heard	
43. v	van, have	
44. w	win, one, why, squid, suede	
45. x	box, socks	
46. y	yes, onion	
47. z	zoo, dogs, Xerox®	
48. zh	measure, vision, garage	

Overview

Unit 1 introduces the alphabet letters, sounds, key words used to memorize alphabet letters, alphabet consonant and vowel breakdown of the alphabet, introduction of short and long vowel sounds, and auditory discrimination.

Objectives

Part 1 The Alphabet

Students will:

1. Learn the alphabet.
2. Learn the letter sounds.

Part 2 Consonants and Vowels

Students will:

1. Become acquainted with the concept of vowels and consonants constituting the letters of the alphabet.
2. Become acquainted with short and long vowel sounds and their diacritical marks.

Part 3 Auditory Discrimination

Students will:

1. Say, hear, and match the sound of the beginning consonant in each key word and subsequent words with the same beginning consonant.

Instruction

Part 1 The Alphabet (pp.32-36)

1. Pages 32-33: Direct student(s) to say and trace the letters of the alphabet.
2. Page 34: Direct students to say the sounds of the letters. On problematic letters, model the letter sounds and have student imitate until the pronunciation is correct, allowing for accent/ regional differences.
3. Pages 35-36: To help students learn the alphabet sounds and letter-name correspondence, use associative (key) words. Note that short vowel-words (*apple*), are associated with alphabet letters as are hard *c* (*cat*) and *g* (*go*). If repetition and review are needed, make flash cards with the letter on one side and illustration on the back. Say the letter sound, have them repeat, and say the word.
4. To teach the alphabet, sing the alphabet song: "*Abcdefg...hijklmnop...qrs...tuv...w,x,y and z*. Now I know my *abc's*. Won't you come and play with me?" You may want to omit the question at the end of the song.

Part 2 Consonants and Vowels (pp.37-39)

1. Introduce consonants and vowels. The 5 vowels: *a, e, i, o, u*, and sometimes *y*, using

the chart on page 37. Of the 26 letters in the alphabet, 5 are vowels, and the remaining 21 letters are consonants. Define consonants and vowels and model the sounds in each group. Use the following page, short and long vowels, to help introduce this concept. (See glossary.)

Again, the long vowel sounds are the letter names: Say, "They say their own names." Have students repeat the sounds. Direct them to say and trace the letters in the "Trace" column.

2. Page 38: This page is an introduction to short and long vowel sounds: thus, there is no work to be done on this page. Introduce short and long sounds, their associative words, the breve and macron as short and long diacritical marks, and the pug and dachshund illustrations as symbols of short and long sounds respectively.

Instruct students in the pronunciation of the short vowel sounds: ă as in *at*, *cat*, or *apple*; ĕ: Picture a rubber band stretching your mouth sideways in *egg*, *pen*, and *elephant*; ĭ as in *in* and *sit*; the short o sounds like what the doctor with a tongue depressor says when she wants to examine your throat: "Say ŏ." Key words are *on* and *hot*. Short u sounds like what people say when they forget what they were going to say, as in *uh*, or *umm*. Key words are *up* and *sun*.

Repetition may be necessary to pronounce short *a, e,* and *i,* but mastery is not essential in Unit 1 because students practice saying and writing short-vowel words in Units 2 and 3. And, in Unit 4, they will focus on short vowel sounds in words they have practiced in Units 1-3.

3. Page 39 Alphabet Review
Direct the learner to say and write the consonants, directing his attention to the say and write symbols, the megaphone and hand with pencil writing on a tablet. If he needs help filling in the numbered boxes, refer him to pages 32 and 33. Then, direct your learner to say and write the vowels. After he completes both charts, have him read the alphabet in order, numbers 1-26.

Resources:
1. Use the dictionary, phone book, or other directories that are listed in alphabetical order to help students learn to alphabetize and use these reference tools efficiently.
2. "Vowel Spellings by Mouth Position" by Louisa Moats (1996) helps students form vowel sounds and note subtle differences among them.
3. Zaner-Bloser materials include manuscript and cursive letter formation and practice.

Instruction
Part 3 Auditory Discrimination: Beginning Sounds (pp. 40-45)
1. Inform him that in each exercise, the first example is completed, and symbols and picture clues are there to help him complete lessons successfully. It is important that he see, say, circle, and write the words; speaking quietly or whispering is fine.

30

2. On page 40, review the directions with your student: "Say the name of the 1st picture in each row. Say the name of each picture in that row. Circle the words that begin with the same sound." Direct his attention to the symbols of the megaphone for *say*, the circle around the word *circle*, and the train engine for *begin*. The same directions are within the chart, at the top of each exercise, with the additional direction to *write* the correct word on the line. Point out that key words are the first word in each row and are separated from the other words by a bold line. Go over the completed example with your student, row, #1, emphasizing the *m* sound in *man*, the key word, and *mat*. See if he can hear the difference among *m, n,* and *s*. Note that *mat*, the correct answer, is circled and printed on the line. If he cannot discriminate among the sounds or associate the sounds with their letters, repeat until he succeeds.

3. Last, direct the student to complete the lesson. In row #2, he should say *ham*, then *hat, man,* and *cat*. Since *hat* begins with the same sound as the key word *ham*, he should circle the word *hat* and write it on the line underneath the word *hat*. You may want to have him complete a page or two at your desk so you can check his comprehension of the directions, his auditory discrimination, and can be sure he is using the VAKT technique.

Unit 1, Part 1: The Alphabet

Directions: Say and trace.

1.	Aa	A a
2.	Bb	B b
3.	Cc	C c
4.	Dd	D d
5.	Ee	E e
6.	Ff	F f
7.	Gg	G g
8.	Hh	H h
9.	Ii	I i
10.	Jj	J j
11.	Kk	K k
12.	Ll	L l
13.	Mm	M m
14.	Nn	N n
15.	Oo	O o
16.	Pp	P p
17.	Qq	Q q
18.	Rr	R r

19.	Ss	S s
20.	Tt	T t
21.	Uu	U u
22.	Vv	V v
23.	Ww	W w
24.	Xx	X x
25.	Yy	Y y
26.	Zz	Z z

The Alphabet

Directions: Read and say .

Alphabet letter	Sounds like	Vowel Illustration
1. A, a	ā say	
2. B, b	bē	
3. C, c	sē	
4. D, d	dē	
5. E, e	ē key	
6. F, f	ĕf	
7. G, g	jē	
8. H, h	āch	
9. I, i	ī I, Hi!	
10. J, j	jā	
11. K, k	kā	
12. L, l	ĕl	
13. M, m	ĕm	
14. N, n	ĕn	
15. O, o	ō Oh, no!	
16. P, p	pē	
17. Q, q	kū	
18. R, r	âr	
19. S, s	ĕs	
20. T, t	tē	
21. U, u	ū you	
22. V, v	vē	
23. W, w	dŭb'•ŭl•ū	
24. X, x	ĕks	
25. Y, y	wī	
26. Z, z	zē	

The Alphabet

Directions: Read 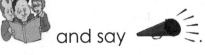 and say .

Alphabet letters	Words	Illustrations
A, a	apple, man	
B, b	boy, bat	
C, c	cat	
D, d	dime, dad	
E, e	elephant, egg	
F, f	fan	
G, g	go, girl	
H, h	hot	
I, i	in	
J, j	jam, jet	
K, k	kiss	

Alphabet letters	Words	Illustrations
L, l	lip	
M, m	man	
N, n	no	
O, o	on, hot	
P, p	pig	
Q, q	quiet	Shhh!
R, r	run	
S, s	sun	
T, t	top	
U, u	up	
V, v	van	
W, w	wet	
X, x	x-ray	
Y, y	yes	
Z, z	zoo	

Part 2: Consonants and Vowels

Directions: Say and trace.

Consonants	Trace	Vowels
	A a	A, a
B, b	B b	
C, c	C c	
D, d	D d	
	E e	E, e
F, f	F f	
G, g	G g	
H, h	H h	
	I i	I, i
J, j	J j	
K, k	K k	
L, l	L l	
M, m	M m	
N, n	N n	
	O o	O, o
P, p	P p	
Q, q	Q q	
R, r	R r	
S, s	S s	
T, t	T t	
	U u	U, u
V, v	V v	
W, w	W w	
X, x	X x	
Y, y	Y y	
Z, z	Z z	

Short and Long Vowels

A, e, i, o, and u are vowels. Vowels have short and long sounds.

Short Vowels

Short vowel sound	Word	Illustration
1. ă	at, cat	
2. ĕ	egg, pen	
3. ĭ	in, sit	
4. ŏ	on, hot	
5. ŭ	up, sun	

Hint: The breve (˘) /brĕv/ on the top of the vowel tells you it has a short vowel sound. Examples: ă, ĕ, ĭ, ŏ, ŭ.

Long Vowels

Long vowels say their /thair/ names.

Long vowel sound	Word	Illustration
1. ā	say	
2. ē	key	
3. ī	I, hi!	
4. ō	oh!	
5. ū	you	

Hint: The macron (¯) /mā'•krŏn/ on the top of the vowel tells you it has a a long vowel sound.

Alphabet Review

Directions: Say and write the consonants.

2.	3.	4.	6.	7.	8.
10.	11.	12.	13.	14.	16.
17	18.	19.	20.	22.	23.
24.	25.	26.			

Directions: Say and write the vowels.

1.	5.	9.	15.	21.

Star (☆) Words

Directions: Read and say.

1. a =   1 (one)   = a man
2. an = 1 (one)   = an apple, an egg
3. the = 1 (one)   = the man
4. I =   me   = I am a man.

Part 3: Auditory Discrimination: beginning sounds

Directions: Say the name of the 1st picture in each row.

Say the name of each picture in that row.

Circle the words that **begin** with the same sound.

Say the word.	Say each word. Circle then write the correct word on the line.		
1. man	no ____	sun ____	mat mat
2. ham	hat ____	man ____	cat ____
3. dog	goat ____	dot ____	dime ____
4. jam	man ____	jet ____	jar ____
5. lamp	leg ____	lip ____	dog ____
6. fan	fill ____	feed ____	man ____

Yes, I Can Read!   Unit 1

Auditory Discrimination: beginning sounds

Directions: Say the name of the 1st picture in each row.
Say the name of each picture in that row.

Circle the words that **begin** with the same sound.

Say the word.	Say each word. Circle then write the correct word on the line.			
1. mail	men men	milk milk	mix mix	gas
2. boat	bus	door	bad	bat
3. sing	gas	sink	six	sick
4. tag	ten	tub	mat	tell
5. sit	mitt	sand	cab	sell

41

Auditory Discrimination: beginning sounds

Directions: Say the name of the 1st picture in each row.
Say the name of each picture in that row.

(Circle) the words that **begin** with the same sound.

Say the word.	Say each word. (Circle) then write the correct word on the line.			
1. pig	sun _____	(pan) pan	saw _____	good good
2. cat	tag _____	cab _____	pen _____	can _____
3. nail	saw _____	neck _____	no _____	cab _____
4. rat	rib _____	rug _____	mitt _____	can _____
5. run	red _____	bad _____	sit _____	rat _____

Auditory Discrimination: beginning sounds

Directions: Say the name of the 1st picture in each row.

Say the name of each picture in that row.

Circle the words that **begin** with the same sound.

Say the word.	Say each word. Circle then write the correct word on the line.			
1. jeep	jam ○ jam	jail ○ jail	jaw ○ jaw	stop
2. van	vest	mop	dime	vet
3. gas	grass	car	go	girl
4. wax	web	wash	wood	job
5. well	leg	not	walk	wax

43

Auditory Discrimination: beginning sounds

Directions: Say the name of the 1st picture in each row.
Say the name of each picture in that row.

(Circle) the words that **begin** with the same sound.

Say the word.	Say each word. (Circle) then write the correct word on the line.			
1. kiss	(kit) kit	bad ___	(key) key	jam ___
2. door	jaw ___	dot ___	dog ___	pay ___
3. yes	yell ___	yawn ___	kit ___	rat ___
4. zero	zip ___	no ___	man ___	zoo ___
5. dollar	doll ___	disk ___	dime ___	stop ___

Auditory Discrimination: beginning sounds

Directions: Say the name of the 1st picture in each row.

Say the name of each picture in that row.

Circle the words that **begin** with the same sound.

Say the word.	Say each word. Circle then write the correct word on the line.			
1. cent	left left	circle circle	cell cell	hat ___
2. gel	gem ___	saw ___	gym ___	book ___
3. quiet	quilt ___	circle ___	quiz ___	queen ___
4. x-ray	x-rated ___	gym ___	yield ___	ten ___
5. cell	circle ___	cent ___	dam ___	van ___

Overview

Twenty-one consonants are sequenced in order of frequency of appearance and the reliability of their sounds.

Objectives

Part 1

1. To associate beginning consonant sounds with the letters that make those sounds such as the *s* sound in *sun, sad, sit, stop*, etc.
2. To learn words in the lessons beginning with the 21 consonants in initial position.

Parts 2 Less reliable sounds and their words

1. To learn the sound-symbol correspondence of the hard sound of *g* as in *girl, go, gas*, etc.
2. To learn words in the lesson beginning with the hard sound of *g*.

Part 3

1. To learn the sound-symbol correspondence *q(u)* /kw/ as in *quart, queen, quarter*, etc.
2. To learn that *q* is followed by *u* in English.
3. To learn the words in the lesson beginning in *qu*.
4. To learn the hard sound of *c* /k/ as in *can, cat, cut*, etc.
5. To learn the words in the lesson beginning in *c* /k/.

Part 4

1. To learn the sound-symbol correspondence of *x* /z/ at the beginning of a word as in *Xerox* or *xylophone*.
2. To learn the sound-symbol correspondence of *x* /eks/ at the end of a syllable as in *x-ray*.
3. Read and learn star words *on, in, is, has, he, me*, and *she*.
4. Read and gain a sense of conjugations with *do, run*, and *work* in present and past tense.

Instruction

Part 1

1. On the first page of Unit 2, review the example with your student, reading across the first row, emphasizing the *s* sound /s/ in *sun, sad, sit*, and *stop*. Direct him to note that *sad, sit*, and *stop* are circled and printed on the lines. If he does not know that these words begin with the same letter and sound, repeat or give him other examples until he succeeds.

2. If the student does not know how to pronounce a letter, use the key word in that row and isolate the sound, modeling the pronunciation. Also, instruct him how to form and say the letter using his tongue, teeth, and mouth position. Have him repeat his pronunciation until it is correct. For

example, model and tell him that to form s, almost touch the tongue to the roof of the mouth and model the hissing sound of a snake.

3. Be sure he understands the directions and notes the completed example in the practice exercises that follow the lesson. Direct the student to complete the lesson and exercises. Review directions and exercises with your student. He should be able to proceed with minimal assistance. You may want him to complete a lesson at your desk so you can assess his understanding and can be sure he is using the VAKT technique.

Assessment

Assign a few pages at time, correct completed work, and go over any incorrect answers with the student. Have him read random words aloud in the lessons as well as the sentences following the lessons or exercises, but focus on the sound/letter connection in the exercises. This awareness and ability to make the consonant sounds are more important than learning the words.

Vocabulary Acquisition Strategies

Star words (*is*, *has*), easily confused words (*two*, *to*, *too*), and multiple meaning words (*saw*, *seal*, *hand*) should be read, discussed, used orally in sentences, dictated, etc. Pages with extra space can be used for spelling tests or student's sentences, etc. Make flash cards for troublesome words which the student reviews daily. Each time you see him one-on-one, review the words with him, adding troublesome words so his stack of cards grows. He should also copy the words into his notebook. As soon as he knows enough words, he can create sentences using featured words, or you can dictate sentences for him to write.

Unit 2: Beginning Consonants
Part 1: s, b, m, t, k, h

Beginning Consonants: s

Directions: Say the name of the 1st picture in each row.

Say the name of each picture in that row.

(Circle) the words that **begin** [image] with **s**.

Say the word.	Say each word. (Circle) then write the correct word on the line.			
1. sun	(sad) sad	car ____	(sit) sit	(stop) stop
2. see	say ____	pay ____	send ____	sail ____
3. sad	sand ____	stop ____	saw ____	ten ____
4. sink	sell ____	seal ____	bus ____	salt ____

Beginning Consonants: s

Directions: Look at the picture. (Circle) the word that matches the

picture. Say and write it on the line.

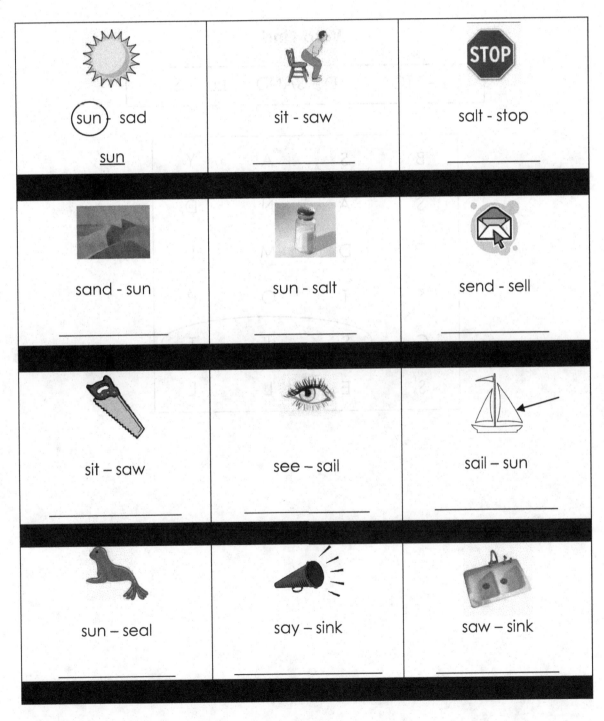

(sun) - sad	sit - saw	salt - stop
sun		
sand - sun	sun - salt	send - sell
sit – saw	see – sail	sail – sun
sun – seal	say – sink	saw – sink

Beginning Consonants: s

Directions: Find  and (circle) the words.

Word Find

SIT – STOP – SAD – SAND – SELL – SAY

B	S	A	Y
S	A	N	D
T	D	M	L
S	T	O	P
G	S	I	T
S	E	L	L

50

Yes, I Can Read!   Unit 2

Beginning Consonants: b

Directions: Say the name of the 1st picture in each row.
Say the name of each picture in that row.

Circle the words that **begin** with **b.**

Say the word.	Say each word. Circle, then write the correct word on the line.			
1. boat	(bus) bus	hot _____	(bed) bed	(bath) bath
2. bush	sun _____	bag _____	milk _____	baby _____
3. box	bag _____	boil _____	sit _____	ax _____
4. bed	bank _____	boat _____	book _____	tub _____
5. bill	bath _____	bed _____	cup _____	ball _____

Beginning Consonants: b

Directions: Match the word and its picture.

chair

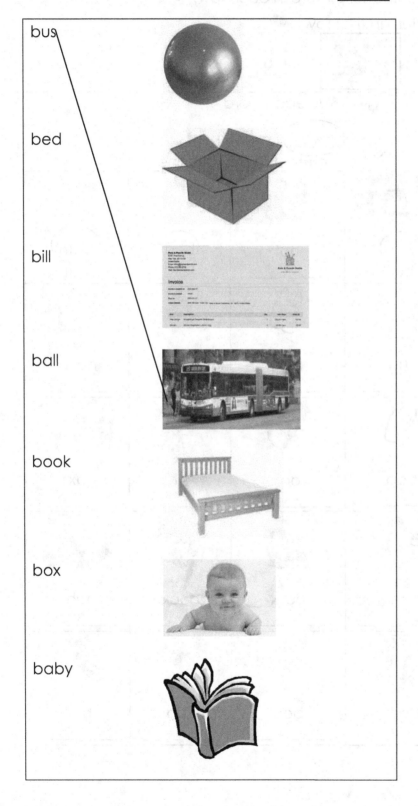

bus

bed

bill

ball

book

box

baby

Beginning Consonants: b

Directions: Say and trace.

1. The book is on the bus.

2. The ball is in the box.

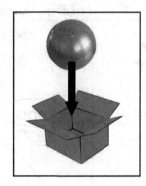

3. The baby is on the bed.

Yes, I Can Read!   Unit 2

Beginning Consonants: m

Directions: Say the name of the 1st picture in each row.
Say the name of each picture in that row.
Circle the words that **begin**  with **m**.

Say the word.	Say each word. Circle then write the correct word on the line.			
 1. man	4 four	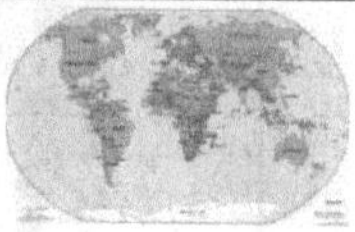 map (map)	 milk (milk)	 no
 2. mop	 mix	6 six	 pan	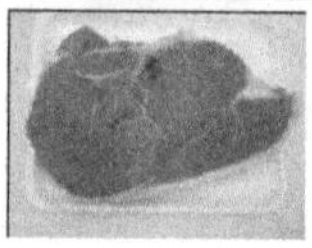 meat
 3. mat	 map	 sit	 man	 fan
 4. mug	 men	 mitt	 sit	 jug

54

Beginning Consonants: m

Directions: 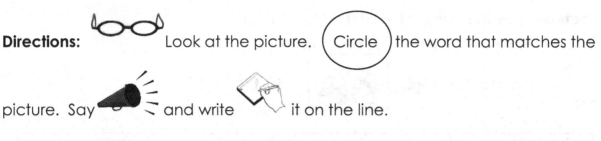 Look at the picture. (Circle) the word that matches the

picture. Say and write it on the line.

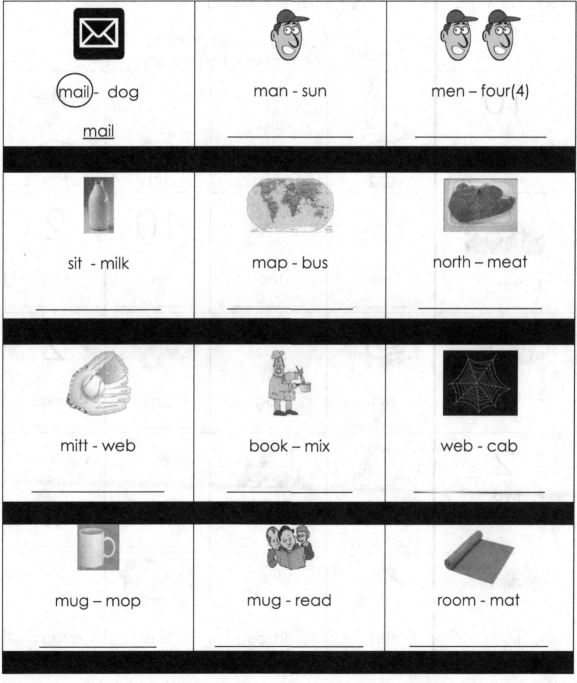

(mail) - dog <u>mail</u>	man - sun _____	men – four(4) _____
sit - milk _____	map - bus _____	north – meat _____
mitt - web _____	book – mix _____	web - cab _____
mug – mop _____	mug - read _____	room - mat _____

Yes, I Can Read!   Unit 2

Beginning Consonants: t

Directions: Say the name of the 1st picture in each row.
Say the name of each picture in that row.

(Circle) the words that **begin** with **t**.

Say the word.	Say each word. (Circle) then write the correct word on the line.			
10 1. ten	(tag) <u>tag</u>	sit ____	(tot) <u>tot</u>	(top) <u>top</u>
2. tub	tell ____	tool ____	**10** ten ____	**2** two ____
3. tea	tent ____	tag ____	box ____	**2** two ____
2 4. two	twins ____	cab ____	toss ____	toe ____
5. top	tell ____	trace ____	bus ____	tag ____

56

Beginning Consonants: t

Say the word.	Say each word. Circle then write the correct word on the line.			
6. tent	**10** ten _____	pet _____	sit _____	take _____
7. tea	tall _____	trace _____	dog _____	mat _____
8. tall	bat _____	tell _____	**10** ten _____	man _____

Star (☆) Words: Read and say.

on /ŏn/ = The dog is on the mat.

in /ĭn/ = The dog is in the tent.

is /ĭz/ = The dog is two (2).

has /hăz/ = The dog has a tag.

Beginning Consonants: t

Star (☆) Words:

two (2)
to
too

Directions: Say, trace, and read.

1. Bill has two (2) dogs.

2. The dogs have to run.

3. The dogs have to sit too.

4. Bill has to pay bills.

5. Take the tea to Tom.

6. Take the tea to Bill too.

Directions: Find and (circle) the words.

Word Find

| TELL – TOP – TEA – TEN – TAN |

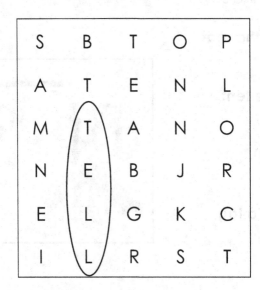

S	B	T	O	P
A	T	E	N	L
M	T	A	N	O
N	E	B	J	R
E	L	G	K	C
I	L	R	S	T

Beginning Consonants: k

Directions: Say the name of the 1st picture in each row. 📢

Say the name of each picture in that row. 📢

(Circle) the words that **begin**  with **k.**

Say the word. 📢	Say each word. 📢 (Circle) then write the correct word on the line.			
 1. kiss	 (kick) kick	 bus bus	 sun _____	 (king) king
 2. kit	 kick	 keg	 sit	 kiss
 3. kid	 kit _____	ten _____	 kite _____	 mitt _____
 4. keg	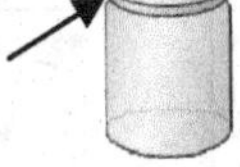 lid _____	 king _____	 kit _____	 sad _____

Beginning Consonants: h

Directions: Say the name of the 1st picture in each row.
Say the name of each picture in that row.

Circle the words that **begin**  with **h.**

Say the word.	Say each word. Circle then write the correct word on the line.			
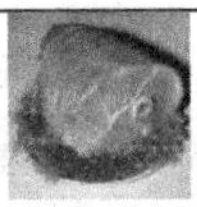 1. ham	 mat _____	 hill (hill)	 hen (hen)	 hit (hit)
 2. hit	 van _____	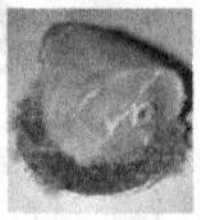 ham _____	 him _____	 hat _____
 3. hand	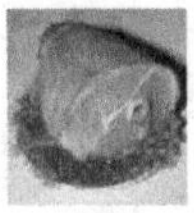 ham _____	 hat _____	 moon _____	 hot _____
 4. hill	sand _____	 hand _____	 hot _____	ten _____

Beginning Consonants: h

Directions: Say the name of the 1st picture in each row.
Say the name of each picture in that row.

Circle the words that **begin** with **h.**

Say the word.	Say each word. Circle then write the correct word on the line.		
5. hat	hot	hop	help
6. hit	hip	hill	bus
7. hen	help	see	ham
8. hot	hit	mat	hand
9. house	help	hand	milk

61

Beginning Consonants: h

 10. hug	 him	 hop	 hot
 11. head	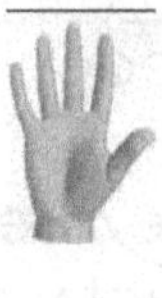 hand	 mop	 her
 12. hand	 hug	 top	 house

Star (☆) words: Say and trace.

1. he he

2. me me

3. she she

Beginning Consonants: h

Directions: 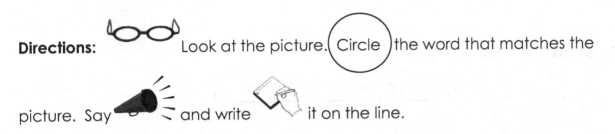 Look at the picture. Circle the word that matches the

picture. Say and write it on the line.

(him) - hat __him__	hot - hug _____	hill - tub _____
hat - hot _____	hat - he _____	hat - hand _____
hot - head _____	hen - me _____	him - help _____
hat - hip _____	hog - hit _____	hand - house _____

Beginning Consonants: h

Directions: Fill in the missing word.

> hand – hot – him – ham

1. Hand the book to _ i _.

2. The meat is _ _ m.

3. The pot is _ _ t.

4. H_ _ _ me the pan, please.

Directions: Say and trace.

1. The pot is hot.

2. Her hand is big.

Yes, I Can Read!   Unit 2

Beginning Consonants: Review

Directions: Look at the picture. (Circle) the word that matches the

picture. Say and write it on the line.

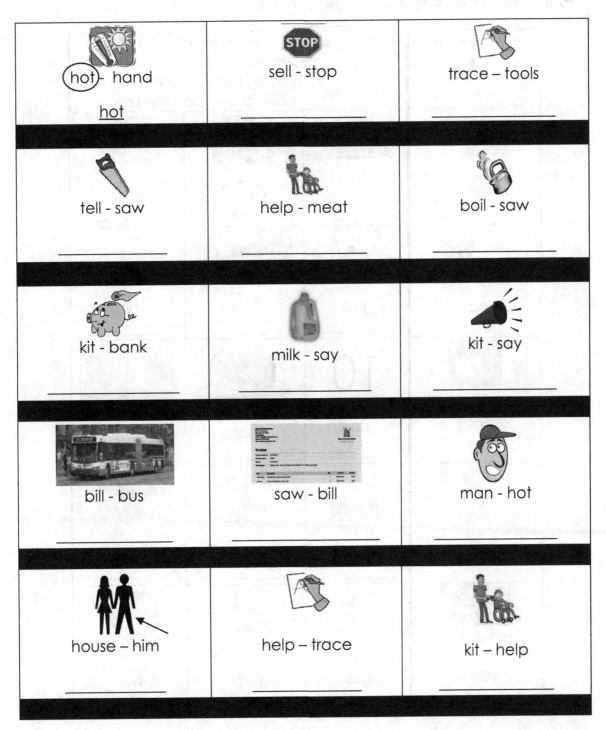

(hot) - hand hot	sell - stop	trace – tools
tell - saw	help - meat	boil - saw
kit - bank	milk - say	kit - say
bill - bus	saw - bill	man - hot
house – him	help – trace	kit – help

Unit 2, Part 2: g, n, d, l, f, j

Beginning Consonants: g

Directions: Say the name of the 1st picture in each row.

Say the name of each picture in that row.

Circle the words that **begin** with **g**.

Say the word.	Say each word. Circle then write the correct word on the line.		
1. girl	hat	go _go_	dog
2. gas	give	bus	pin
3. goat	ten	hat	gate
4. grill	green	gum	go
5. go	gas	gap	hot

Yes, I Can Read!   Unit 2

Beginning Consonants: g

Directions: Say the name of the 1st picture in each row.
Say the name of each picture in that row.
Circle the words that **begin**  with **g**.

Say the word.	Say each word. Circle then write the correct word on the line.			
 6. gate	 gift ___	 box ___	 go ___	 goat ___
 7. give	 grass ___	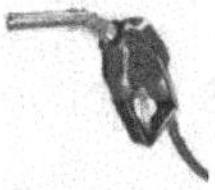 gas ___	 girl ___	 man ___
 8. girl	 book ___	ten ___	 go ___	 green ___

67

Beginning Consonants: g

Star (☆) words:

Directions: Say and write

good
_____

1. Gil gives Mom a gift.

2. Mom gives a gift to Gil.

3. Gil and Mom get good gifts.

chair

Directions: Match the word and its picture.

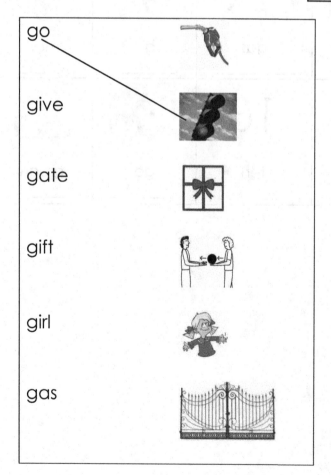

go

give

gate

gift

girl

gas

Beginning Consonants: n

Directions: Say the name of the 1st picture in each row.

Say the name of each picture in that row.

(Circle) the words that **begin** with **n**.

Say the word.	Say each word. (Circle) then write the correct word on the line.		
1. net	(nut) nut	(nap) nap	baby _____
2. nest	no _____	not _____	nut _____
3. neck	bag _____	bank _____	not _____
4. nap	net _____	go _____	nun _____
5. name	gas _____	nest _____	need _____

69

Beginning Consonants: n

Directions: Say the name of the 1st picture in each row.

Say the name of each picture in that row.

(Circle) the words that **begin** with **n**.

Say the word.	Say each word. (Circle) then write the correct word on the line.		
6. no	need	row	net
7. name	nun	no	gas
8. nest	nose	name	hat
9. need	nail	nuts	sun
10. net	no	pan	nap

Beginning Consonants: n

Directions: Say the name of the 1st picture in each row.
Say the name of each picture in that row.

Circle the words that **begin** with **n**.

Say the word.	Say each word. Circle then write the correct word on the line.		
11. nun	nose	me	sing
12. neck	nails	help	ten
13. nut	neck	hat	name

Beginning Consonants: n

Directions: Find and (circle) the words.

Word Find

~~NET~~ – NOSE – NAME – NOT – NAP - NO

N	O	N	A	M	E	W
E	N	O	S	E	J	V
T	K	V	L	O	R	X
Y	N	A	P	B	E	R
E	B	C	N	O	T	G

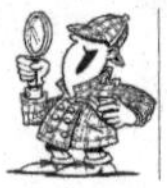

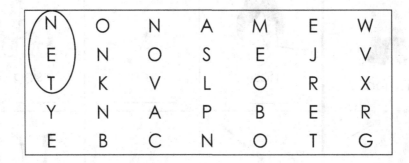

Sight Words

Directions: Say and trace.

1. my my
2. my hen my hen
3. mine mine
4. The hen is mine. The hen is mine.
5. your /yôr/ your
6. your dog your dog
7. yours / yôrz/ yours
8. The dog is yours. The dog is yours.
9. my nose my nose
10. your neck your neck

Beginning Consonants: n

Directions: Match the word and its picture.

Beginning Consonants: d

Directions: Say the name of the 1st picture in each row.

Say the name of each picture in that row.

Circle the words that **begin** with **d**.

Say the word.	Say each word. Circle then write the correct word on the line.			
1. dog	milk _____	bus _____	(doll) doll	(dime) dime
2. duck	boat _____	desk _____	door _____	gas _____
3. dad	disc _____	door _____	bank _____	dig _____
4. desk	dad _____	deck _____	dog _____	bed _____
5. disk	dime _____	door _____	name _____	bat _____

74

Beginning Consonants: d

Directions: Look at the picture. (Circle) the word that matches the

picture. Say and write it on the line.

 duck - (dime) dime	 door - dig _____	dad – disk _____
desk - dog _____	 deck - dog _____	 deck – dog _____

Directions: Fill in the missing word.

dad – dog – door – do – duck – dish

1. The _ _g is at the _oo_.

2. The _og's d_sh is in the den.

3. The _ _ck is wet.

4. D_ _ is in the house.

Beginning Consonants: d

Directions: Say and read.

Do

Today Present	Yesterday Past	Past with have/has
I do	I did	I have done
you do	you did	you have done
he, she, it does	he, she, it did	he, she, it has done
we do	we did	we have done
you do	you did	you have done
they do	they did	they have done

Directions: Say and read.

I did a good job. I did my best. My dad gave me a dime to run the dog.

Directions: Say and trace.

1. I do my job.

2. You did your job.

3. I did see my dad.

4. I do pay my bills.

5. I do!

6. The meat is done.

7. I, _____, (your name) do a good job!

Beginning Consonants: l

Directions: Say the name of the 1st picture in each row.

Say the name of each picture in that row.

(Circle) the words that **begin** with **l**.

Say the word.	Say each word. (Circle) then write the correct word on the line.			
1. lips	saw	(lid) lid	(leg) leg	pan
2. lid	lock	hat	leaf	man
3. lamp	leaf	lips	lid	give
4. leg	lamp	bed	left	desk
5. leaf	book	lock	leg	lab
6. left	lift	lid	dime	sink

Beginning Consonants: l

Directions: Fill in the missing word:

lamp – left

1.   Turn off the _amp.

2.   Turn the _amp to the l_ _ t.

3.   Turn on the _amp.

4.   The desk _ _ _ p is on the desk.

Directions: Say and trace.

1. My job is in a lab.

2. The leaf is green.

3. Lift your left leg.

Beginning Consonants: f

Directions: Say the name of the 1st picture in each row. 🔈

Say the name of each picture in that row. 🔈 (Circle) the words that **begin**
with **f**.

Say the word. 🔈	Say each word. 🔈 (Circle) then write the correct word on the line.		
1. fan	pan	(fat) fat	(feed) feed
2. fill	fast	full	tea
3. fog	fan	dog	fire
4. fat	fan	fast	hat
5. fun	run	fog	fill
6. fast	4 four	duck	face
7. full	duck	face	food

79

Beginning Consonants: f

Directions: Say and read.

1. Feed the baby.

2. We fed the baby.

3. He feeds the baby.

4. She feeds the baby.

5. They feed the baby.

Directions: Fill in, read, and say. .

fun – fill – four – fast – fan – for

1. F_ _l the glass.

2. Run _ast.

3. It is _u_ to run fast.

4. It is hot. Turn on the _an .

5. 1, 2, 3, 4 (_ou_)

6. My bill is _or $4.00.

Beginning Consonants: f

Directions: Find  and (circle) the words.

Word Find

FOOD – FILL – FACE – FAN – FULL

F	I	L	L	B	R	F
O	F	A	C	E	T	O
L	S	F	U	L	L	O
D	F	A	N	V	W	D

Beginning Consonants: j

Directions: Say the name of the 1st picture in each row.
Say the name of each picture in that row.

(Circle) the words that **begin** with **j**.

Say the word.	Say each word. (Circle) then write the correct word on the line.			
1. jam	sad	(Jell-o ®) <u>Jell-o</u>	gas	cup
2. jet	jump	wet	bed	him
3. jump	run	duck	jam	job
4. Jell-o ®	jar	jet	bat	baby
5. jar	milk	jam	box	jeep

Beginning Consonants: j

Directions: Say the name of the 1st picture in each row.
Say the name of each picture in that row.

Circle the words that **begin**  with **j.**

Say the word.	Say each word. Circle then write the correct word on the line.			
 6. jack	 jacks	 jet	 leaf	 jam
 7. jog	 jump	 jar	 jacks	 door
 8. jeep	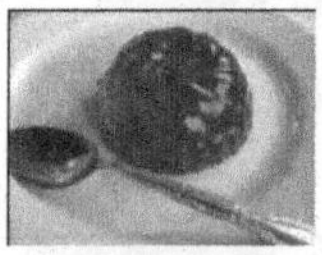 Jell-o®	 Jill	 cup	 jog
 9. Jill	 jog	 hand	 jump	 jeep
 10. jet	 job	 jump	 dig	 book

83

Beginning Consonants: j

Directions: Say and trace.

1.   Jack jogs.

2.   Jill and Jack jam.

3.   The jam is in a glass jar.

4.   Jump up!

5.   I am in a jam.

Directions: Find   and circle the words.

Word Find

JOB - JELL-O® - JAR - JAM - JET

J	J	A	R	J
K	E	S	T	O
M	T	L	B	B
B	C	D	L	T
J	A	M	P	O

Beginning Consonants: Review g, n, d, l, f, j

Directions: Look at the picture. (Circle) the word that matches the

picture. Say and write it on the line.

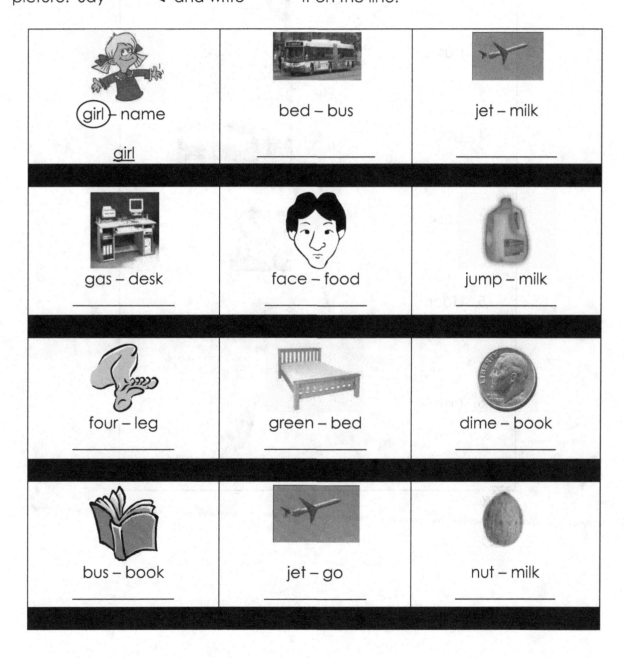

girl – name

girl

bed – bus

_____

jet – milk

_____

gas – desk

_____

face – food

_____

jump – milk

_____

four – leg

_____

green – bed

_____

dime – book

_____

bus – book

_____

jet – go

_____

nut – milk

_____

Beginning Consonants: Review

Directions: Match the word and picture.

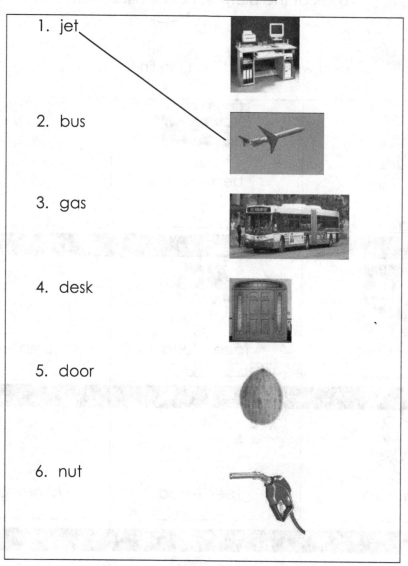

1. jet

2. bus

3. gas

4. desk

5. door

6. nut

Beginning Consonants: Review

Directions: Say and trace.

1. Jill has a lock.

2. Jill locks the door.

Directions: Say, circle, and fill in.

1. Did you sit on the bus? Yes/No, I sat/did not sit on the bus.

2. Did you lock the door? Yes/No, I did/did not I _ _ _
   the d _ _ _.

Star (☆) Words

Say the word.	Illustration	Trace the word.
1. eat		eat
2. drink		drink
3. and	+	and

Directions: Read and say.

1. Jack eats ham and nuts.

2. Jill drinks milk in a cup.

Unit 2, Part 3: p, r, v, w, q, c

Beginning Consonants: p

Directions: Say the name of the 1st picture in each row. 🔊

Say the name of each picture in that row. 🔊

Circle the words that **begin** [image] with **p**.

Say the word. 🔊	Say each word. 🔊 Circle then write the correct word on the line.			
1. pig	(pin) pin	gas _____	(pen) pen	(pan) pan
2. pass	pot _____	pet _____	pill _____	pail _____
3. pit	sink _____	pot _____	pan _____	pass _____
4. pin	pill _____	gas _____	pen _____	pan _____

88

Beginning Consonants: p

Directions: Fill in the missing word.

┌─────────────────────────┐
│ pan-pet-pass-pig-pit │
└─────────────────────────┘

1. Do not _ _ss a school bus.

2. A _ig is big.

3. The _an is hot.

4. Dig a _it.

5. P_t the dog.

6. The dog is my _e_ .

Directions: Find and (circle) the words.

Word Find

┌──┐
│ G̶A̶S̶ – PASS – PILL – PAN – PET - PAIL │
└──┘

R	P	E	T	G
P	I	L	L	A
P	A	N	B	S
A	O	M	S	T
I	P	A	I	L
I	P	A	S	S

Yes, I Can Read!   Unit 2

Beginning Consonants: r

Directions: Say the name of the 1st picture in each row.

Say the name of each picture in that row.

Circle the words that **begin** with **r**.

Say the word.	Say each word. Circle then write the correct word on the line.			
1. rib	bus	rim (rim)	red (red)	hand
2. run	rim	rib	rain	leg
3. red	read	rat	rain	nose
4. rain	run	red	man	fan
5. rim	tag	rib	read	turn
6. ram	rain	pen	bat	baby
7. red	rash	tea	red	job

90

Beginning Consonants: r

Directions: Say and trace the words.

1.   The tea bag is on the rim.

2.   It is fun to run.

3.   I see a rat !

4.   Ribs are good.

5.   It is my rib.

6.   Read the book.

Directions: Say and read.

Run

Today Present	Yesterday Past
I run	I ran
you run	you ran
he, she, it runs	he, she, it ran
we run	we ran
you run	you ran
they run	they ran

Beginning Consonants: r

Directions: Find  and (circle) the words.

Word Find

| RAT – RIB – RUN – RAN – RASH |

R	A	T	F	T	R	S
O	A	B	T	N	A	U
R	S	Y	D	J	S	V
L	R	A	N	R	H	I
A	W	R	I	B	T	R
B	C	T	D	T	O	B
R	U	N	C	D	E	V

Directions: Say and read.

I have a rash on my face and neck. I cannot eat eggs or nuts, and I did. I ate

eggs and nuts.

Beginning Consonants: v

Directions: Say the name of the 1st picture in each row.

Say the name of each picture in that row.

(Circle) the words that **begin** with **v**.

Say the word.	Say each word. (Circle) then write the correct word on the line.			
1. van	rash ____	**a, e, i, o, u** (vowels) vowels	(vest) vest	face ____
2. vet	band ____	van ____	vent ____	cup ____
3. vat	boy ____	nuts ____	vest ____	vent ____
a, e, i, o, u 4. vowels	zoo ____	bus ____	tape ____	vest ____
5. vote	vest ____	vet ____	girl ____	book ____
6. vest	pan ____	vote ____	**a, e, i, o, u** vowels	job ____

Beginning Consonants: v

Directions: Find  and (circle) the words.

Word Find

~~VAN~~ - VET – VOWELS – VOTE – VEST

V	O	T	E	R	M	V
M	N	T	O	K	S	E
V	O	W	E	L	S	S
V	E	T	E	W	V	T
X	V	N	V	K	L	O
V	A	N	U	U	M	S

Directions: Say and trace the words.

1. Can you vote? Yes, I can vote.

2. A, e, i, o and u are /âr/ vowels.

Yes, I Can Read!   Unit 2

Beginning Consonants: w

Directions: Say the name of the 1st picture in each row.
Say the name of each picture in that row.
(Circle) the words that **begin**  with **w**.

Say the word.	Say each word. (Circle) then write the correct word on the line.			
 1. wet	 pig	 leg	 (well) well	 dime
 2. wool	 wag	 pot	 sink	 web
 3. wood	 win	 wax	 book	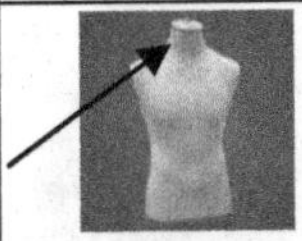 neck
 4. wag	 work	 well	 bus	 wax

95

Beginning Consonants: w

Directions: Match the word to its picture.

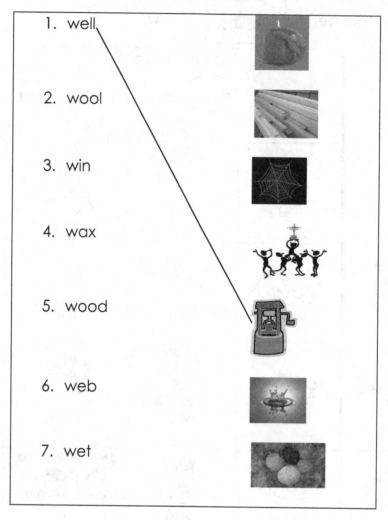

1. well

2. wool

3. win

4. wax

5. wood

6. web

7. wet

Wow! Good job!

Beginning Consonants: w

Directions: Read and say.

Work

Today Present	Yesterday Past	Tomorrow Future
I work	I worked	I shall work
you work	you worked	you will work
he, she, it works	he, she, it worked	he, she, it will work
we work	we worked	we shall work
you work	you worked	you will work
they work	they worked	they will work

Directions: Say and trace the words.

1. I work at Walmart ®.

2. He works at Walmart ®.

3. They worked at Lowe's ®.

4. I will work at Lowe's ®.

5. She worked at McDonald's ®.

6. We worked at Dunkin' Donuts ®.

Beginning Consonants: q

Directions: Say the name of the 1st picture in each row.
Say the name of each picture in that row.

(Circle) the words that **begin** with **q**.

Say the word.	Say each word. Circle then write the correct word on the line.		
1. quart	(queen) / queen	fat	lid
2. quarter	quart	queen	no
3. quilt	quart	quiz	quarter
4. quiet	bag	glasses	quilt
5. quill	quilt	quiet	quarter

Beginning Consonants: q

Directions: Look at the picture. (Circle) the word that matches the

picture. Say and write  it on the line.

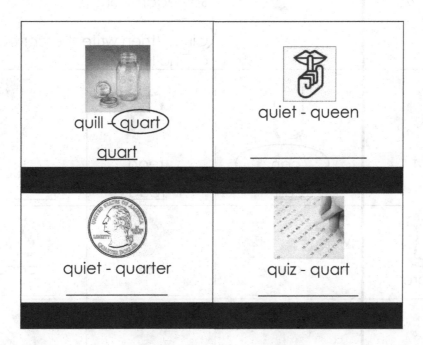

quill - (quart)

quart

quiet - queen

_____

quiet - quarter

_____

quiz - quart

_____

Directions: Say, trace, and read.

1. The quiet queen is on a quilt on the grass.

2. A quart of /ŭv/ milk is a quarter.

Beginning Consonants: c

Directions: Say the name of the 1st picture in each row.
Say the name of each picture in that row.

Circle the words that **begin** with **c**.

Say the word.	Say each word. Circle then write the correct word on the line.		
1. cat	(can) can	read read	quart _____
2. core	car _____	box _____	candy _____
3. cup	box _____	cut _____	card _____
4. can	cat _____	cup _____	car _____
5. call	corn _____	man _____	coffee _____

Beginning Consonants: c

Directions: Match the word and the picture.

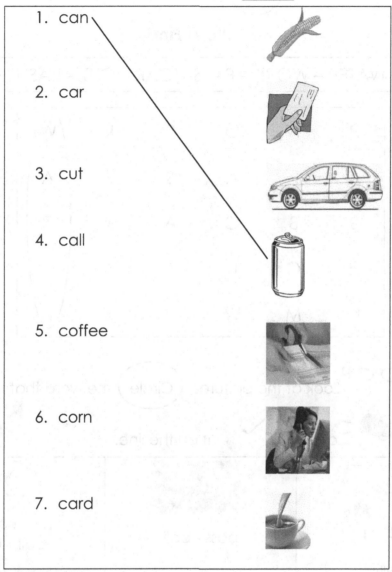

1. can

2. car

3. cut

4. call

5. coffee

6. corn

7. card

Directions: Say and trace the words.

1. The core of the apple is left.
2. The cat is in the box.
3. It is not a quarter for a cup of /ŭv/ coffee.
4. The candle is wax.
5. My car is a van.

Review: p, r, v, w, g, c

Directions: Find and (circle) the words.

Word Find

~~WATER~~ – WORK – PASS – CAR – CUT – RASH

R	W	O	R	K	W
A	P	A	S	S	A
S	B	C	A	R	T
H	C	U	T	A	E
N	M	W	V	B	R

Directions: Look at the picture. (Circle) the word that matches the

picture. Say and write it on the line.

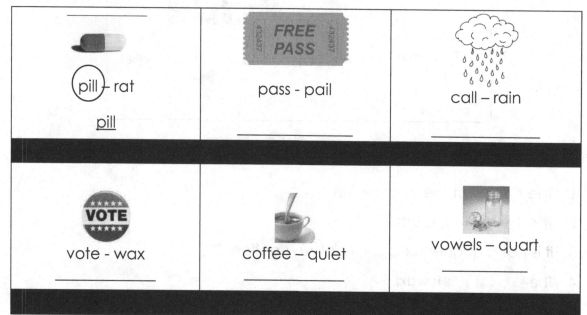

(pill) – rat

pill

_____

pass – pail

_____

call – rain

_____

vote – wax

_____

coffee – quiet

_____

vowels – quart

_____

Review: p, r, v, w, g, c

Directions: Say, trace, and read.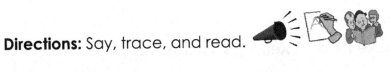

1. Pass the van.

2. Pass the milk, please /plēz/.

3. Rain is wet.

4. Water is wet.

5. Read the vowels: a, e, i, o, u.

Unit 2, Part 4: x, y, z

Beginning Consonants: x

- The sound of x in x-ray is /ĕks/.

- If x begins a word, it sounds like /z/ as in Xerox® or xylophone.

- At the end of a syllable, it sounds like /ks/ as in box, or /ĕgz/ as in exit, exam, or exist.

Say the word.	Illustration	Trace the word.
1. Xerox®		Xerox®
2. x-ray		x-ray
3. xylophone		xylophone

chair

Directions: Match the word to its picture.

Xerox®

xylophone

x-ray

Yes, I Can Read!   Unit 2

Beginning Consonants: y

Directions: Say the name of the 1st picture in each row.

Say the name of each picture in that row.

(Circle) the words that **begin** [image] with **y**.

Say the word	Say each word (Circle) then write the correct word on the line.		
1. yes	(yawn) yawn	(you) you	10 ten _____
2. yo-yo	quart _____	✔ yes _____	rim _____
3. yell	yawn _____	yarn _____	tree _____
4. yam	mail _____	✔ yes _____	yawn _____
5. yard	you _____	jump _____	yarn _____
6. yarn	yard _____	yam _____	you _____

105

Review: beginning consonants: z

Directions: Say the name of the 1st picture in each row.

Say the name of each picture in that row.

Circle the words that **begin** with **z**.

Say the word.	Say each word. Circle then write the correct word on the line.		
1. zip	(zipper) zipper	(zero) zero	cat _____
2. zebra	zoo _____	zip _____	0 zero _____
3. zig-zag	zipper _____	help _____	zoo _____
4. zoo	zoom _____	band _____	cup _____

Directions: Say, trace, and read.

Dad: Zip up your wool coat. We will go see a zebra at the zoo.

Boy: Yes, I will zip up my wool coat and go to the zoo to see a zebra.

Beginning Consonants: z

Directions: 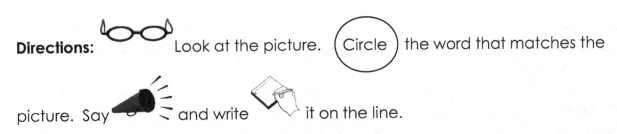 Look at the picture. (Circle) the word that matches the

picture. Say and write it on the line.

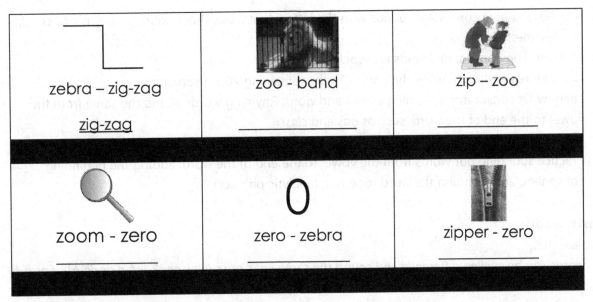

zebra – zig-zag	zoo - band	zip – zoo
<u>zig-zag</u>	_____	_____
zoom - zero	zero - zebra	zipper - zero
_____	_____	_____

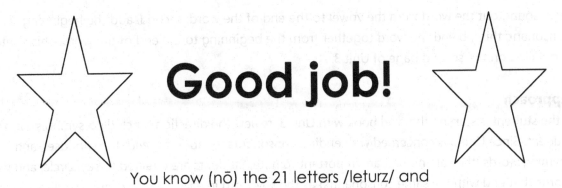

Good job!

You know (nō) the 21 letters /leturz/ and

sounds (sowndz) that begin words. /wurdz/.

Overview

Unit 3 focuses on ending consonants and recognition of rhyming words, including variant spellings as in *egg* and *leg*.

Objectives

Students will:

1. Associate ending consonant sounds with the letters that make those sounds such as *s* or *ss* /s/as in *class*, *mess*, and *dress*, etc.
2. Learn ending consonant sounds and spellings.
3. Learn words in these lessons that end with the remaining 20 consonants.
4. Learn what constitutes a rhyming sound and word: Rhyming words sound the same from the vowel to the end of the word, such as *gas* and *class*.
5. Practice onsets and rimes (word families), such as *mess* and *dress*.
6. Practice sounding out words from the vowel to the end of the word, adding the beginning consonant, and blending the word together. (analytic phonics)

Instruction

Explain that:

1. words can be spelled differently and sound the same i.e., *s* or *ss* /s/; *k* or *ck* /k/; *d* or *dd* /d/; *f* or *ff* /f/.
2. words can end in *ll*, but not *l*.
3. words can end in *ve* but not *v*.

If the student does not know a word after looking at the page heading, key word, using picture clues, and trying to read the featured word, practice the following with him:

First, sound out the word from the vowel to the end of the word; second, add the beginning consonant; third, blend the word together from the beginning to the end of the word. This strategy is detailed on the second page of Unit 3.

Approach

If the student is starting the workbook with Unit 3, review the directions, including symbols, with the student. Since Unit 3 is concerned with ending consonants, symbols for *end* (the caboose), and rhyming words (the cat and hat) are important to note. Students are directed to say, circle, and write words that end with the same consonant(s) as the key word in each row. They are also directed to say, circle, and write words that rhyme. If he has worked in Unit 2, he will be familiar with the page format.

Assessment

Assign a few pages at a time, correct completed work, and go over any incorrect answers with the student. Have him read random words aloud from the lessons, as well as the sentences following the lessons or exercises, but focus on the sound/letter(s) connection of the ending consonants in these exercises. He should also be able to identify rhyming words.

Vocabulary Acquisition Strategies

Multiple Meaning Words

Multiple meaning words (*stem, sock, check*, etc.) should be read, discussed, and used orally in sentences to check for comprehension, dictated, etc.

Flash Cards

Make flash cards for troublesome words which the student reviews daily. Each time you see him one-on-one, review the words with him, adding troublesome words so his stack of cards grows. When you are certain he has mastered a word, remove it from the stack and give it to him to save. He should also copy the words into his notebook. As soon as he knows enough words, he can create written sentences using featured words, or you can dictate sentences for him to write.

Note: *W* is omitted in Unit 3 as an ending consonant because when *w* is preceded by *a, e,* or *o*, it is a vowel. Examples of *w* as a vowel are included in Unit 6 lessons as vowel teams, specifically diphthongs: *ow* (*low, cow*), *aw* (*saw*), and *ew* (*stew, few*). *Sew* is another example of a word which contains *w* as a vowel.

Unit 3: Ending Consonants and Rhyming Words

Part 1: s, ss, b, m, t, k, g, n

Ending Consonants: s, ss

Directions: Say the name of the 1st picture in each row.
Say the name of each picture in that row.

Circle the words that **end** with **s** or **ss**.

Say the word.	Say each word. Circle, then write the correct word on the line.		
1. class	(mess) mess	tag _____	rib _____
2. dress	grass _____	kiss _____	chess _____
3. kiss	gas _____	glass _____	mess _____
4. gas	class _____	chess _____	mess _____
5. grass	pass _____	gas _____	glass _____

Ending Consonants: s, ss

Directions: Look at the picture. (Circle) the word that matches the

picture. Say and write it on the line.

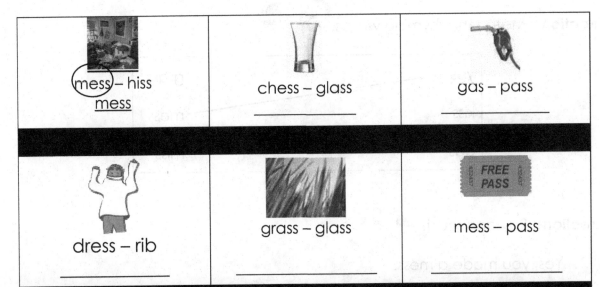

(mess) – hiss	chess – glass	gas – pass
mess	_____	_____
dress – rib	grass – glass	mess – pass
_____	_____	_____

Rhymes: **cat** and **hat**.

Pat, the fat cat, sat on the mat.

Words that rhyme sound the same from the vowel to the end of the word.

Pat =   ăt + P = Pat

fat =   ăt + f = fat

cat =   ăt + c = cat

sat =   ăt + s = sat

mat =   ăt + m = mat

Ending Consonants: s, ss

Rhyming words are not always spelled the same. But, they must **sound** the same from the vowel to the end of the word if they are rhyming words.

Directions: Match the rhyming words.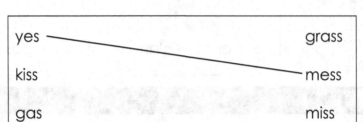

yes ———————————————————— grass

kiss ————————————————— mess

gas   miss

Directions: Say and read.

1. Yes, you made a mess.

2. Kiss me so I will not miss you.

3.   I spilled gas on the grass.

4. Please, pass the gas can to me.

Yes, I Can Read!   Unit 3

Rhyming Words: ess, as, ass

Directions: Say the name of the first picture in each row.  (Circle) the words in each row that **rhyme** with the 1st word.

1. mess	can	(dress) dress	(chess) chess
2. gas	class	pass	sad
3. kiss	miss	hiss	class
4. grass	dress	boat	gas
5. glass	gas	grass	sun

Rhyming Words: as, ass

Directions: Match the word to its picture.

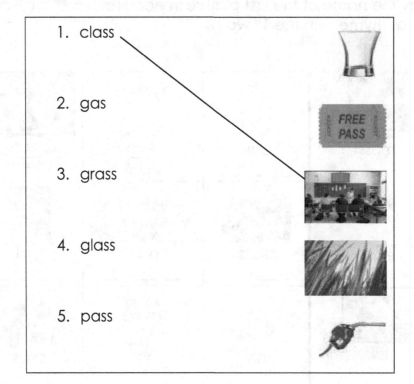

1. class

2. gas

3. grass

4. glass

5. pass

Ending Consonants: b

Directions: Say the name of the 1st picture in each row.
Say the name of each picture in that row. (Circle) the words that **end**
with **b**.

Say the word.	Say each word. (Circle) then write the correct word on the line.		
1. tub	cab cab	milk	cob cob
2. cob	lab _____	tub _____	bus _____
3. sub	tub _____	jet _____	scrub _____
4. cab	tab _____	rib _____	crib _____
5. sob	rob _____	cob _____	mob _____

Yes, I Can Read!   Unit 3

Rhyming Words: ab, ob

Directions: Say the name of the first picture in each row.  Circle the words in each row that **rhyme** with the 1st word.  Write them on the line.

 1. cab	 bat	 lab _lab_	 tab _tab_	 tag
 2. lab	 tab	 jab	 bed	 ran
 3. jab	 cab	 cob	 ran	 lab
 4. nab	 job	 sub	 lab	 tub
 5. mob	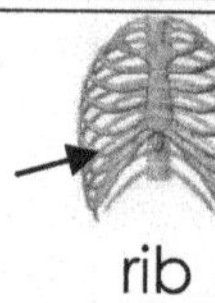 rib	 sob	 swim	 rob
 6. cob	 pig	 bus	 job	 cat
 7. sob	 sun	 mob	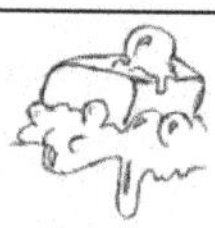 soap	 can

116

Ending Consonants: b

Directions: Say and trace.

1. Scrub the tub.
2. The lab is in a cab.

Directions: Say and write the words that **rhyme**.

lab-tab-cob-sub-crib-mob-rob

tub	cab	rib	sob
1.	1.	1.	1.
	2.		2.
			3.

Can you think of more?

_____

_____

Yes, I Can Read!   Unit 3

Ending Consonants: m

Directions: Say the name of the 1st picture in each row. 📢
Say the name of each picture in that row. 📢 (Circle) the words that **end**
with **m**.

Say the word. 📢	Say each word. 📢 (Circle) then write the correct word on the line.		
1. trim	(rim) rim	(swim) swim	(drum) drum
2. gum	boat ___	clam ___	stem ___
3. hem	chum ___	gum ___	drum ___
4. bum	slim ___	them ___	ham ___
5. him	them ___	trim ___	dam ___
6. skim	stem ___	swim ___	ham ___

118

Ending Consonants: m

7. jam	bus	dam	swam
8. slim	gum	glass	slam
9. bum	trim	hum	gum
10. slam	stem	clam	jam

Ending Consonants: m

Directions: Look at the picture. (Circle) the word that matches the

picture. Say and write it on the line.

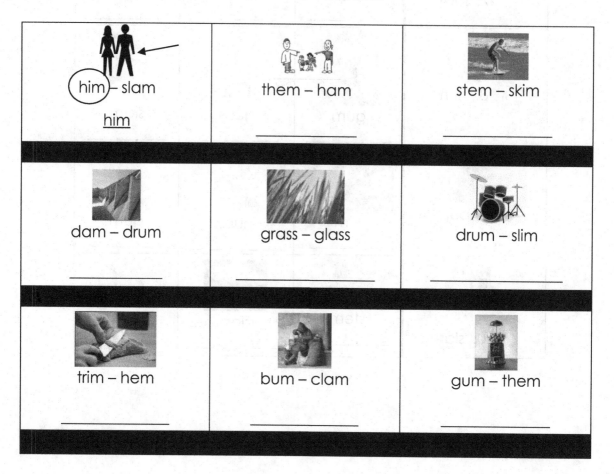

(him) – slam him	them – ham _____	stem – skim _____
dam – drum _____	grass – glass _____	drum – slim _____
trim – hem _____	bum – clam _____	gum – them _____

Directions: Say and trace.

1. Do not slam the door.
2. A clam is good to eat.
3. Skim milk has no fat.
4. I will not swim at the dam.

swim

I swim.

I swam.

I will swim.

Ending Consonants: m

 Add the **rhyming** words to their lists:

~~clam~~ – ~~stem~~ – ~~trim~~ – ~~drum~~ – swim – gum – hem – them – swam – him

-am	-em	-im	-um
1. clam	1. stem	1. trim	1. drum
2.	2.	2.	2.
	3.	3.	

Can you think of more?

_____

_____

Ending Consonants: t

Directions: Say the name of the 1st picture in each row.

Say the name of each picture in that row. (Circle) the words that **end** with **t**.

Say the word.	Say each word. (Circle) then write the correct word on the line.		
1. hot	(mitt) mitt	(spot) spot	frog _____
2. nut	cot _____	net _____	cat _____
3. pit	sit _____	kit _____	mitt _____
4. dot	cat _____	spot _____	pot _____

Directions: Fill in the missing words.

coat – mat – spot – cat – rat – net

1. The _oat has a sp _ _ on it.
2. The c_t has a r_t.
3. The r_t is in the n_t.
4. The cat is on the m_t.

sit – pot – jet – hot

5. They s_t on the mat.
6. The p_t is h_t.
7. The j_t is fast.

Ending Consonants: k

Directions: Say the name of the 1st picture in each row. 🔊
Say the name of each picture in that row. 🔊 (Circle) the words that **end**
 with **k**.

Say the word. 🔊	🔊 Say each word. (Circle) then write the correct word on the line.		
1. neck	(rock) rock	(deck) deck	(check) check
2. clock	gas	sock	snack
3. lock	duck	tusk	rib
4. crack	pack	sit	rack
5. book	back	they	lock
6. pack	them	sock	job

Ending Consonants: k

chair

Directions: Match the word to its picture.

1. book

2. clock

3. back

4. sock

5. lock

6. check

Directions: Say and trace.

1. A pack on the back is a backpack.

2. Lock the door.

Yes, I Can Read!   Unit 3

Ending Consonants: Review

Directions: Say the name of the 1st picture in each row.
Say the name of each picture in that row. Circle the words that **end**
with the same sound.

Say the word.	Say each word. Circle then write the correct word on the line.		
 1. dress	 (kiss) kiss	 left _____	 (gas) gas
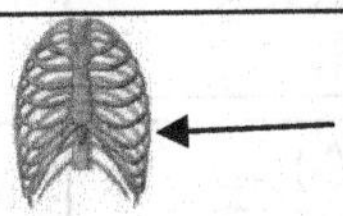 2. rib	 check	 tub	 cab
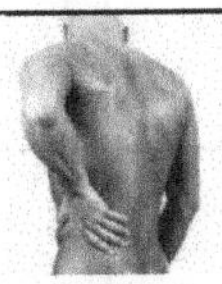 3. back	 clock	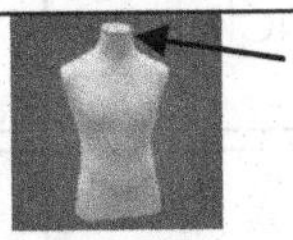 neck	 glass
 4. pot	nut	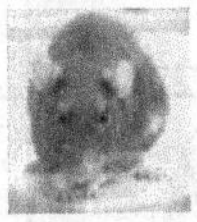 rat	 lock
 5. job	left	 cab	 pot

125

Ending Consonants: Review

Directions: Say the name of the first picture in each row.  Circle the words in each row that **rhyme** with the 1st word.

1. check	(neck) neck	run ___	(deck) deck	(peck) peck
2. tack	snack	pig	crack	pack
3. rack	tack	crack	book	boat
4. lock	bed	rock	dock	bag
5. sick	lick	job	tick	work

Directions: Read and say.

Jack has a snack in his pack. His backpack is on the rack. At his job, he locks

his backpack in his locker.

Ending Consonants: g

Directions: Say the name of the 1st picture in each row.

Say the name of each picture in that row. (Circle) the words that **end** with **g**.

Say the word.	Say each word. (Circle) then write the correct word on the line.		
1. hog	(pig) pig	(egg) egg	(leg) leg
2. big	bag _____	bus _____	pin _____
3. dog	hog _____	log _____	rug _____
4. frog	leg _____	bed _____	dog _____
5. plug	big _____	tug _____	left _____

Rhyming Words: og

Directions: Match the word to its picture.

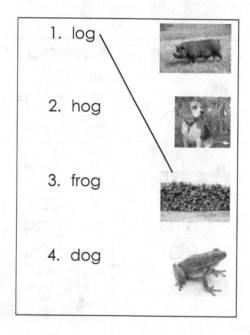

1. log

2. hog

3. frog

4. dog

Directions: Say and read.

A dog, a frog, and a hog sat on a log.

Ending Consonants: n

Directions: Say the name of the 1st picture in each row.
Say the name of each picture in that row. (Circle) the words that **end**
with **n**.

Say the word.	Say each word. (Circle) then write the correct word on the line.		
1. pan	(pen) pen	(run) run	egg ___
2. pin	tan ___	sun ___	pig ___
3. fan	bun ___	pan ___	gun ___
4. can	bag ___	rug ___	pin ___
5. in	pin ___	pen ___	man ___

Good job!

Part 2: d, dd, f, ff, ll, p, v, ve, w, x, zz

Ending Consonants: d, dd

Directions: Say the name of the 1st picture in each row.
Say the name of each picture in that row. Circle the words that **end** with **d** or **dd**.

Say the word.	Say each word. Circle then write the correct word on the line.		
1. bed	cat ___	(bad) bad	+ (add) add
2. sad	bleed ___	gas ___	lid ___
3. kid	mud ___	read ___	red ___
4. bird	kid ___	wood ___	bleed ___

Ending Consonants: d, dd

Directions: Match the word to its picture.

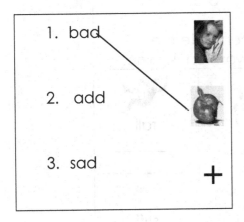

1. bad
2. add
3. sad

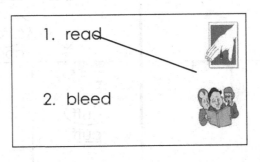

1. read
2. bleed

Directions: Say, trace, and read.

Ted has a red bed.

Ed reads.

Ending Consonants: f, ff

Directions: Say the name of the 1st picture in each row.

Say the name of each picture in that row. (Circle) the words that **end** with **f** or **ff**.

Say the word.	Say each word. Circle then write the correct word on the line.		
1. half	(cuff) <u>cuff</u>	(cliff) <u>cliff</u>	fall _____
2. puff	off _____	bleed _____	stiff _____
3. off	read _____	stuff _____	chef _____
4. sniff	half _____	cliff _____	bus _____

Directions: Say and trace.

half   one half   1/2

Ending Consonants: f, ff

Directions: Fill in the missing word.

off – roof – shelf – half - sniff

1. Flip _____ the light.

2. The top of the house is the _____.

3. I like half and _____ in my coffee.

4. Sn_____ the milk.

5. The books are on the sh_____.

Directions: Say and write the rhyming words on the line.

bluff – cliff – sniff –cuff – elf – stuff – shelf – stiff – self

-elf	-uff	-iff
1. elf	1. bluff	1.cliff
2._____	2. _____	2._____
3. _____	3.._____	3. _____

Ending Consonants: ll

Directions: Say the name of the 1st picture in each row. 🔊

Say the name of each picture in that row. 🔊 (Circle) the words that **end**
with **ll**.

Say the word. 🔊	Say each word. 🔊 (Circle) then write the correct word on the line.		
1. doll	(call) <u>call</u>	(tall) <u>tall</u>	sit ___
2. hall	bleed ___	small ___	cab ___
3. bull	mall ___	roll ___	hill ___
4. bill	hill ___	spill ___	glass ___
5. ball	fall ___	small ___	hall ___
6. grill	roll ___	read ___	spill ___

Ending Consonants: ll

Directions: Match the word to its picture.

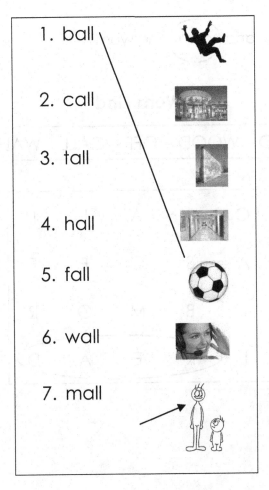

1. ball

2. call

3. tall

4. hall

5. fall

6. wall

7. mall

Directions: Say, trace, and read.

1. Jill has a small doll, and Lil has a tall doll.

2. Roll the ball in the hall.

3. Bill grills meat on his grill.

Ending Consonants: ll

Directions: Find  and  the words.

Word Find

READ – WOOD – OFF – CALL – WALL

```
C   W   A   L   L

A   S   O   F   F

L   B   M   O   R

L   R   E   A   D
```

Yes, I Can Read!   Unit 3

Ending Consonants: p

Directions: Say the name of the 1st picture in each row.
Say the name of each picture in that row. (Circle) the words that **end**
with **p**.

Say the word.	Say each word. (Circle) then write the correct word on the line.		
1. mop	(map) map	(cap) cap	cliff _____
2. top	up _____	mop _____	lap _____
3. shop	sip _____	lap _____	top _____
4. lip	tip _____	map _____	small _____
5. up	grill _____	cup _____	tap _____
6. cup	quiet _____	up _____	sip _____

137

Ending Consonants: p

Directions: Match the word to its picture.

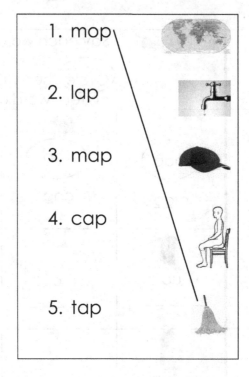

1. mop

2. lap

3. map

4. cap

5. tap

Directions: Say, trace, and read.

1. Lift your cup to your lips and sip.

2. Ron lifts his cup to his lips and sips his tea.

3. Sam works on his laptop in class.

Ending Consonants: v, (ve)

Directions: Say the name of the 1st picture in each row.
Say the name of each picture in that row. (Circle) the words that **end**
with **ve**. *

Say the word.	Say each word. Circle then write the correct word on the line.		
1. love	tall _____	drive drive	glove glove
2. grave	shave _____	wave _____	small _____
3. shove	give _____	shave _____	clock _____
4. dive	glove _____	top _____	brave _____
5. dove	cave _____	move _____	shave _____

* Note: Words that end in the **v** sound are spelled **ve**.

Ending Consonants: v, (ve)

Directions: Match the word to its picture.

chair

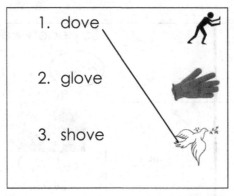

1. dove

2. glove

3. shove

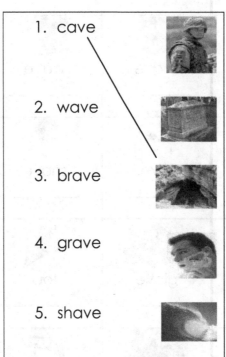

1. cave

2. wave

3. brave

4. grave

5. shave

Ending Consonants: x

Directions: Say the name of the 1st picture in each row.

Say the name of each picture in that row. (Circle) the words that **end** with **x**.

Say the word.	Say each word. (Circle) then write the correct word on the line.		
6 1. six	(fix) fix	(ax) ax	(box) box
2. mix	box _____	read _____	fox _____
3. fax	mall _____	swim _____	six _____
4. ax	ox _____	fix _____	fax _____

Directions: Say, trace, and read.

The OX is in the box with the fox.

Ending Consonants: zz

Directions: Say the name of the 1st picture in each row.
Say the name of each picture in that row. (Circle) the words that **end**
with **z** or **zz**.

Say the word.	Say each word. (Circle) then write the correct word on the line.		
1. buzz	(Oz) Oz	(Dr. Oz ®) Dr. Oz	leg _____
2. jazz	fizz _____	buzz _____	top _____
3. fuzz	jazz _____	fizz _____	a e i o u vowels _____

Directions: Find and (circle) the words.

Word Find

~~FAX~~ – SIX – MIX – JAZZ – BUZZ

S	I	X	W	B	F
T	M	C	K	U	A
R	M	I	X	Z	X
E	N	S	R	Z	A
J	A	Z	Z	V	R

Ending Consonants: zz

Directions: Fill in, say, and trace.

> fuzz – Liz – buzz

1. _____ is a girl.

2. Bees _____ in the hive.

3. FUZZ is on his chin.

4. Tom shaves the fuzz on his face.

Good job!

Yes, I (name) _____ can read!

Teacher's Guide   Unit 4 Short Vowels: Closed Syllables: 1st Syllable

Overview

The first of the six syllables is introduced in Unit 4. Its defining characteristics are a vowel which has a short sound and a syllable which ends in a consonant. Short vowel sounds, including *y*, are practiced. Blending is also introduced and practiced. Word families are listed together in lessons.

Objectives

To learn:

1. the definition of a syllable: a word or word part that has a single vowel sound, and usually has a vowel. A word has at least one syllable and has meaning, such as *me* or *a*.
2. the short vowel sounds.
3. the breve (˘) over a vowel indicates a short vowel sound.
4. associate the symbol of the pug, a short dog, with short vowel sounds and the closed syllable.
5. that one vowel sound equals one syllable.
6. that the closed syllable, the first syllable, contains a short vowel sound and ends with a consonant.
7. that they will be underlining vowel sounds . This concept lays the groundwork for dividing words into syllables and decoding unfamiliar words.
8. to blend from the vowel to the end of the word (rime), then tack on the beginning consonant (onset), and read the word.
9. the concept of word families, words that are spelled and sound the same from the vowel to the end of a word.

Instruction

1. Read through the first page of Unit 4 with your student, making sure he understands the concepts.
2. Review and practice the short vowel sounds, both in isolation and in words, using the chart. See the Unit 1 Teacher's Guide for mouth position, distinct vowel sounds, and their associations. Elicit additional words from your student, and listen for correct pronunciation.
3. Model and have your student practice the blending method at the bottom of the page and as follows:
   1. Sound out the word from the vowel to the end of the word (rime).
   2. Add the beginning consonant (onset).
   3. Blend the word together.
   4. Read the word.
      Using the same procedure, replace the beginning consonant with other consonants and sound out each word. Have the student repeat unit his pronunciation is correct. Using letter cards, switch consonants at the beginning of each word family to make new words. Direct the student to read each new word after the substitution is made.
4. Review the format, then the content, of the lessons, noting the blending method at the bottom of each page. The learner should utilize the blending method, aloud, to sound out words in the lesson if it is necessary. It also provides blending practice. To complete the lesson the student should say the word, note the illustration and phonetic pronunciation ("Sounds like" column), to help him decode

the word. In the fourth column, he is to say and trace the larger (18-point), light gray word. In the last column, he is to say the word, write it on the line, and underline the vowel sound.

5. After the student has finished the short *a* lesson, you can work on additional short *a* word families or wait until he finishes all of the Unit 4 lessons before extending the lessons. Blending and word family practice reinforces the student's short vowel sound knowledge. Furthermore, it supports the student's vocabulary acquisition.

Word Families

Short *a*: An example of the short *a* word family in the first exercise is *at*: *at, hat, cat, bat, fat, rat,* and *sat*. Ask him to supply additional words in the same word family, using letter cards. Other word families in this lesson are *at* and *ad*. To expand on the lesson, supply a word family or ask your student for another such as *ap*: *map, sap, rap, cap, nap, lap, trap, clap,* etc. Other word families include *ab, ad, ag, am, an,* and *ap*.

Short *e*: Emphasize the short *e* sound in each word family. Continue with word families for short *e*: *eg, en, es,* and *et,* that are in the lesson and *ex* and *ell* which are not. Words for *ex*: *hex, Mex, Tex, Rex, sex*. Words for the *ell* word family include *bell, dell, fell, sell, tell,* and *yell*.

Short *i* word families in the lesson are *it, in, id, ill, ilk, ix,* and *im*. Those that are not in the lesson include *ib, ick, ig, ip, iss, ip,* etc.

Short *o* word families in Unit 4 are *on, ot, op, ock,* and *ox*. Those that are not in the lesson include *ob, od,* and *og*.

Short *u* word families include *ut, un, up, us, ub, ud,* and *um*. Those that are not in a lesson include *uck, uff, ug,* etc.

Assessment

Correct assigned pages and review problem areas with your student. He should be able to read words in each lesson and the sentences in the review exercise at the end of Unit 4.

Unit 4: Short Vowels: Closed Syllables: 1ˢᵗ Syllable

A syllable /sĭl´•ŭ•bŭl/ is a word or word part. It has 1 vowel sound. 1 vowel sound = 1 underline = 1 syllable

Examples:

<u>a</u>t

c<u>a</u>t

The closed syllable has a short vowel sound and ends with a consonant.

Examples:

up

sun

Hint: The breve (˘) /brĕv/ on the top of the vowel tells you it has a short vowel sound.

Short vowel sound	Word	Illustration
ă	at, cat	
ĕ	egg, pen	
ĭ	in, sit	
ŏ	on, hot	
ŭ	up, sun	

Directions: Sound out the word from the vowel to the end. Then say the beginning consonant. Then sound out the word.

Examples:

hat   ă t   h   h ă t

bat   ă t   b    b ă t

Short Vowels: a /ă/

Word	Illustration	Sounds like	Say and trace the word.	Say and write the word and underline the vowel sound.
1. at		ăt	at	<u>a</u>t
2. hat		hăt	hat	_____
3. cat		kăt	cat	_____
4. bat		băt	bat	_____
5. fat		făt	fat	_____
6. rat		răt	rat	_____
7. sat		săt	sat	_____
8. ad		ăd	ad	_____
9. add	+	ăd	add	_____
10. sad		săd	sad	_____

ăt

Word	at	Blend
cat	at	c + at
rat	at	r + at

Short Vowels: e /ĕ/

Word	Illustration	Sounds like	Say 📢 and trace 👆 the word.	Say 📢 and write ✍ the word and underline the vowel sound.
1. egg		ĕg	egg	egg
2. pen		pĕn	pen	_____
3. yes		yĕs	yes	_____
4. leg		lĕg	leg	_____
5. net		nĕt	net	_____
6. ten	10	tĕn	ten	_____
7. help		hĕlp	help	_____
8. pet		pĕt	pet	_____
9. let		lĕt	let	_____
10. bed		bĕd	bed	_____

📢 ĕt

Word	et	Blend
net	et	n + et
pet	et	p + et
let	et	l + et

Short Vowels: i /ĭ/

Word	Illustration	Sounds like	Say and trace the word.	Say and write the word and underline the vowel sound.
1. it		ĭt	it	it
2. mitt		mĭt	mitt	_____
3. sit		sĭt	sit	_____
4. in		ĭn	in	_____
5. pin		pĭn	pin	_____
6. lid		lĭd	lid	_____
7. hill		hĭl	hill	_____
8. milk		mĭlk	milk	_____
9. six		sĭks	six	_____
10. swim		swĭm	swim	_____

 ĭd

Word	ĭd	Blend
lid	id	l + id
kid	id	k + id

Short Vowels: o /ŏ/

Word	Illustration	Sounds like	Say and trace the word.	Say and write the word and underline the vowel sound.
1. on		ŏn	on	<u>o</u>n
2. hot		hŏt	hot	_____
3. pot		pŏt	pot	_____
4. not		nŏt	not	_____
5. top		tŏp	top	_____
6. stop		stŏp	stop	_____
7. lock		lŏk	lock	_____
8. sock		sŏk	sock	_____
9. clock		klŏk	clock	_____
10. box		bŏks	box	_____

ŏt

Word	ŏt	Blend
pot	ot	p + ot
hot	ot	h + ot
not	ot	n + ot

150

Short Vowels: u /ŭ/

Word	Illustration	Sounds like	Say and trace the word.	Say and write the word and underline the vowel sound.
1. cut		kŭt	cut	c<u>u</u>t
2. sun		sŭn	sun	_____
3. run		rŭn	run	_____
4. up		ŭp	up	_____
5. cup		kŭp	cup	_____
6. us		ŭs	us	_____
7. bus		bŭs	bus	_____
8. tub		tŭb	tub	_____
9. mud		mŭd	mud	_____
10. gum		gŭm	gum	_____

ŭn

Word	ŭn	Blend
sun	un	s + un
run	un	r + un

151

Short Vowels: Review

Directions: Look at the picture. (Circle) the word that matches the

picture. Say and write it on the line.

10 (ten) - hat <u>ten</u>	 milk - leg _____	 bus - box _____
   hill - help _____	 swim - pen _____	 sad - tub _____
   gas - pet _____	 clock - lock _____	 sock - on _____

Short Vowels: y

The vowels are a, e, i, o, u and sometimes /sūm'• tīmz/ y. When y is within

/wĭth•ĭn'/ a word, it mostly /mōst'•lē/ sounds like a short i /ĭ/ as in gym.

When y does <u>not</u> begin ⊘ a word, it is a vowel. *

Word	Illustration	Sounds like	Say 🔊 and trace ✍ the word.
1. gym		jĭm	gym
2. syrup		sĭr'• ŭp	syrup
3. syringe		sĭr•ĭnj'	syringe
4. symbol	chair	sĭm'•bŭl	symbol
5. cymbals		sĭm'•bŭlz	cymbals
6. pyramid		pîr'•ŭ•mĭd	pyramid
7. syllable	syl	sĭl'•ŭ•bŭl	syllable

* If y begins a word, it is a consonant.

Short Vowels: Review

Directions: Say and read.

1. His mitt is in the gym.

2. Ten bats and six mitts are in the gym.

3. The man in the cap has a bat.

4. Tug on the rug.

5. Pat, a fat cat, sat on a mat.

6. The hen has an egg.

7. Mud is on the man's leg.

---

8. The ham is in the hot pot.

9. The lid is on the big hot pot.

10. It is hot.

11. If he is not sick, Rick is on the job at six a.m.

12. The tot gets a bath in the tub.

13. Ted is in bed.

14. The hat is on the bed.

15. If he is not sick, Ron gets up at six a.m. for his job.

 Good job! Go on!

Overview

Long vowel sounds in words are introduced with the quiet *e* syllable, the second syllable type. Its defining characteristic is a silent *e* at the end of a word which is preceded by a long vowel as in *tape*.

Objectives

To learn:

1. the long vowel sounds.
2. the 2nd syllable, which is the quiet *e* syllable and contains long vowel sounds.
3. that the macron indicates a long vowel sound.

To understand:

4. that the silent *e* at word's end makes the preceding vowel long.
5. that the *e* that ends a word in this syllable should not be underlined because it does not make a vowel sound.
6. that the headers on each page indicate the word family spelling and its phonetic pronunciation in slash marks, such as the word family *ake* /āk/ as in *lake*, *take*, etc.

Instruction

1. Draw students' attention to the dachshund symbol, (a long dog) to visualize and associate with long vowel sounds and the macron which indicates the same in phonetic pronunciations.
2. Use the information on the first page of Unit 5 to teach the quiet *e* syllable. To help him or her remember, say: "The *e* at the end of the word is silent, or quiet, but it has a job to do. It makes the preceding vowel long." Emphasize that the long vowel is underlined because it makes a sound, while the *e* at the end of the word is not underlined because it does not make a sound.
3. Draw your student's attention to page headers that indicate the featured word family in each lesson, such as the word family *ake* and its phonetic pronunciation /āk/. If the learner can read the completed example, he or she may be able to complete the lesson independently. In doing the lesson, if the learner struggles to read a word, lead him to do the following: First, practice sounding out the word from the vowel to the end of the syllable; second, tack on the beginning consonant or blend; and third, read the word aloud.

   Students should complete assigned lessons and subsequent exercises, one lesson at a time at first. If learners can read but fail to comprehend any word(s) in a lesson after using the picture clues, discuss the word until it is understood, use it in a sentence, recall synonyms, make flash cards, etc. If the word has more than one meaning, and your learner understands how it is most often used, discuss its other meanings.

4. On page 193, read aloud with your student and have him repeat the conjugation of the verb *drive*, reading down the first column, then the second, and finally the third column. Discuss the tenses and the changing verb forms. This drill helps familiarize students with tenses and proper usage,

especially of irregular verbs. The learner can then complete the exercise following the conjugation chart. He or she should read the sentence aloud as words are traced. Then the student should read the completed sentence aloud. Subvocalizing is fine.

Assessment

Students should be able to read featured words aloud and read the sentences at the end of the lessons.

Vocabulary Acquisition Strategies

Multiple Meaning Words

Multiple meaning words in Unit 5 are too numerous to list, but the following words are illustrated and/or used in sentences to indicate their different meanings: *broke, spoke, fire, cube, plume,* and *phone.* Additional multiple meaning words in Unit 5 include but are not limited to the following: *case, crane, wake, ape, base, date, state, blade, grade, shade, save, wave, grave, fine, time, pipe, swipe, hide, side, ride, slide, like, file, drive, tire, dope, tube, use,* and *crude.* Multiple meaning words can be read, discussed, used in sentences, etc.

Flash Cards

Make flash cards for troublesome words which the student reviews daily. Each time you see her one-on-one, review the words with her, adding troublesome words to her stack of cards and to the vocabulary list in her notebook. When you are certain she has mastered a word, remove it from the stack and give it to her to save. As you know, words of encouragement and congratulations go a long way, so be generous with them. As soon as she knows enough words, she can create written sentences using featured words, or you can dictate sentences for her to write. Extra space on workbook pages can be used for dictation and/or spelling practice.

Unit 5: Long Vowels : Quiet e

Long vowels say their /thair/ names.

Example:

Vowel	Sounds like	Illustration
1. a	say	
2. e	key	
3. i	I, hi!	
4. o	oh!	
5. u	you	

Some long vowels have a quiet e at the end of the word. The e is quiet, and the vowel that comes before it is long.

Example: tape   /tāp/

cake   /kāk/

The words tape and cake have 1 vowel sound, so they have 1 syllable. They are one-syllable words. The quiet e at the end does not get an underline /ŭn'•dŭr•līn/.

> 1 vowel sound = 1 syllable = 1 underline

Examples: tape
cake

Hint: The macron (‾) /mā'•krŏn/ on the top of the vowel tells you it has a a long vowel sound.

Long Vowels: ake /āk/

Word	Illustration	Sounds like	Say and trace the word.	Say and write the word and underline the vowel sound.
1. lake		lāk	lake	lake
2. take		tāk	take	_____
3. make		māk	make	_____
4. wake		wāk	wake	_____
5. brake		brāk	brake	_____
6. flake		flāk	flake	_____
7. shake		shāk	shake	_____
8. snake		snāk	snake	_____

Long Vowels: a_e

Directions: Look at the picture. Circle the word that matches the picture. Say and write it on the line.

| tape - brake | lake - wake | brake - flake |
| tape | _____ | _____ |

| flake - snake | cane - lake | brake - take |
| _____ | _____ | _____ |

Long Vowels: ale /āl/

Word	Illustration	Sounds like	Say and trace the word.	Say and write the word and underline the vowel sound.
1. male		māl	male	m<u>a</u>le
2. sale		sāl	sale	_____
3. tale		tāl	tale	_____
4. scale		skāl	scale	_____

Directions: Say and trace.

1. A man is a male.
2. The ham is on the scale.

Long Vowels: ame /ām/

Word	Illustration	Sounds like	Say and trace the word.	Say and write the word and underline the vowel sound.
1. game		gām	game	g<u>a</u>me
2. name		nām	name	_____
3. same		sām	same	_____
4. flame		flām	flame	_____
5. frame		frām	frame	_____

Directions: Trace and write.

My name is _____ _____.

Long Vowels: ane /ān/

Word	Illustration	Sounds like	Say and trace the word.	Say and write the word and underline the vowel sound.
1. cane		kān	cane	c<u>a</u>ne
2. mane		mān	mane	_____
3. lane		lān	lane	_____
4. pane		pān	pane	_____
5. crane		krān	crane	_____

Long Vowels: a_e

Directions: Look at the picture. (Circle) the word that matches the picture. Say and write it on the line.

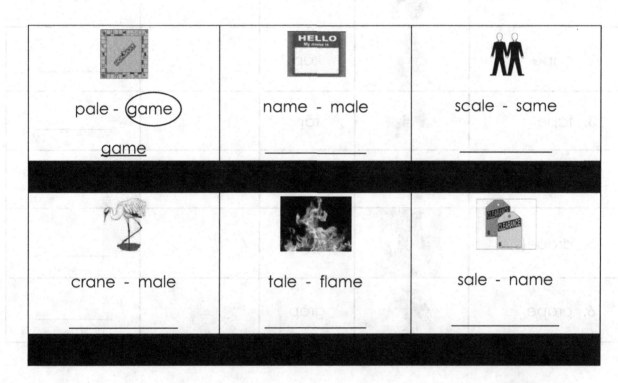

pale - (game)	name - male	scale - same
game	_____	_____
crane - male	tale - flame	sale - name
_____	_____	_____

Directions: Fill in the missing word and read the sentence.

| cane – lane – crane – plane |

1. Run up the l _ _ _.

2. The cr_ _ _ is big.

3. He needs a c_ _ _ to walk.

4. The jet pl_ _ _ is fast.

Long Vowels: ape /āp/

Word	Illustration	Sounds like	Say and trace the word.	Say and write the word and underline the vowel sound.
1. ape		āp	ape	<u>a</u>pe
2. cape		kāp	cape	_____
3. tape		tāp	tape	_____
4. shape		shāp	shape	_____
5. drape(s)		drāp (s)	drape(s)	_____
6. grape		grāp	grape	_____

Directions: Say and trace.

1. This is a box shape.

2. Tape the box shut.

3. Jan has a cape.

Long Vowels: a_e

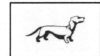

Directions: Find and circle the words.

Word Find

~~SALE~~ – SCALE – TAKE – SAME – MAKE – BRAKE

S	C	A	L	E	T
A	M	A	K	E	A
L	S	A	M	E	K
E	B	R	A	K	E

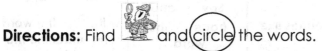

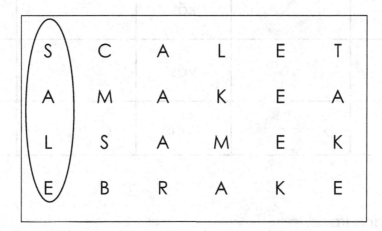

Long Vowels: ase /ās/

Word	Illustration	Sounds like	Say and trace the word.	Say and write the word and underline the vowel sound.
1. base		bās	base	b<u>a</u>se
2. case		kās	case	_____
3. vase		vās	vase	_____
4. chase		chās	chase	_____

Directions: Say and trace.

1. Run to the base.

2. Chase the dog.

Long Vowels: ate /āt/

Word	Illustration	Sounds like	Say and trace the word.	Say and write the word and underline the vowel sound.
1. ate		āt	ate	<u>a</u>te
2. date		dāt	date	_____
3. gate		gāt	gate	_____
4. late		lāt	late	_____
5. mate		māt	mate	_____
6. rate		rāt	rate	_____
7. plate		plāt	plate	_____
8. skate		skāt	skate	_____
9. state		stāt	state	_____
10. crate		krāt	crate	_____

Long Vowels: ate /āt/

Directions: Say and trace.

1. Dan skates.

2. I ate on the plane.

3. I met my date at 8 o'clock.

4. The duck sits with his mate.

Directions: Match the word and picture.
chair

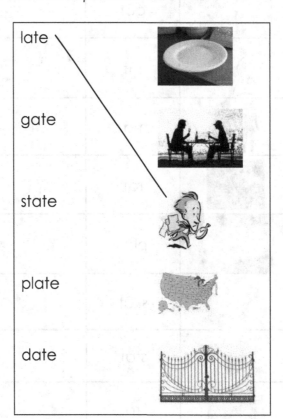

late

gate

state

plate

date

Long Vowels: ade /ād/

Word	Illustration	Sounds like	Say and trace the word.	Say and write the word and underline the vowel sound.
1. blade		blād	blade	bl<u>a</u>de
2. grade		grād	grade	_____
3. shade		shād	shade	_____
4. spade		spād	spade	_____
5. trade		trād	trade	_____

Directions: Say and trace.

1. That blade will cut.
2. An "A" is a good grade.
3. It is hot. Sit in the shade.
4. This card is a spade.
5. Ron will sell or trade his car.
6. Pull the shade or close the drapes.

 Good job, (your name) _____.
You rate an "A"!

Long Vowels: ave /āv/

Word	Illustration	Sounds like	Say and trace the word.	Say and write the word and underline the vowel sound.
1. save		sāv	save	s<u>a</u>ve
2. wave		wāv	wave	_____
3. shave		shāv	shave	_____
4. grave		grāv	grave	_____
5. crave		krāv	crave	_____
6. brave		brāv	brave	_____

Long Vowels: ave /āv/

Directions: Look at the picture. (Circle) the word that matches the

picture. Say and write it on the line.

rave - (brave)	shave - crave	shave - wave
brave	_____	_____
shave - wave	wave - grave	crave - brave
_____	_____	_____

Long Vowels: ine /īn/

Word	Illustration	Sounds like	Say and trace the word.	Say and write the word and underline the vowel sound.
1. line	————	līn	line	l<u>i</u>ne
2. nine	9	nīn	nine	———
3. pine		pīn	pine	———
4. vine		vīn	vine	———
5. mine		mīn	mine	———
6. fine		fīn	fine	———
7. wine		wīn	wine	———
8. whine		wīn	whine	———
9. shine		shīn	shine	———
10. twine		twīn	twine	———

Long Vowels: ine /īn/

Directions: Look at the picture. (Circle) the word that matches the picture. Say and write it on the line.

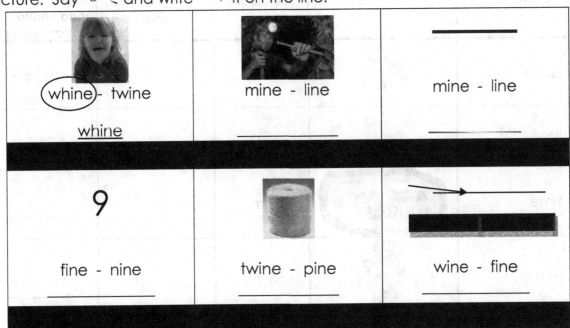

(whine) - twine	mine - line	mine - line
whine	_____	_____
9		
fine - nine	twine - pine	wine - fine
_____	_____	_____

Directions: Say and trace.

1. I am fine.
2. This box is mine.

Directions: Trace, fill in, and read.

1. How do you feel? Do you feel fine?

    Yes, I feel fine.

2. Is twine a thin rope?

    Yes, tw_ _ _ is a th_ _ rope.

3. Can you tie the box with rope or twine?

    Yes, I can tie the b_ _ with _ _ _ _ _.

 Good job, (your name) _____.
You shine!

Long Vowels: ime /īm/

Word	Illustration	Sounds like	Say and trace the word.	Say and write the word and underline the vowel sound.
1. dime		dīm	dime	d<u>i</u>me
2. lime		līm	lime	_____
3. time		tīm	time	_____
4. mime		mīm	mime	_____
5. crime		krīm	crime	_____
6. prime		prīm	prime	_____

Directions: Fill in the blanks.

prime – lime – dime – time

1. Gum is a d_ _ _.
2. The t_ _ _ is 2 p.m.
3. A l_ _ _ is green.
4. Pr_ _ _ rib is beef.

Long Vowels: ipe /īp/

Word	Illustration	Sounds like	Say and trace the word.	Say and write the word and underline the vowel sound.
1. pipe		pīp	pipe	p<u>i</u>pe
2. ripe		rīp	ripe	_____
3. wipe		wīp	wipe	_____
4. gripe		grīp	gripe	_____
5. swipe		swīp	swipe	_____

Directions: Say and trace.

1. A ripe apple is good.

2. Swipe your card.

Long Vowels: ide /īd/

Word	Illustration	Sounds like	Say and trace the word.	Say and write the word and underline the vowel sound.
1. hide		hīd	hide	h<u>i</u>de
2. side		sīd	side	_____
3. wide		wīd	wide	_____
4. glide		glīd	glide	_____
5. tide		tīd	tide	_____
6. ride		rīd	ride	_____
7. slide		slīd	slide	_____

Directions: Say and trace.

1. We slide on a sled.

2. The baby is on his side.

3. The skates glide on the ice.

Long Vowels: ike /īk/

Word	Illustration	Sounds like	Say and trace the word.	Say and write the word and underline the vowel sound.
1. bike		bīk	bike	bi_ke
2. hike		hīk	hike	_____
3. Mike		mīk	Mike	_____
4. like		līk	like	_____
5. strike		strīk	strike	_____

Directions: Say and trace.

1. Ride your bike.

2. I like your bike.

3. Mike is a man.

4. Hike up the hill.

Long Vowels: i_e

Directions: Match the word and picture.

chair

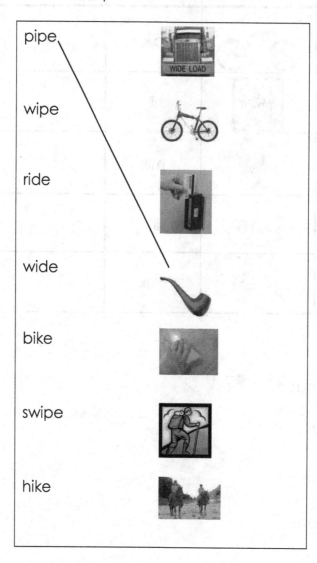

pipe

wipe

ride

wide

bike

swipe

hike

Long Vowels: ile / īl/

Word	Illustration	Sounds like	Say and trace the word.	Say and write the word and underline the vowel sound.
1. file		fīl	file	f<u>i</u>le
2. pile		pīl	pile	_____
3. tile		tīl	tile	_____
4. mile		mīl	mile	_____
5. smile		smīl	smile	_____

Directions: Say and trace.

1. I can run a mile.

2. The pile of books is on the desk.

3. File the bills.

Long Vowels: ite /īt/

Word	Illustration	Sounds like	Say and trace the word.	Say and write the word and underline the vowel sound.
1. kite		kīt	kite	kite
2. bite		bīt	bite	_____
3. white		wīt	white	_____
4. write		rīt	write	_____

Directions: Say and trace.

1. Bite the apple.

2. Fly your kite.

3. Write your name: _____ _____.

180

Long Vowels: ive /īv/

Word	Illustration	Sounds like	Say and trace the word.	Say and write the word and underline the vowel sound.
1. dive		dīv	dive	d<u>i</u>ve
2. five	5	fīv	five	_____
3. hive		hīv	hive	_____
4. drive		drīv	drive	_____

Directions: Fill in the blank.

> dive – drive – five - hive

1. I like to dr_ _ _ my car.

2. Bees go in the h_ _ _.

3. It is f_ _ _ o'clock.

4. D_ _ _ into the lake.

Long Vowels: i_e

Directions: Find  and circle the words.

Word Find

DRIVE – DIVE – SMILE – MILE – TILE

S	O	A	W	C	D	D
M	I	L	E	V	R	I
I	N	U	S	C	I	V
L	T	I	L	E	V	E
E	O	M	B	D	E	W

Long Vowels: ife /īf/

Word	Illustration	Sounds like	Say and trace the word.	Say and write the word and underline the vowel sound.
1. knife		nīf	knife	kn<u>i</u>fe
2. wife		wīf	wife	_____

Directions: Say and trace.

1. Cut it with a knife.

2. This is my wife, Mrs. Torres /Tôr´•ĕz/; we have a good life.

Long Vowels: ice /īs/

Word	Illustration	Sounds like	Say and trace the word.	Say and write the word and underline the vowel sound.
1. ice		īs	ice	i̲ce
2. mice		mīs	mice	_____
3. rice		rīs	rice	_____
4. lice		līs	lice	_____
5. nice		nīs	nice	_____
6. price		prīs	price	_____
7. spice		spīs	spice	_____
8. twice	x2	twīs	twice	_____

Directions: Say and trace.

1. The price of the dress is $25.
2. I like ice in my tea.
3. Be nice to the cat.
4. We ran the mile twice: we ran 2 miles.
5. Mice eat rice.

Long Vowels: ire /īr/

Word	Illustration	Sounds like	Say and trace the word.	Say and write the word and underline the vowel sound.
1. fire		fīr	fire	f<u>i</u>re
2. tire		tīr	tire	_____
3. wire		wīr	wire	_____
4. hire		hīr	hire	_____

fire

fire

Directions: Say and trace.

1. I will hire you for the job, not fire you.
2. Cut the wire for the lamp.
3. My car has a new tire.
4. Fire is hot.

Long Vowels: i_e

Directions: Say and trace.

1. A man and his wife went for a ride.
2. It is five after nine.
3. A knife will cut the vine.
4. Mike wipes his boots.

Directions: Look at the picture. Say and write the word.

hive – price – knife – rice – mile – smile – line – pile

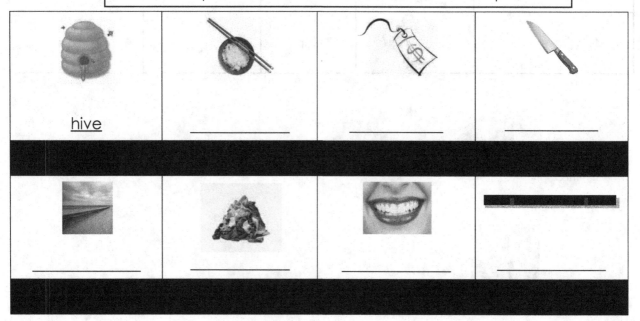

hive

_____

_____

_____

_____

_____

_____

Directions: Say and read.

Mike likes to hike with his bike. He has a bite of rice. He naps under a pine tree. He dives in the lake. Mike smiles.

Long Vowels: oke   /ōk/

Word	Illustration	Sounds like	Say and trace the word.	Say and write the word and underline the vowel sound.
1. Coke®		kōk	Coke	C<u>o</u>ke
2. joke		jōk	joke	_____
3. smoke		smōk	smoke	_____
4. broke		brōk	broke	_____
5. choke		chōk	choke	_____
6. spoke		spōk	spoke	_____
7. stroke		strōk	stroke	_____

Directions: Look at the picture. Say and write the word.

<u>smoke</u>	_____	_____
_____	_____	_____

Long Vowels: oke /ōk/

Directions: Say and trace.

Past tense

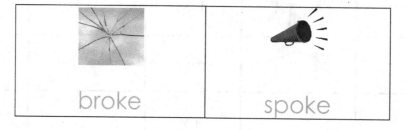

broke

spoke

Directions: Say and read.

1. I broke a glass.

2. Ann spoke to Al.

3. The spoke on my bike broke.

4. I am broke.

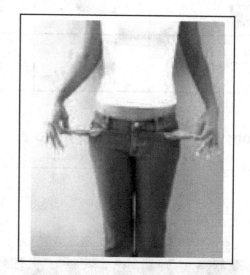

Long Vowels: obe /ōb/

Word	Illustration	Sounds like	Say and trace the word.	Say and write the word and underline the vowel sound.
1. robe		rōb	robe	r<u>o</u>be
2. lobe		lōb	lobe	_____
3. globe		glōb	globe	_____
4. probe		prōb	probe	_____

Directions: Match the word and picture.   chair

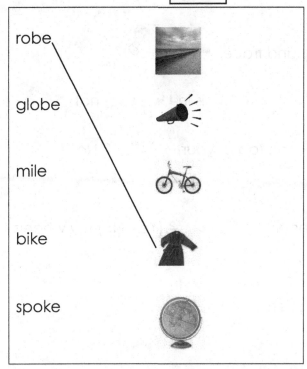

robe

globe

mile

bike

spoke

Long Vowels: ome /ōm/

Word	Illustration	Sounds like	Say and trace the word.	Say and write the word and underline the vowel sound.
1. home		hōm	home	h<u>o</u>me
2. dome		dōm	dome	_____
3. Nome		nōm	Nome	_____
4. Rome		rōm	Rome	_____
5. chrome		krōm	chrome	_____

Directions: (Circle) say and trace.

1. The pope's home is in Rome, not Nome.

2. Is a dome on top of your home? No. A dome is not on top of my home.

3. Are your wheels chrome? (Yes, No) my wheels (are, are not) chrome.

4. My house is my home.

Long Vowels: ote /ōt/

Word	Illustration	Sounds like	Say and trace the word.	Say and write the word and underline the vowel sound.
1. note		nōt	note	n<u>o</u>te
2. vote		vōt	vote	_____
3. wrote		rōt	wrote	_____
4. quote		kwōt	quote	_____
5. tote		tōt	tote	_____

Directions: Say and trace.

1. Write a note.

2. I will stop at the shop to get grapes.

Directions: Read and say.

1. I wrote a note to tell you I went to vote.

2. Do not quote me.

3. Take a tote bag with you.

Long Vowels: ove /ōv/

Word	Illustration	Sounds like	Say and trace the word.	Say and write the word and underline the vowel sound.
1. dove 		dōv	dove	d<u>o</u>ve
2. drove		drōv	drove	_____
3. wove		wōv	wove	_____
4. cove		kōv	cove	_____
5. clove		klōv	clove	_____
6. grove		grōv	grove	_____
7. stove		stōv	stove	_____

Long Vowels: ive /īv/

Drive

Today Present	Yesterday Past	Past with have/has
I drive	I drove	I have driven
you drive	you drove	you have driven
he, she, it drives	he, she, it drove	he, she, it has driven
we drive	we drove	we have driven
you drive	you drove	you have driven
they drive	they drove	they have driven

Directions: Say and trace.

1. I drive to work.

2. Drive the car.

3. Al drives the car well.

4. We drove to the cove in 1 car.

5. I drove to the cove in my car.

6. He and she drove to the cove.

7. They will drive the van.

8. Clive drives fast.

Long Vowels: o_e

Directions: Look at the picture. Circle the word that matches the picture. Say and write it on the line.

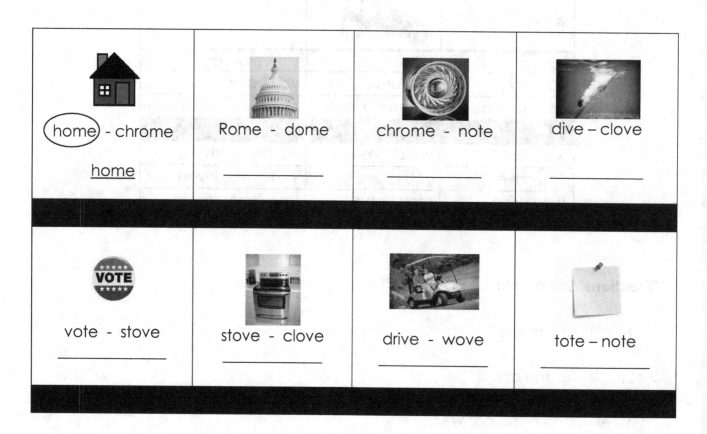

(home) - chrome	Rome - dome	chrome - note	dive – clove
home	_____	_____	_____
vote - stove	stove - clove	drive - wove	tote – note
_____	_____	_____	_____

Long Vowels: ope /ōp/

Word	Illustration	Sounds like	Say and trace the word.	Say and write the word and underline the vowel sound.
1. rope		rōp	rope	rope
2. pope		pōp	pope	_____
3. dope		dōp	dope	_____
4. scope		skōp	scope	_____
5. slope		slōp	slope	_____

Directions: Say and trace.

1. The pope's home is not in Nome. It is in Rome.

2. The pope is in Rome, not Nome.

3. A slope is a slant.

4. The side of the hill is a slant, or a slope.

Long Vowels: ole /ōl/

Word	Illustration	Sounds like	Say and trace the word.	Say and write the word and underline the vowel sound.
1. hole		hōl	hole	h<u>o</u>le
2. mole		mōl	mole	_____
3. pole		pōl	pole	_____
4. stole		stōl	stole	_____
5. whole		hōl	whole	_____

Directions: Say and trace.

1. The dog dug a hole.

2. Is that a mole on your face?

3. The flag is up the pole.

Directions: Match the word and picture. chair

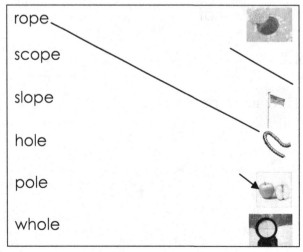

rope

scope

slope

hole

pole

whole

Long Vowels: one /ōn/

Word	Illustration	Sounds like	Say 📢 and trace ✍ the word.	Say 📢 and write ✍ the word and underline the vowel sound.
1. bone		bōn	bone	b<u>o</u>ne
2. cone		kōn	cone	_____
3. zone	SPEED ZONE AHEAD	zōn	zone	_____
4. stone		stōn	stone	_____
5. phone		fōn	phone	_____

Directions: Match the word and picture. | chair |

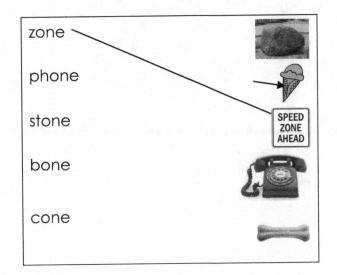

zone

phone

stone

bone

cone

Long Vowels: one /ōn/

Directions: Say, trace, and write.

1. The dog has a _____ (phone, bone).

2. I spoke to Rose on my cell _____ (phone, bone).

3. Phone your mom.

4. Phone your boss.

5. Ribs have bones.

6. Tim fell and broke a bone, a rib.

Long Vowels: ose /ōz/

Word	Illustration	Sounds like	Say and trace the word.	Say and write the word and underline the vowel sound.
1. nose		nōz	nose	n<u>o</u>se
2. hose		hōz	hose	_____
3. rose		rōz	rose	_____
4. close		klōz	close	_____
5. chose		chōz	chose	_____
6. those		thōz	those	_____

Directions: Say and trace.

1. I chose those roses.

2. Your nose is on your face.

3. Please close the door.

4. The hose has a hole in it.

Long Vowels: Review o_e

Directions: Look at the picture. Circle the word that matches the picture. Say and write it on the line.

(nose) - hose **nose**	hose - close _____	those - nose _____
pole - hole _____	hole - phone _____	zone - mole _____
cove - stove _____	wrote - note _____	home - robe _____

Directions: Circle, fill in, say, and write.

I dug a hole. Have you dug a hole? Yes or no?

(Yes or No), I (have, have not) _____ a _____.

Long Vowels: Review o_e

Directions: Find  and (circle) the words.

Word Find

| ~~BONE~~ – PHONE – NO – ZONE – WHOLE - HOSE |

W	L	R	U	S	S	B
H	O	S	E	T	T	W
O	Q	P	H	O	N	E
L	U	B	K	V	X	L
E	R	O	S	E	O	M
Z	O	N	E	H	B	N
R	M	E	W	C	N	O

Long Vowels: ube /ūb/

Word	Illustration	Sounds like	Say and trace the word.	Say and write the word and underline the vowel sound.
1. cube		kūb	cube	c_ube
2. tube		tōob	tube	_____
3. lube		lōob	lube	_____

Directions: Say and trace.

1. I will get a lube job on my car.

2. The tire has a tube in it.

3. I like ice cubes in my tea, in my iced tea.

4. A cube has six sides.

ice cube

cube

Long Vowels: uke /ūk/ /o͞ok/

Word	Illustration	Sounds like	Say and trace the word.	Say and write the word and underline the vowel sound.
1. Duke®		do͞ok	Duke	Duke
2. nuke		no͞ok	nuke	_____
3. Luke		lo͞ok	Luke	_____
4. cuke		kūk	cuke	_____

Long Vowels: use /ūz/

| 1. use | | ūz | use | use |
| 2. fuse | | fūz | fuse | _____ |

Directions: Say and trace.

1. Place the fuse in the fuse box.

2. The fuse box uses fuses.

3. I use my cell to phone home.

4. I use tools at work.

Long Vowels: ute /ūt/, /o͞ot/

Word	Illustration	Sounds like	Say 📢 and trace ✍ the word.	Say 📢 and write ✍ the word and underline the vowel sound.
1. cute		kūt	cute	c<u>u</u>te
2. mute		mūt	mute	_____
3. flute		flo͞ot	flute	_____
4. brute		bro͞ot	brute	_____
5. chute		sho͞ot	chute	_____

Directions: Fill in the blanks.

> cute – chute – brute - flute

1. The Ch_ _ _ s and Ladders© game is fun.

2. Ben is a br_ _ _ .

3. Pat has a fl_ _ _ .

4. Pups are c_ _ _ .

Long Vowels: une /o͞on /

Word	Illustration	Sounds like	Say and trace the word.	Say and write the word and underline the vowel sound.
1. tune		to͞on	tune	t<u>u</u>ne
2. June		Jo͞on	June	_____
3. prune		pro͞on	prune	_____

Directions: Fill in the blanks.

June – prune – tune

1. A pr_ _ _ is a fruit.

2. It is hot in J_ _ _ .

3. Hum a t_ _ _ .

Directions: Say and trace.

Luke and Duke are cute.

Long Vowels: ude /ōod/

Word	Illustration	Sounds like	Say and trace the word.	Say and write the word and underline the vowel sound.
1. nude		nōod	nude	n<u>u</u>de
2. dude		dōod	dude	_____
3. rude		rōod	rude	_____
4. crude		krōod	crude	_____
5. prude		prōod	prude	_____

Directions: Say and trace.

1. A crude dude is rude.

2. A rude dude is crude.

Long Vowels: ume /ūm/, /o͞om/

Word	Illustration	Sounds like	Say and trace the word.	Say and write the word and underline the vowel sound.
1. fume		fūm	fume	f<u>u</u>me
2. flume		flo͞om	flume	_____
3. plume		plo͞om	plume	_____

Directions: Say and trace.

1. Ride the flume.
2. The mad lad fumes. To be mad is to fume.
3. My car needs a lube job. Its fumes smell.
4. A plume of smoke rose from the fire.

5.

plume

plume

Long Vowels: Review u_e

Directions: Look at the picture. (Circle) the word that matches the picture. Say and write it on the line.

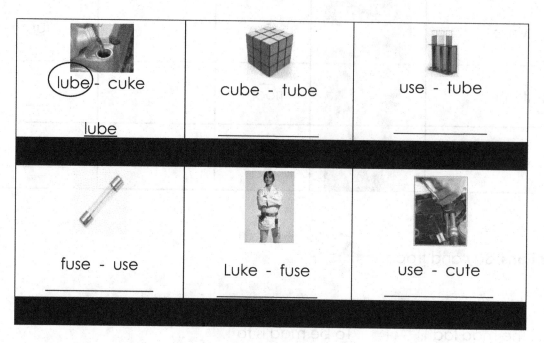

(lube)- cuke	cube - tube	use - tube
lube	_____	_____
fuse - use	Luke - fuse	use - cute
_____	_____	_____

Directions: Fill in or trace the word.

> tune – flute – prune – cubes– June - fuse

1. A pr_ _ _ is a fruit.
2. June plays a t_ _ _ on her fl_ _ _.
3. The fuse box is on the wall.
4. Ice cubes are /âr/ in the glass.

 **Congratulations! Good job!**

Overview

Unit 6 focuses on the vowel team, the third syllable. Its defining characteristic is two vowels together making one sound. Conjugations include *see*, *feed*, and *take*.

In Part 1, long vowel sounds constitute the vowel teams. Examples include *rain*, *feet*, *read*, *road*, and *yield*.

Part 2 features vowel teams with sliding sounds as does Part 3's ew and ey. These are also referred to as diphthongs, which resemble a "glide" from one sound to the other as in *oi* (*oil*), *oy* (*toy*), *ou* (*house*), *ow* (*now*), *au* (*sauce*), *aw* (*saw*), and *ay* (*tray*).

Part 3 includes ten vowel teams, some of which are diphthongs, as *ew* (*stew*), *ew* (*few*), and *ey* (*they*). It begins with long and open sounds of *oo* as in *boot* and *book*, and there are four additional spellings for the long *oo* sound as in *blue*, *stew*, *fruit*, and *soup*.

Part 3 also focuses on the last two of the three sounds of *ea*: the short *e* sound as in *head*, and long *a* sound as in *steak*. The first, the long *e* sound as in *pea*, is covered in Part 1. See Appendix A for additional *ea* words.

Objectives

Students should learn that:

1. the vowel team is the third syllable and that its defining characteristic is two vowels together making one sound.
2. the vowel teams in Part 1 have long vowel sounds.
3. one vowel sound is underlined once.

Students should be able to:

1. Complete the lessons, tracing, writing the words, and underlining vowel sounds as directed.
2. Complete the exercises following the lessons.
3. Read the featured words in the lessons.

Instruction

1. Read through the first page of Unit 6 with your students, pointing out the long vowel sounds and phonetic representations in the "Sounds like" column. In many vowel teams, such as those on this page, the first vowel is long and the second is silent. A good way to remember that is "When two vowels go walking, the first one does the talking."
2. Review the concept of a syllable being a word or word part that usually has a vowel and has one vowel sound.

3. Conjugations in Unit 6: *see*, *feed*, and *take*: Point out that some verbs are irregular in that they change their form and spelling when one expresses different tenses, as in *see*, *saw*, and *seen*. Practice correct usage aloud with students.

Assessment

After completing the lessons, students should be able to read the words in those lessons, the sentences following the exercises, and complete the practice activities following the lessons. By assigning a few pages at a time, correcting those pages, and having your student read aloud, you will assess his level of mastery, including strengths and weaknesses. Spend time on any areas or sounds that need additional work before continuing.

Vocabulary Acquisition Strategies

Multiple Meaning Words

Point out and discuss multiple meaning words in the lessons. *Beam* and *bowl* are illustrated to depict their meanings. Others are too numerous to mention, but they include *aid*, *rail*, *sail*, *tail*, *trail*, *nail*, *train*, *drawn*, *deep*, *sheet*, *coat*, *saw*, *goal*, *chief*, *pool*, *blue*, and *break*.

Word Families

Point out word families such as *rail*, *sail*, *tail*, *nail*, *trail*, etc. Ask if the student can think of additional word families. Point out that looking for word families or word chunks in words not only helps them decode words but also helps build their vocabulary.

Synonyms and Antonyms

Furnish similar and opposite-meaning words when they are encountered, such as *pail* and its synonym *bucket*.

Homonyms

Discuss homonyms as they are encountered, such as the following: *peel -peal*, *week- weak*, *feet-feat*, *beet-beat*, *meet-meat*, *sea-see*, *flea-flee*, *steal-steel*, *heal-heel*, *road-rode*, *loan-lone*, etc.

Note: *W* is a vowel when it follows *a*, *e*, or *o*, as in *cow*, *tow*, *saw*, *yawn*, *sew*, *few*, etc. *W* is a consonant if it is followed by a vowel in the same syllable, as in *won*, *win*, *was*, *want*, *winter*, *window*, etc.

Unit 6, Part 1: Vowel Teams

The vowel team, or beam team, is the 3rd syllable. The first vowel is long and the second vowel is quiet, or silent. When 2 vowels are together, they usually make 1 sound.

 Remember: A long vowel says its name. (When two vowels go walking, the first one does the talking.)

Examples:

Vowel Team	Word	Illustration	Vowel Sounds	Sounds like
ai	rain		ā	rān
	tail		ā	tāl
ee	tree		ē	trē
	feet		ē	fēt
ea	pea		ē	pē
	read		ē	rēd
oa	oats		ō	ōts
	road		ō	rōd

The two vowels work together to make one sound, so they get one underline.
rain   r<u>ai</u>n   tree   tr<u>ee</u>
These words have 1 vowel sound, so they are 1-syllable words.

A syllable is a word or word part that has a vowel sound. A vowel team is 2 vowels that work together to make 1 sound.

Part 1: ai, ee, ea, oa, ie

Vowel Teams: ai /ā/

Word	Illustration	Sounds like	Say and trace the word.	Write the word and underline the vowel sound.
1. aid		ād	aid	<u>ai</u>d
2. aim		ām	aim	_____
3. rail		rāl	rail	_____
4. sail		sāl	sail	_____
5. tail		tāl	tail	_____
6. mail		māl	mail	_____
7. pail		pāl	pail	_____

Vowel Teams: ai /ā/

Word	Illustration	Sounds like	Say and trace the word.	Write the word and underline the vowel sound.
8. nail		nāl	nail	n<u>ai</u>l
9. jail		jāl	jail	_____
10. trail		trāl	trail	_____
11. snail		snāl	snail	_____
12. frail		frāl	frail	_____
13. rain		rān	rain	_____
14. train		trān	train	_____

Vowel Teams: ai /ā/

Star (☆) words:

Word	Illustration	Sounds like	Say and trace the word.	Write the word and underline the vowel sound.
1. laid		lād	laid	l<u>ai</u>d
2. paid		pād	paid	_____
3. raid		rād	raid	_____

Vowel Teams: ai

Directions: Trace. Then say and read.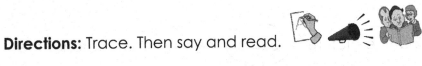

 lay = to put or set

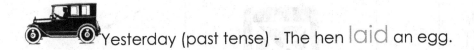 Yesterday (past tense) - The hen laid an egg.

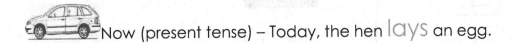 Now (present tense) – Today, the hen lays an egg.

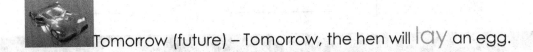 Tomorrow (future) – Tomorrow, the hen will lay an egg.

Yesterday, Mom laid the baby down for his nap.

Today, Mom lays down the baby for his nap.

Tomorrow, Mom will lay down the baby for his nap.

Yesterday, Tom paid his bill.

Today, Tom pays his bill.

Tomorrow, Tom will pay his bill.

Vowel Teams: ai

Directions: Look at the picture. (Circle) the word that matches the

picture. Say and write it on the line.

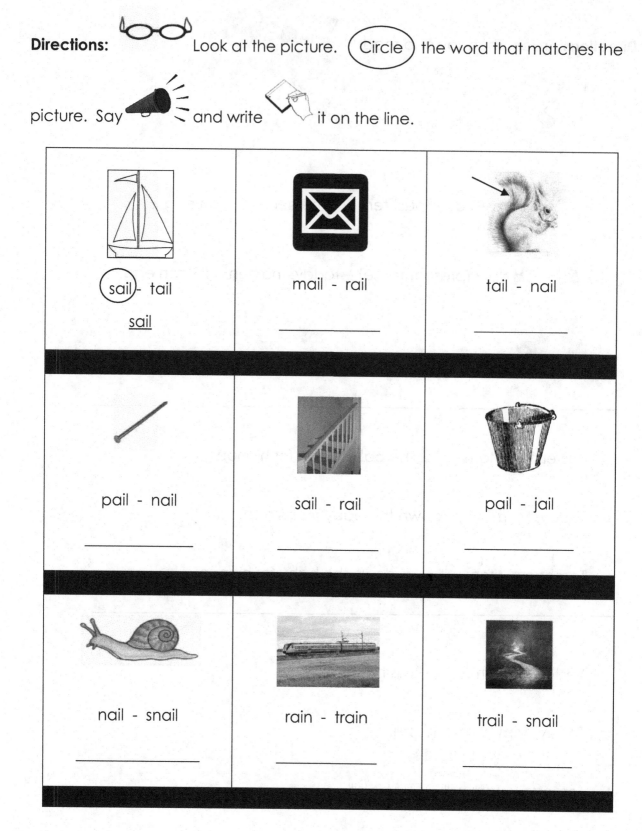

(sail) - tail <u>sail</u>	mail - rail _____	tail - nail _____
pail - nail _____	sail - rail _____	pail - jail _____
nail - snail _____	rain - train _____	trail - snail _____

Vowel Teams: ai

Directions: Fill in, read, and say.

paid – train – aid – nail – mail

1. Bill gets first _ _d for his cut.

2. Pat aims as he hits the n_ _ _ .

3. The tr_ _ _ is on time.

4. Matt likes to get m_ _ _.

5. Ted p_ _ _ his bill on time.

tail – trail – pail – snail – rain

6. Jog on the tr_ _ _ in the woods.

7. The dog wags its t_ _ _.

8. The sn_ _ _ is in the bay.

9. The kids place the snail in the p_ _ _.

10. The wet kids jog on the trail in the sun and r_ _ _.

Vowel Teams: ee

Word	Illustration	Sounds like	Say and trace the word.	Write the word and underline the vowel sound.
1. bee		bē	bee	b<u>ee</u>
2. see		sē	see	_____
3. fee		fē	fee	_____
4. tree		trē	tree	_____
5. free		frē	free	_____
6. three	3	thrē	three	_____

Vowel Teams: ee

Word	Illustration	Sounds like	Say 📣 and trace ✍ the word.	Write ✍ the word and underline the vowel sound.
1. feed		fēd	feed	f<u>ee</u>d
2. seed		sēd	seed	_____
3. weed		wēd	weed	_____
4. need		nēd	need	_____
5. deed		dēd	deed	_____
6. bleed		blēd	bleed	_____
7. speed		spēd	speed	_____

Vowel Teams: ee

Directions: Say, trace, and read.

I see three bees in the weeds.

The cut will bleed.

The wee tree grew from a seed.

The fee is three dollars. It is not free.

Kim feeds the baby.

Vowel Teams: ee

Directions: Read and say.

See

Today Present	Yesterday Past	Past with have/has	Tomorrow Future
I see	I saw	I have seen	I shall see
you see	you saw	you have seen	you will see
he, she, it sees	he, she, it saw	he, she, it has seen	he, she, it will see
we see	we saw	we have seen	we shall see
you see	you saw	you have seen	you will see
they see	they saw	they have seen	they will see

Directions: Say and trace.

1. See the tree.

2. Jan sees the tree.

3. I saw the tree.

4. Jan saw the tree.

5. We saw the rain.

6. They saw the train.

7. I have seen the trail.

8. You have seen the trail.

9. He has seen the trail.

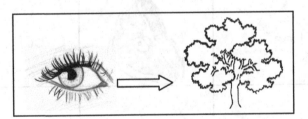

Vowel Teams: ee

Word	Illustration	Sounds like	Say 📢 and trace ✍ the word.	Write ✍ the word and underline the vowel sound.
1. teen		tēn	teen	t<u>ee</u>n
2. seen		sēn	seen	_____
3. green		grēn	green	_____
4. queen		kwēn	queen	_____
5. beef		bēf	beef	_____
6. reef		rēf	reef	_____

Vowel Teams: ee

Directions: Fill in, read, and say.

feed – green – queen – speed

1.   Drive at a safe sp_ _ _.

2.   Bob will f _ _ _ his dog.

3.   The top of the tree is gr_ _ _.

4.   The weeds and grass are gr_ _ _ too.

5.   I see a qu_ _ _ bee in the hive.

Vowel Teams: ee

Directions: Read and say.

Feed

Today Present	Yesterday Past	Past with have/has	Tomorrow Future
I feed	I fed	I have fed	I shall feed
you feed	you fed	you have fed	you will feed
he, she, it feeds	he, she, it fed	he, she, it has fed	he, she, it will feed
we feed	we fed	we have fed	we shall feed
you feed	you fed	you have fed	you will feed
they feed	they fed	they have fed	they will feed

Directions: Say, trace, and read.

1. I feed three cats.

2. You fed three dogs.

3. He has fed three dogs.

4. We shall feed three kids.

Vowel Teams: ee

Word	Illustration	Sounds like	Say and trace the word.	Write the word and underline the vowel sound.
1. eel		ēl	eel	eel
2. heel		hēl	heel	_____
3. peel		pēl	peel	_____
4. reel		rēl	reel	_____
5. peek		pēk	peek	_____
6. week	Sun. Mon. Tues. Wed. Thurs. Fri. Sat.	wēk	week	_____
7. cheek		chēk	cheek	_____
8. creek		krēk	creek	_____

Vowel Teams: ee

Directions: Say, trace, and read.

1. Reel in that eel.

2. The heel is part of the foot.

3. Peel the skin off the peach.

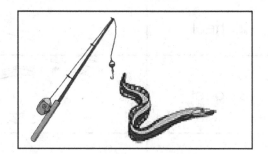

4. You have 2 cheeks on your face.

5. A week has seven (7) days.

6. Three eels are in the creek!

7. A bee is in the tree.

 **Great job!**

Vowel Teams: ee

Word	Illustration	Sounds like	Say and trace the word.	Write the word and underline the vowel sound.
1. feet		fēt	feet	f<u>ee</u>t
2. beet		bēt	beet	_____
3. meet		mēt	meet	_____
4. greet		grēt	greet	_____
5. sheet		shēt	sheet	_____
6. sleet		slēt	sleet	_____
7. sweet		swēt	sweet	_____
8. street		strēt	street	_____

Vowel Teams: ee

Word	Illustration	Sounds like	Say 📣 and trace ✍ the word.	Write ✍ the word and underline the vowel sound.
9. jeep		jēp	jeep	<u>jee</u>p
10. beep		bēp	beep	_____
11. weep		wēp	weep	_____
12. deep		dēp	deep	_____
13. keep		kēp	keep	_____
14. sleep		slēp	sleep	_____
15. sheep		shēp	sheep	_____
16. sweep		swēp	sweep	_____
17. steep		stēp	steep	_____

Vowel Teams: ee

Directions: Say, trace, and read.

1. The three sheep sleep under the tree.

2. The well is deep.

3. Pat keeps the cat.

4. Matt needs a pen.

5. His pager beeps.

6. Lee sweeps the steps.

7. It is nice to meet you.

Vowel Teams: ee /ē/

Review

Directions: Fill in the missing words and read the sentences.

meet – jeep – sleep – sleet – feet – street – sweep – sheep – sheet

1.   His f_ _ _ are wet.

2.   I sl_ _ p in a bed.

3.   Sw_ _ _ with a broom.

4.   Put a sh_ _t on the bed.

5.   Kit and Ben will m_ _ _ at six.

6.   The j_ _ _ is on the str_ _ _.

7.   A sh_ _p bleets.

8.   Ice and rain are sl_ _ _t.

Vowel Teams: ea /ē/

Word	Illustration	Sounds like	Say and trace the word.	Write the word and underline the vowel sound.
1. tea		tē	tea	t<u>ea</u>
2. pea		pē	pea	_____
3. sea		sē	sea	_____
4. flea		flē	flea	_____
5. plea		plē	plea	_____
6. please		plēz	please	_____
7. read		rēd	read	_____
8. bead		bēd	bead	_____
9. lead		lēd	lead	_____

Vowel Teams: ea

Directions: Fill in, read, and say.

tea – read – pea – please – flea

1.   Juan likes his t_ _.

2.   A p_ _ is green.

3.   The dog has a fl_ _.

4.   R_ _ _the book.

5.   Pl_ _ _ _ r_ _ _ the book.

Vowel Teams: ea /ē/

Word	Illustration	Sounds like	Say 📢 and trace ✍ the word.	Write ✍ the word and underline the vowel sound.
1. beak		bēk	beak	b<u>ea</u>k
2. leak		lēk	leak	_____
3. peak		pēk	peak	_____
4. weak		wēk	weak	_____
5. speak		spēk	speak	_____
6. steal		stēl	steal	_____
7. meal		mēl	meal	_____
8. heal		hēl	heal	_____
9. seal		sēl	seal	_____

Vowel Teams: ea /ē/

Directions: Look at the pictures. (Circle) the word that matches the picture. Say and write it on the line.

tea - flea

tea

flea - pea

_____

read - bead

_____

read - lead

_____

tea - sea

_____

leak - weak

_____

beak - weak

_____

meal - seal

_____

steal - seal

_____

Vowel Teams: ea /ē/

Directions: Fill in the missing words and read the sentences.

tea – sea – read – seal – leak

1.   Bea swims in the S_ _.

2.   Drink hot t_ _.

3.   R_ _ _ to the baby.

4.   The pipe has a l_ _ _.

5.   S_ _ _ the jar.

6.   The S_ _l is in the sea.

Vowel Teams: ea /ē/

Word	Illustration	Sounds like	Say 📢 and trace ✍ the word.	Write ✍ the word and underline the vowel sound.
1. team		tēm	team	te<u>a</u>m
2. ream		rēm	ream	_____
3. beam		bēm	beam	_____
4. seam		sēm	seam	_____
5. cream		krēm	cream	_____
6. dream		drēm	dream	_____
7. gleam		glēm	gleam	_____

Vowel Teams: ea /ē/

Directions: Say, trace, and read.

1. The gym team is good on the beam.

2. The cream is the fat of the milk.

3. The top has a seam.

4. The dream team is good.

5. The beam is steel.

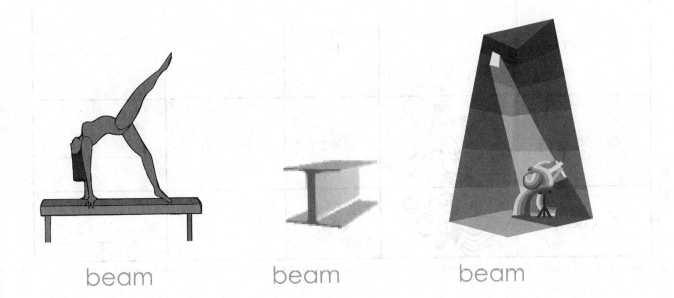

beam   beam   beam

Vowel Teams: ea /ē/

Word	Illustration	Sounds like	Say and trace the word.	Write the word and underline the vowel sound.
1. bean		bēn	bean	b<u>ea</u>n
2. mean		mēn	mean	_____
3. clean		klēn	clean	_____
4. dean		dēn	dean	_____
5. lean		lēn	lean	_____
6. leap		lēp	leap	_____
7. cheap		chēp	cheap	_____

Vowel Teams: ea /ē/

Word	Illustration	Sounds like	Say 📢 and trace ✍ the word.	Write ✍ the word and underline the vowel sound.
1. eat		ēt	eat	<u>ea</u>t
2. meat		mēt	meat	_____
3. heat		hēt	heat	_____
4. beat		bēt	beat	_____
5. seat		sēt	seat	_____
6. neat		nēt	neat	_____
7. cleat		klēt	cleat	_____
8. cheat		chēt	cheat	_____
9. pleat		plēt	pleat	_____

Vowel Teams: ea /ē/

10. treat		trēt	treat	_____
11. wheat		wēt	wheat	_____

Directions: Say, trace, and read.

1.   Beat the heat with a fan.

2.   Beat the eggs.

3.   Lean meat is best.

4.   Tom is a mean man.

5.   Peas, beans and meat can be a meal.

6.   Please sweep the mat.

7.   Please keep the house neat and clean!

Vowel Teams: ea /ē/

Directions: Look at the pictures. Circle the word that matches the

picture. Say and write it on the line.

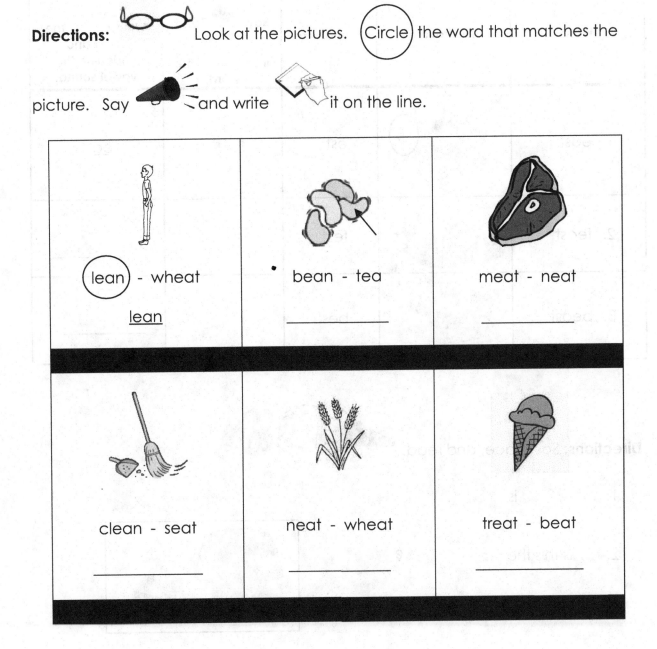

lean - wheat

lean

bean - tea

_____

meat - neat

_____

clean - seat

_____

neat - wheat

_____

treat - beat

_____

Neat! You can read!

241

Vowel Teams: ea /ē/

Word	Illustration	Sounds like	Say and trace the word.	Write the word and underline the vowel sound.
1. east		ēst	east	e̲ast
2. feast		fēst	feast	_____
3. beast		bēst	beast	_____

Directions: Say, trace, and read.

1.   Veal is beef.

2.   Is this the real deal?

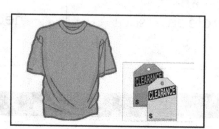

3.   This wee pup gets the least.

4.   It is a good deal: it is cheap.

Vowel Teams: ea /ē/

Directions: 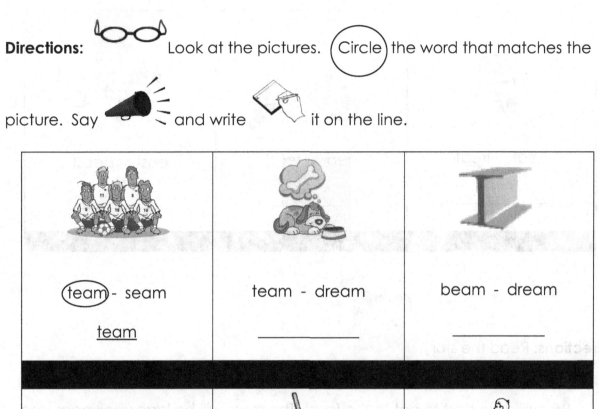 Look at the pictures. Circle the word that matches the

picture. Say and write it on the line.

(team) - seam team	team - dream _____	beam - dream _____
leap - bean _____	clean - lean _____	lean - meat _____
seat - eat _____	seat - heat _____	meat - heat _____

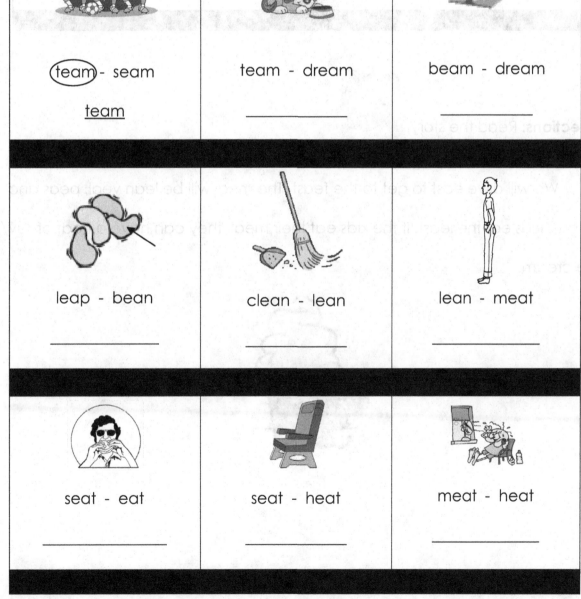

Vowel Teams: ea /ē/

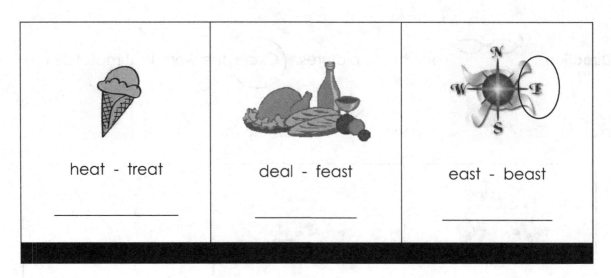

heat - treat	deal - feast	east - beast
_____	_____	_____

Directions: Read the story.

We will drive east to get to the feast. The meal will be lean veal, peas and beans. Kids eat the least. If the kids eat their meal, they can have a treat of /ŭv/ ice cream.

Vowel Teams: oa /ō/

Word	Illustration	Sounds like	Say 📢 and trace ✍ the word.	Write ✍ the word and underline the vowel sounds.
1. boat		bōt	boat	b<u>oa</u>t
2. coat		kōt	coat	_____
3. goat		gōt	goat	_____
4. oats		ōts	oats	_____
5. float		flōt	float	_____
6. bloat		blōt	bloat	_____
7. gloat		glōt	gloat	_____

Vowel Teams: oa /ō/

Directions: Say, trace, and read.

1. Boats float on the sea.

2. Oats and wheat are grains.

3. This coat feels hot in May.

4. Dan gloats if he wins.

5. Goats eat grass.

Vowel Teams: oa /ō/

Word	Illustration	Sounds like	Say  and trace the word.	Write the word and underline the vowel sound.
1. road		rōd	road	r<u>oa</u>d
2. toad		tōd	toad	_____
3. load		lōd	load	_____
4. goal		gōl	goal	_____
5. coal		kōl	coal	_____

Directions: Read and say.

Ted drives the load of coal on the road. That is his goal. The toad must get off the road. That is his goal.

Vowel Teams: oa /ō/

Word	Illustration	Sounds like	Say 📣 and trace ✍ the word.	Write ✍ the word and underline the vowel sound.
1. foam		fōm	foam	f<u>oa</u>m
2. roam		rōm	roam	_____
3. loan		lōn	loan	_____
4. moan		mōn	moan	_____
5. groan		grōn	groan	_____

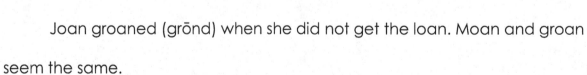

Directions: Read and say.

Joan groaned (grōnd) when she did not get the loan. Moan and groan

seem the same.

Vowel Teams: oa /ō/

Word	Illustration	Sounds like	Say 🔊 and trace ✍ the word.	Write ✍ the word and underline the vowel sound.
1. toast		tōst	toast	t<u>oa</u>st
2. roast		rōst	roast	_____
3. coast		kōst	coast	_____
4. boast		bōst	boast	_____
5. soap		sōp	soap	_____

Vowel Teams: oa /ō/

Directions: Look at the picture. (Circle) the word that matches the

picture. Say and write it on the line.

boat - (coat)

coat

boat - goat

_____

goat - coat

_____

goal - coal

_____

coal - goal

_____

road - toad

_____

moan - loan

_____

moan - foam

_____

toast - coast

_____

Vowel Teams: oa /ō/

roast - toast	roast - coast	oats - goal
_____	_____	_____
gloat - float	toad - road	load - road
_____	_____	_____

Directions: Say, trace, and read.

1. Bob ran with the ball to the goal.

2. It was his goal to load the coal.

3. Please take a bath with soap.

4. Feed the goat oats and wheat.

Vowel Teams: oa /ō/

Directions: Find  and (circle) the words.

Word Find

~~ROAST~~ – LOAD – COAT – COAL – TOAST – SOAP

B	C	T	C	O	A	T	R
C	O	A	L	N	V	W	O
L	O	A	D	X	K	M	A
S	O	S	O	A	P	L	S
D	M	L	T	O	A	S	T

Vowel Teams: ie /ē/

Word	Illustration	Sounds like	Say 📢 and trace ✍ the word.	Write ✍ the word and underline the vowel sound.
1. yield		yēld	yield	y<u>ie</u>ld
2. field		fēld	field	_____
3. chief		chēf	chief	_____
4. grief		grēf	grief	_____
5. thief		thēf	thief	_____
6. brief		brēf	brief	_____
7. piece		pēs	piece	_____

Vowel Teams: ie /ē/

Directions: Read and say.

1. Be brief.

2. Bill takes his briefcase to work.

3. The bean field is green. Its yield is green beans.

Directions: Match the word to its picture.

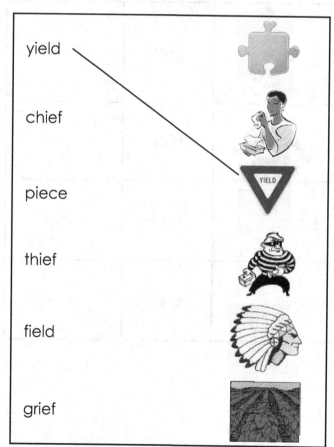

yield

chief

piece

thief

field

grief

Vowel Teams: ei /ē/

Star (☆) Words

Word	Illustration	Sounds like	Say 📢 and trace ✍ the word.	Write ✍ the word and underline the vowel sounds.
1. receive		rē •sēv'	receive	_____
2. receipt		rē •sēt'	receipt	_____

Directions: Read and say.

Save your receipt!

☆ **Neat!** ☆

Part 2: Vowel Teams with Sliding Sounds

Remember: In a vowel team, the two vowels team up to make one (1) vowel sound.

> 1 vowel sound = 1 underline

Some teams have a sliding sound.
Examples:

Say	Sounds like	Word
p ay	pā	pay
h ay	hā	hay
k ow	kou	cow
m ow	mō	mow
b oy	boi	boy
j aw	jaw	jaw

If a word has one (1) vowel sound to underline, it is a 1-syllable word.

Example:
pay= 1-syllable word

Yes, I Can Read!   Unit 6

Vowel Teams: ay /ā/

Word	Illustration	Sounds like	Say and trace the word.	Write the word and underline the vowel sound.
1. hay		hā	hay	h<u>ay</u>
2. jay		jā	jay	_____
3. ray		rā	ray	_____
4. bay		bā	bay	_____
5. day		dā	day	_____
6. lay		lā	lay	_____
7. May		mā	May	_____
8. pay		pā	pay	_____
9. say		sā	say	_____

Vowel Teams: ay /ā/

Word	Illustration	Sounds like	Say and trace the word.	Write the word and underline the vowel sound.
10. way		wā	way	w<u>ay</u>
11. gay		gā	gay	_____
12. clay		klā	clay	_____
13. play		plā	play	_____
14. gray		grā	gray	_____
15. tray		trā	tray	_____
16. stay		stā	stay	_____

Vowel Teams: ay /ā/

Directions: Look at the pictures. (Circle) the word that matches the

picture. Say and write it on the line.

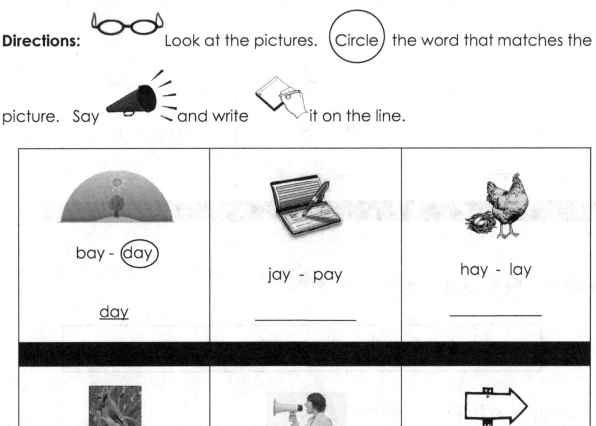

bay - (day)	jay - pay	hay - lay
day	_____	_____

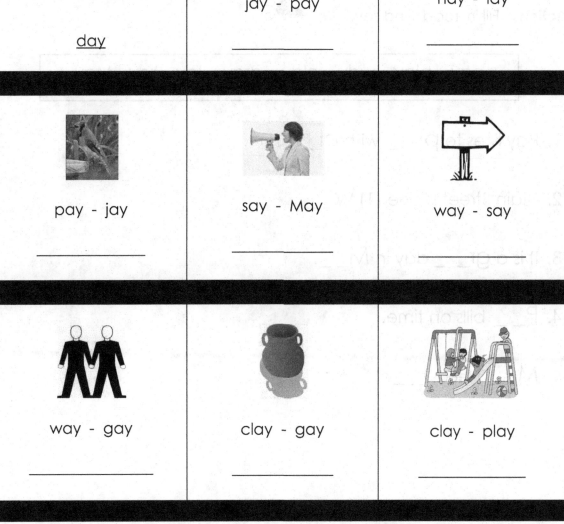

pay - jay	say - May	way - say
_____	_____	_____
way - gay	clay - gay	clay - play
_____	_____	_____

Vowel Teams: ay /ā/

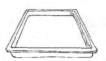		
tray - clay	tray - stay	stay - day
_____	_____	_____

Directions: Fill in, read, and say.

pay – play – way – clay – gray - Jay – ray - May

1. Ray likes to pl_ _ with cl _ _.

2. Main Street is one (1) w_ _.

3. It is a gr_ _ day in M_ _.

4. P_ _ bills on time.

5. M_ _ I feed J_ _?

Vowel Teams: ou /ou/

Word	Illustration	Sounds like	Say 📢 and trace ✍ the word.	Write ✍ the word and underline the vowel sound.
1. out		out	out	<u>ou</u>t
2. house		hous	house	_____
3. mouse		mous	mouse	_____
4. ouch		ouch	ouch	_____
5. couch		kouch	couch	_____
6. pouch		pouch	pouch	_____
7. loud		loud	loud	_____

Vowel Teams: ou /ou/

Word	Illustration	Sounds like	Say 📢 and trace ✍ the word.	Write ✍ the word and underline the vowel sound.
1. mouth		mouth	mouth	m<u>ou</u>th
2. round		round	round	_____
3. pound		pound	pound	_____
4. sound		sound	sound	_____
5. mound		mound	mound	_____
6. pout		pout	pout	_____
7. grout		grout	grout	_____

Directions: Read and say.

1. Pat put Kim in a pouch. Pat and Kim went out of the house. The mouse hid under the couch. The cat went under the couch. Ouch!

2. Tim has 1 pound of grout for the tile. He has round tiles. The tiles are piled in a mound.

3. Kris is sad. Kris's mouth is down in a pout.

Vowel Teams: ou /ou/

Directions: Look at the pictures. Circle the word that matches the

picture. Say and write it on the line.

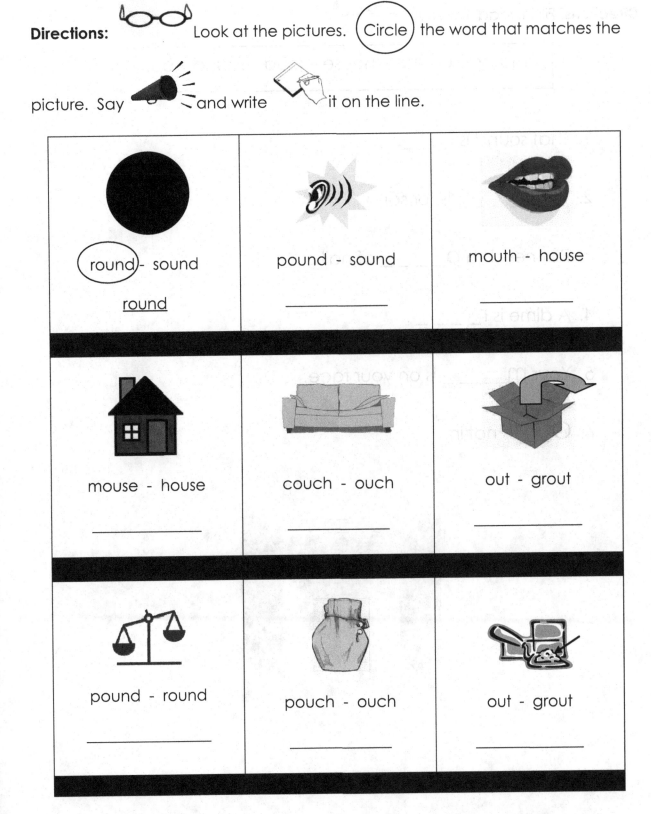

round - sound

round

pound - sound

_____

mouth - house

_____

mouse - house

_____

couch - ouch

_____

out - grout

_____

pound - round

_____

pouch - ouch

_____

out - grout

_____

Vowel Teams: ou /ou/

Directions: Fill in, read, and say.

| mouth – pound – house – loud – round – out |

1. That sound is l_ _ _.

2. The h_ _ _ _ is for sale.

3. Pat needs a p_ _ _ _ of nails.

4. A dime is r_ _ _ _ .

5. Your m_ _ _ _ is on your face.

6. O_ _ is not in.

Vowel Teams: ow /ō/

Word	Illustration	Sounds like	Say and trace the word.	Write the word and underline the vowel sound.
1. bow		bō	bow	b<u>ow</u>
2. mow		mō	mow	_____
3. tow		tō	tow	_____
4. low		lō	low	_____
5. row		rō	row	_____
6. snow		snō	snow	_____

Directions: Read and say.

1.   Please place a bow on the gift.

2.   Place the desks in a row.

3.   Tim mows the grass.

4.   Al rows the boat.

5.   Sal tows the car.

Vowel Teams: ow /ō/

Word	Illustration	Sounds like	Say 🔊 and trace ✍ the word.	Write ✍ the word and underline the vowel sound.
1. bowl		bōl	bowl	b<u>ow</u>l
2. blow		blō	blow	_____
3. flow		flō	flow	_____
4. glow		glō	glow	_____
5. slow		slō	slow	_____
6. crow		krō	crow	_____
7. grow		grō	grow	_____

Vowel Teams: ow /ō/

Directions: Say, trace, and read.

1. Drive slowly (slō'• lē) in a school zone.

2. Tim bowls for fun.

3. The sun glows as it rises.

4. Ed eats rice in his bowl.

5. Please read out loud.

6. You can read slowly.

bowl   bowl

Vowel Teams: ow /ō/

Star (⭐) Words

Word	Illustration	Sounds like	Say 📢 and trace ✍️ the word.	Write ✍️ the word and underline the vowel sound.
1. show		shō	show	_____
2. own		ōn	own	_____

Directions: Say, trace, and read.

1. Al owns the boat. It is on loan to his pal Pat.

2. Please show me the snow.

3. Kids grow fast.

4. The crows are big and black.

5. Jim owns his own home.

Vowel Teams: ow /ou/

Word	Illustration	Sounds like	Say 🔊 and trace ✏️ the word.	Write ✏️ the word and underline the vowel sound.
1. cow		kou	cow	c<u>ow</u>
2. down		doun	down	_____
3. town		toun	town	_____
4. brown		broun	brown	_____
5. clown		kloun	clown	_____
6. crown		kroun	crown	_____
7. owl		oul	owl	_____
8. scowl		skoul	scowl	_____

Vowel Teams: ow /ou/

Directions: Read.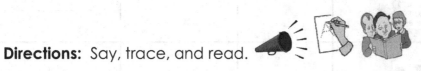

h + ow = how

How is Bob? Bob is fine.

n + ow = now

Now is the time.

Directions: Say, trace, and read.

1. How now, brown cow?

2. The brown cow went down the hill to town.

3. The owl has a scowl on its face.

4. The clown has a crown.

5. Bob and Tom went downtown.

Vowel Teams: oi /oi/

Word	Illustration	Sounds like	Say and trace the word.	Write the word and underline the vowel sound.
1. coin		koin	coin	c<u>oi</u>n
2. join		join	join	_____
3. point		point	point	_____
4. boil		boil	boil	_____
5. coil		koil	coil	_____
6. broil		broil	broil	_____

Vowel Teams: oi /oi/

Directions: Say, trace, and read.

1. A cape is a point of land. Please point to it on a map.

2. Bess needs coins to do her wash.

3. His dog Ted points at crows. Ted is a pointer.

4. Please broil the meat. The coil in the broiler gets red hot. Please broil the meat and boil an egg.

Vowel Teams: oi /oi/

Word	Illustration	Sounds like	Say and trace the word.	Write the word and underline the vowel sound.
1. soil		soil	soil	s<u>oi</u>l
2. spoil		spoil	spoil	_____
3. noise		noiz	noise	_____
4. poise		poiz	poise	_____
5. moist		moist	moist	_____

Directions: Trace, read, and say.

1. Moist soil is a bit wet.

2. The snake coils. It has poison in its bite.

3. The cake is moist. It has oil in it.

Vowel Teams: oy /oi/

Word	Illustration	Sounds like	Say 📣 and trace ✍ the word.	Write ✍ the word and underline the vowel sound.
1. boy		boi	boy	b<u>oy</u>
2. toy		toi	toy	_____
3. joy		joi	joy	_____
4. soy		soi	soy	_____
5. Roy		roi	Roy	_____

Directions: Trace then read out loud.

1. Roy has soy milk with his lunch.

2. Roy is a boy's name.

Vowel Teams: oy /oi/

Directions: Look at the pictures. (Circle) the word that matches the

picture. Say and write it on the line.

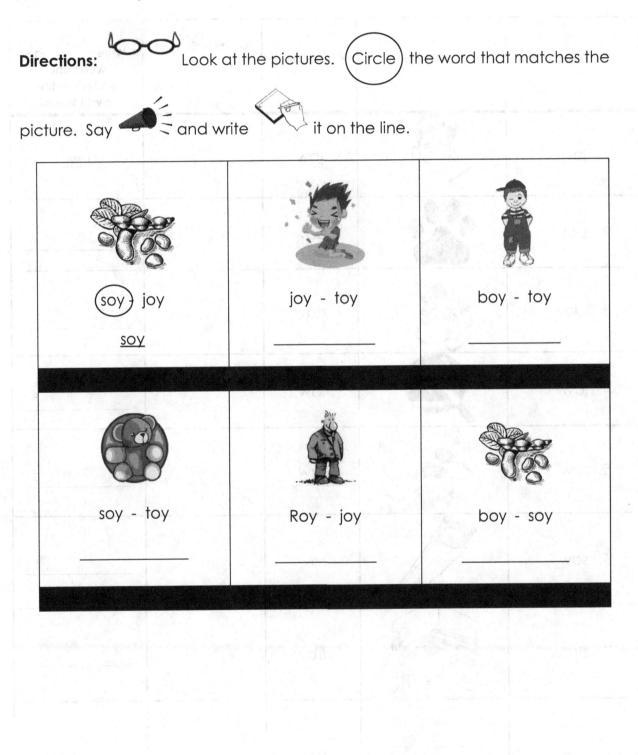

(soy) joy	joy - toy	boy - toy
soy	_____	_____
soy - toy	Roy - joy	boy - soy
_____	_____	_____

Vowel Teams: aw /aw/

Word	Illustration	Sounds like	Say and trace the word.	Write the word and underline the vowel sound.
1. jaw		jaw	jaw	jaw
2. paw		paw	paw	_____
3. claw		klaw	claw	_____
4. law		law	law	_____
5. raw		raw	raw	_____
6. saw		saw	saw	_____
7. draw		draw	draw	_____
8. straw		straw	straw	_____

Vowel Teams: aw /aw/

Directions:  Look at the pictures. (Circle) the word that matches the picture. Say ⟍ and write ⟍ it on the line.

straw - (law) __law__	paw - draw _____	claw - jaw _____
raw - saw _____	jaw - claw _____	saw - law _____

Vowel Teams: aw /aw/

Directions: Read and say.

My cat Pat has a jaw and four paws with claws. I saw her eat raw fish that she held in her claws. Pat sleeps on a bed of straw.

_____

Draw your pet or a pet in this space.

Vowel Teams: aw /aw/

Word	Illustration	Sounds like	Say and trace the word.	Write the word and underline the vowel sound.
1. gnaw		naw	gnaw	gn<u>aw</u>
2. hawk		hawk	hawk	_____
3. yawn		yawn	yawn	_____
4. lawn		lawn	lawn	_____
5. dawn		dawn	dawn	_____
6. fawn		fawn	fawn	_____
7. pawn		pawn	pawn	_____
8. drawn		drawn	drawn	_____
9. prawn		prawn	prawn	_____
10. crawl		krawl	crawl	_____
11. shawl		shawl	shawl	_____

Vowel Teams: aw /aw/

Directions: Say, trace, and read.

1. A cat has claws.

2. A dog has four (4) paws.

3. Dogs gnaw on bones.

4. Ken saw a fawn at dawn. He was in awe. He has drawn the fawn he saw.

5. Hawks eat raw meat.

6. Circle the correct answer. Is a pawn used in chess? (Yes, No) a

   pawn (is, is not) used in chess.

Vowel Teams: aw /aw/

Word	Illustration	Sounds like	Say  and trace the word.	Write the word and underline the vowel sound.
1. sauce		saws	sauce	s<u>au</u>ce
2. aunt		awnt	aunt	_____
3. August		awgust aw'•gŭst	August	_____

Directions: Read and say.

In August, Aunt Bea puts sauce on the ribs and broils them.

☆ Wow! Good job! ☆

Vowel Teams: aw /aw/

Directions: Find  and (circle) the words.

Word Find

~~SAUCE~~ – SOIL – JAW – AUNT – HAWK – SAW – BOY

O	S	A	U	C	E
J	S	A	W	L	A
A	B	O	Y	K	U
W	M	J	I	O	N
H	A	W	K	L	T

Part 3: More vowel teams

Vowel Teams: oo /o͞o/

 A vowel team makes 1 vowel sound.

1 vowel= 1 underline

Word	Illustration	Sounds like	Say and trace the word.	Write the word and underline the vowel sound.
1. boot		bo͞ot	boot	bo͞ot
2. root		ro͞ot	root	_____
3. shoot		sho͞ot	shoot	_____
4. noon		no͞on	noon	_____
5. moon		mo͞on	moon	_____
6. spoon		spo͞on	spoon	_____
7. food		fo͞od	food	_____
8. roof		ro͞of	roof	_____

Yes, I Can Read!   Unit 6

Vowel Teams: oo /o͞o/

Word	Illustration	Sounds like	Say and trace the word.	Write the word and underline the vowel sound.
1. too		to͞o	too	t<u>oo</u>
2. school		sko͞ol	school	_____
3. stool		sto͞ol	stool	_____
4. pool		po͞ol	pool	_____
5. tool		to͞ol	tool	_____
6. cool		ko͞ol	cool	_____
7. spool		spo͞ol	spool	_____
8. tooth		to͞oth	tooth	_____

Vowel Teams: oo /ōo/

Directions: Trace. Then read and say.

1.   Stay cool in the pool.

2.   You can go too.

3.   Rose is in school too.

4.   The leg on the stool is loose.

5.   We have food in school at noon.

chair

Directions: Match the word and picture.

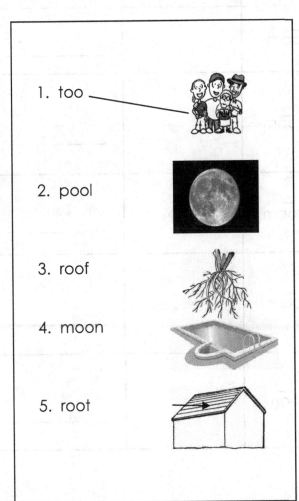

1. too

2. pool

3. roof

4. moon

5. root

Yes, I Can Read!   Unit 6

Vowel Teams: oo /o͞o/

Word	Illustration	Sounds like	Say and trace the word.	Write the word and underline the vowel sound.
1. goose		go͞os	goose	g<u>oo</u>se
2. moose		mo͞os	moose	_____
3. loose		lo͞os	loose	_____
4. room		ro͞om	room	_____
5. bloom		blo͞om	bloom	_____
6. broom		bro͞om	broom	_____
7. zoom		zo͞om	zoom	_____
8. gloom		glo͞om	gloom	_____

Vowel Teams: oo /o͞o/

Directions:  Look at the pictures. (Circle) the word that matches the

picture. Say 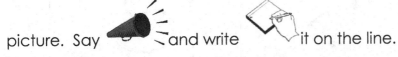 and write it on the line.

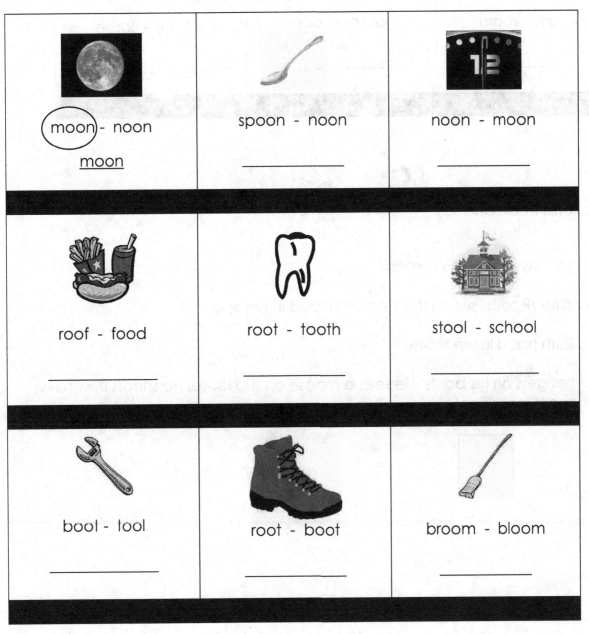

(moon)- noon

moon

spoon - noon

_____

noon - moon

_____

roof - food

_____

root - tooth

_____

stool - school

_____

bool - tool

_____

root - boot

_____

broom - bloom

_____

Vowel Teams: oo /o͞o/

broom - room	goose - room	school - loose
_____	_____	_____

Directions: Read and say.

1. Bess sweeps with a broom.

2. Ruth /R͞ooth/ sits on the stool with food in her spoon.

3. Ruth has a loose tooth.

4. Les gets on his boots. He sees a moose on the loose. He shoots it with his zoom lens /lĕnz/.

Vowel Teams: oo /o͝o/

A lot of words with oo sound like oo as in book or cook.

Word	Illustration	Sounds like	Say 📢 and trace ✍ the word.	Write ✍ the word and underline the vowel sound.
1. book		bŏok	book	b<u>oo</u>k
2. cook		kŏok	cook	_____
3. look		lŏok	look	_____
4. brook		brŏok	brook	_____
5. took		tŏok	took	_____
6. wood		wŏod	wood	_____

Directions: Read out loud.

Ray takes the brook trout from the brook. He looks for a cookbook. Ray cooks the brook trout as he reads the cookbook.

Vowel Teams: oo /o͝o/

Directions: Say, trace, and read out loud.

Take

Today Present	Yesterday Past	Past with have/has	Tomorrow Future
I take	I took	I have taken	I shall take
you take	you took	you have taken	you will take
he, she, it takes	he, she, it took	he, she, it has taken	he, she, it will take
we take	we took	we have taken	we shall take
you take	you took	you have taken	you will take
they take	they took	they have taken	they will take

Directions: Read out loud.

1. I take the bus to school.

2. You took a cab to school.

3. He has taken his pet goose to school.

4. We will take our books to school.

Vowel Teams: ue, /o͞o/

One more vowel team that sounds like oo:

Word	Illustration	Sounds like	Say  and trace the word.	Write the word and underline the vowel sound.
1. clue		klo͞o	clue	cl<u>ue</u>
2. blue		blo͞o	blue	_____
3. flue		flo͞o	flue	_____

Directions: Say, trace, and read.

1. The kids look for a clue until they are blue in the face.

2. Ted put the wood in the stove and made a fire. The smoke went up the flue.

Vowel Teams: ew, /oo/

Word	Illustration	Sounds like	Say and trace the word.	Write the word and underline the vowel sound.
1. stew		stoo	stew	st<u>ew</u>
2. blew		bloo	blew	_____
3. dew		doo	dew	_____
4. flew		floo	flew	_____
5. chew		choo	chew	_____
6. crew		kroo	crew	_____
7. drew		droo	drew	_____
8. grew		groo	grew	_____

292

Vowel Teams: ew, /o͞o/

Directions: Trace and read.

1. The gray goose flew.

2. Beef stew makes a good meal.

3. The new game is fun to play.

4. Dew was on the grass.

5. The wind blew the trees.

Directions: Trace and read out loud.

1. Lew drew a blue sky and dew on green grass.

2. A goose flew in the sky.

3. A moose is in the grass.

4. The crew sailed (sāld) in the new sailboat. The wind blew them on the lake.

5. The baby grew fast.

Vowel Teams: ui, /o͞o/

Word	Illustration	Sounds like	Say  and trace the word.	Write the word and underline the vowel sound.
1. fruit		fro͞ot	fruit	fr<u>ui</u>t
2. suit		so͞ot	suit	_____
3. juice		jo͞os	juice	_____

Vowel Teams: ou, /o͞o/

1. soup		so͞op	soup	_____
2. you		yo͞o	you	_____

Directions: Say, trace, and read.

1. Do you like fruit juice?

   Yes, I like fruit juice, but I like fruit best.

2. You look nice in your new suit.

Vowel Team: Review

oo = boot

ue = clue

ew = stew

ui = fruit

ou = soup

Directions: Read and say.

Pat and Jane sat on stools in his room to play Clue®. Then Pat and Jane went in the pool to swim and get cool. At noon, Pat and Jane had lunch. They ate soup, stew, and fruit. Pat lost his loose tooth in the stew. He did not chew well.

☆ **Good for you!** ☆

Vowel Teams: ew, / ū /

Word	Illustration	Sounds like	Say and trace the word.	Write the word and underline the vowel sound.
1. mew		mū	mew	m<u>ew</u>
2. pew		pū	pew	_____
3. few		fū	few	_____

Directions: Read and say.

1. Few cats just mew a few times.

2. Please sit in a pew.

Directions: Look at the pictures. Say the word and write it on the line.

Vowel Teams: ea /ĕ/

Ea can sound like ĕ as in egg, elephant, or head.
(For the ea that sounds like ē, as in team, see Unit 6, Part 1)

Word	Illustration	Sounds like	Say and trace the word.	Write the word and underline the vowel sounds.
1. head		hĕd	head	h<u>ea</u>d
2. bread		brĕd	bread	_____
3. dead		dĕd	dead	_____
4. dread		drĕd	dread	_____
5. read		rĕd	read	_____
6. feather		fĕth'•ûr	feather	_____
7. leather		lĕth'•ûr	leather	_____
8. Heather		Hĕth'•ûr	Heather	_____

Directions: Read.

Heather has brown leather boots.

See Appendix A for a list of ea words.

Vowel Teams: ea /ā/

The 3rd sound of ea is ā as in break and steak.

Word	Illustration	Sounds like	Say and trace the word.	Write the word and underline the vowel sound.
1. break		brāk	break	br<u>ea</u>k
2. steak		stāk	steak	_____
3. great		grāt	great	_____

Directions: Read and say.

　　The team of cooks baked bread, broiled steak, steamed peas, boiled beets, and made tea. They cooked a great meal.

See Appendix A for more ea words.

Vowel Teams: ea /ĕ/, /ā/

Directions: Look at the pictures. (Circle) the word that matches the

picture. Say and write it on the line.

dead - (head)

head

bread - head

_____

bread - dead

_____

feather - dread

_____

dread - head

_____

read - dread

_____

steak - break

_____

break - great

_____

great - steak

_____

Vowel Teams: ey /ā/

Word	Illustration	Sounds like	Say  and trace the word.	Write the word and underline the vowel sound.
1. they		thā	they	th<u>ey</u>
2. grey		grā	grey	_____
3. greyhound		grā'•hound	greyhound	_____

Directions: Trace. Then read and say.

1. They take the greyhound to the lake on this grey day in May .

Great Job!

Now you know the third (3rd) syllable, the vowel team, the beam team!

 You can read lots of words now!

Overview

Unit 7 begins with one-syllable words which are open syllables and progresses to two- and three-syllable words which contain open syllables. Accent and the schwa sound are explained. And, prefixes *un-* and *re-* are taught.

Objectives

Students learn that:

1. the open syllable, the fourth syllable, ends with a vowel that has a long sound. (This syllable type is different from the quiet *e* syllable, the second syllable, in that the latter ends with a silent *e* which is preceded by a vowel.)

2. *Y* in the middle or end of a word is a vowel. At the end of a one-syllable word, it sounds like long *i*, as in *sky*. At the end of a two- syllable word or longer, it sounds like long *e*, as in *baby* or *happy*.

Instruction

1. Discuss information on the first page of Unit 7, calling attention to long vowel sound characteristics: They say their own names. Call attention to the dachshund and the macron as associative clues for long vowel sounds.

2. Review the definition of a syllable: a word or word part that has a vowel sound and usually has a vowel.

3. Review the definition of a word: a syllable or syllables that have meaning, as in *a*, meaning *one*, and *go*, meaning *move*.

4. If the student cannot read the words in the first exercise, beginning with *a*, remind him to use the picture and phonetic clues in the second and third columns as aids. In the fourth column, he should say and trace the word, and in the fifth column, he should write the word and underline its vowel sound.

5. In the next exercise, on page 306, which features *y* at the end of a one-syllable word and its long *i* sound, call attention to the train car (*middle*) and the caboose (*end*) as symbols to help students read the directions. After completing the exercise, students should be able to read the featured words and complete the exercises on the following two pages.

6. On page 309, "Open syllables: accent" features *y* at the end of two-syllable words and its long *e* sound. Additional examples of *y* sounding like long *e* are *berry, happy, very, vary, malady, melody,* and *harmony*. A more uncommon sound of *y* occurs at the end of a two-syllable word: It is long *i*, as in *deny* or *rely*. *Y* in words ending in *ify* also sound like long *i* as in *codify, identify, modify, rectify, sanctify,* and *simplify*.

7. The accent mark is explained with the introduction of two-syllable words. In a word of two or more syllables, one syllable is said louder than the other(s). The accent mark ('), placed at the end of the stressed syllable, indicates which syllable to stress.

Tell students to play with the stress, as they are saying, tracing, writing, or underlining the vowel sounds until they recognize the word. At this level, and until about the middle of the fifth grade reading level, beginning with Unit 10, they will likely have most of the lesson words in their receptive vocabulary even if they cannot yet read them.

This would be an ideal time to teach dictionary usage as students can use the dictionary to find the accent marks within the phonetic pronunciation of each entry word.

8. The schwa sound (ə) is the vowel sound in the one or more unstressed syllables in a word. Its sound is *u* or *uh*, as if one forgot what he was going to say. To demonstrate how the schwa sound works, do the following: Write *pal* on the board and ask what the word is. Students should say *pal* with a short *a* sound. Then write *ace* on the board and ask what the word is. Students will say *ace*, with a long *a*. Then write *palace* on the board and ask for its pronunciation. *Palus* is the way it sounds because the first syllable is stressed, and the second syllable is relaxed, so its vowel sounds like short *u*, the schwa sound.

   In the dictionary, the schwa is represented by a backward, upside down, lower case *e* (ə). Lesson words with the schwa sound on page 311 are provided as examples such as *giant*, *dial*, etc. Dictionary usage at this point, too, is a natural progression as students can look up words like *lion*, *giant*, *dial*, or words of your choice, to note the schwa sound in the phonetic pronunciation. Point out that although two-syllable words or longer have one syllable which is stressed more than others, not all unstressed syllables will have the schwa sound. Some retain their vowel sounds, as in *diet* and *poet*. Because the goal is for students to decode unfamiliar words, refrain from parsing the dictionary pronunciation of words as in *po ĕt* or *po ŭt*. In addition, explain that the schwa sound is represented by a short *u* in the book's "Sounds like" columns because it sounds like a short *u*. The *u* spelling ensures consistency throughout the workbook and makes it easier for students to use with less assistance.

   Following your instruction, students should be able to say and trace the words, write the words and underline the vowel sounds in the fourth and fifth columns in the lessons. Note: Numbers 1-9 are two-syllable words, and their two vowels should be underlined after the word is written in the fifth column. *Idea* should have its *i*, *e* and *a* underlined as it is a three-syllable word. They should complete the practice exercise following the lessons.

Assessment

Students should be able to read all the words in the lessons and read the sentences which follow the lessons. This of course would be one-on-one. A spelling test and/or dictation would be other methods that can be used in a group situation. Students should be able to create and write simple sentences using featured words and those they have learned thus far.

Vocabulary Acquisition Strategies

Lesson Expansion Words

Additional one-syllable words for Unit 7 are as follows: *be, by, flu,* and *no.*

Additional two-syllable words include the following:

a	e	i	o	u
1. April	1. even	1. iPad®	1. coed	1. music
2. apron	2. evil	2. iPhone®	2. open	2. pupil
3. facing	3. fever	3. iPod®	3. over	3. super
4. paper	4. secret	4. iris	4. polar	
		5. iTunes®	5. Poland	
		6. quiet		
		7. silent		
		8. virus		
		9. Wi-Fi®		

Three-syllable words include *cereal, folio, Latino, radio,* and *studio.* Unit 12, "Syllable Division," contains a comprehensive list of open syllable words (See Rule #4).

Multiple Meaning Words

Examples include *fry, dry, try, shy, giant, trial,* and *fuel* respectively.

Word Families

Word families to discuss and add to include the following: *me, he, she, we; to, do;* and *my, cry, fly, sly, fry, dry, shy, sky,* and *spy.*

Homonyms

Buy-by-bye and *flu* and *flew* are homonyms for word study.

Unit 7: Long Vowels  : Open Syllables

The 4th syllable is the open syllable. The vowel is alone /ŭ•lōn´/ as in the words **a** or **I**, or it ends the syllable as in **no**. The vowel sound is long: it says its own name.

Example:

a /ā/ | 1 |

I /ī/ | [figure] |

 Remember: *a* and *I* are syllables *and* words. **A** means one (1). **I** means me. They have 1 vowel sound; they are 1 syllable. They are 1-syllable **words** because they have 1 vowel sound and have meaning.

These words are open syllables. They end in a vowel, and the vowel is long:
> The e sounds like ē:
>> me
>> he
>> she
>> we

Open Syllables

Word	Illustration	Sounds like	Say 📣 and trace ✍ the word.	Write ✍ the word and underline the vowel sound.
1. a		ā	a	a
2. I		ī	I	_____
3. me		mē	me	_____
4. he		hē	he	_____
5. she		shē	she	_____
6. we		wē	we	_____
7. to		tōō	to	_____
8. do		dōō	do	_____
9. go		gō	go	_____

Open Syllables: y /ī/

If y is in the **middle** or at the **end** of a word, it is a vowel.
At the end of a 1-syllable word, y sounds like long i, /ī/.

Word	Illustration	Sounds like	Say and trace the word.	Write the word and underline the vowel sound.
1. my		mī	my	m<u>y</u>
2. cry		krī	cry	_____
3. fly		flī	fly	_____
4. sly		slī	sly	_____
5. fry		frī	fry	_____
6. dry		drī	dry	_____
7. shy		shī	shy	_____
8. sky		skī	sky	_____
9. spy		spī	spy	_____
10. buy		bī	buy	_____

Directions: Fill in the missing words, say, and read.

> dry – sky – fly – buy – by

1. It did not rain, so the road is __ __ __.

2. Jim wants to __uy a new car.

3. The __ __ __ is red at sunset.

4. The jet will __ __ __ in the __ __ __.

5. The sly spy gets __ __.

Open Syllables: y /ī/

Directions: Find 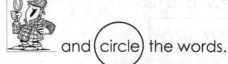 and (circle) the words.

Word Find

A – I – SHE – ME – WE – GO – TO

A	S	M	E	I	T	O
D	H	E	V	N	G	W
W	E	K	(A)	U	O	K

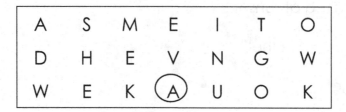

Directions: Read out loud.

1. I go to school.

2. Please read to me.

3. We do a good job!

Directions: Say  and trace.

1. Tom is sly as a fox.

2. I like to fry fish.

3. I try to be at work by 9 a.m.

4. I try to be on time.

5. The boy is by the tree.

6. She is my cat.

7. My car is red.

8. I can do it if I try.

Open Syllables: accent /ăk´•sĕnt/

In a word of 2 or more syllables, say 1 syllable louder than the other. The accent (´) tells you which syllable to stress or say louder.

Example:

baby   /**bā**´• bē/

In baby, the ´ tells you to say bā louder than bē. *

Word	Illustration	Sounds like	Say and trace the word.	Write the word and underline the vowel sounds.
1. baby*		bā´•bē	baby	b<u>a</u>b<u>y</u>
2. lady*		lā´•dē	lady	____
3. pretty		prĭ´•tē	pretty	____
4. funny		fŭn´•ē	funny	____
5. tiny*		tī´•nē	tiny	____
6. tidy*		tī´•dē	tidy	____
7. twenty	20	twĕn´•tē	twenty	____

*The 2 syllables in these words are open syllables.

Open Syllables: y /ē/

Star (☆) words:

many /mĕn´•ē/

plenty /plĕn´•tē/

Directions: Fill in the missing words and read out loud.

| dry – baby – tiny – my – pretty – funny – cry – lady |

The pr__ __ __ __, fun__ __ I __ __ __ __ had a t __ __ __ __ b__ b__.

"Do not c__ __, m__ b__ by, I will see if you are wet or dr__," she said.

_____

Schwa sound /ə/

In a word of 2 or more syllables, the syllable(s) without the accent or stress has a vowel (s) that may say /ŭ/ or /ŭh/. This is the schwa /shwŏ/ sound.

　　Example:

　　lion /lī´• **ŭn**/

The /ŭ/ sound in the 2nd syllable is the schwa /shwŏ/ sound.

On the next page, the schwa sound is the /ŭ/ sound in words like: gi**ant**, di**al**, tri**al**, id**ea**, and cere**al**.*

*If the word has no accent mark, and you cannot read the word, try the stress on each syllable until it sounds like a word you know.

Open Syllables

Word	Illustration	Sounds like	Say and trace the word.	Write the word and underline the vowel sounds.
1. lion		līʹ•ŭn	lion	li on
2. giant		jīʹ•ŭnt	giant	_____
3. dial		dīʹ•ŭl	dial	_____
4. trial		trīʹ•ŭl	trial	_____
5. pliers		plīʹ•ŭrz	pliers	_____
6. diet		dīʹ•ĕt	diet	_____
7. duet		do͞oʹ•ĕt	duet	_____
8. fuel		fūʹ•ĕl	fuel	_____
9. poet		pōʹ•ĕt	poet	_____
10. idea		ī•dēʹ•ŭ	idea	_____
11. cereal		sîrʹ•ē•ŭl	cereal	_____

Open Syllables

Directions: Say, trace, and read.

The giant poet had fruit and cereal at 8:00 a.m. He was on a diet. Then he had an idea for a poem about a lion. The lion went on trial for being truant /trū´•ŭnt/ from school.

Congratulations!

You know the 4th syllable, the open syllable.

Nice job!

Overview

Unit 8 features beginning two-and three-letter consonant blends in Part 1, two-letter ending blends in Part 2, and prefixes *un-* and *re-* in Part 3. Unit 8 covers over sixty pages of words which provide extensive vocabulary acquisition.

Instruction

Review the first page of Unit 8 with your students, explaining that consonant blends may be made up of two or three consonants and may start or end a word. A blend's defining feature is that each letter sound is heard, as the *dr* in *drop* or *tr* as in *train*.

In Unit 8, emphasis is on reading the word from its beginning letter(s), attending to each letter from the beginning to the end of the word, blending the letters together to sound out and read the word. Model saying the consonants and blending them together to sound out and read the word. Students should repeat and practice, thinking and looking at the letters in the word as they pronounce each word, such as *dr* in *drop*. If the student finds it easier to use the following technique, do so with him or her. First, sound out from the vowel to the end of the word, such as *op*. Second, add the blend *dr*. Third, read the word *drop*.

With ending blends in Part 2, emphasize the beginning letters and word families, such as *f, k, m, bl* and *ind* as in *find, kind, mind,* and *blind*. Point out to students that they increase their vocabulary as they become familiar with word families; thus, they should look for word patterns within words to help them decode unfamiliar words.

In Part 3, prefixes are introduced. Review the first page of Part 3 with your students. Define a prefix as a syllable that is added to the beginning of a word to change its meaning. *Un-* is a prefix meaning *not*, and when added to a word, it means the opposite of that word. Review the chart with your students to ensure comprehension. Under the chart, direct them to say aloud the words in the sentence, trace the 18-point word, and read the entire sentence. They should complete all four sentences and then move to the next page where they write the word in the fourth column and underline the vowel sounds. In the fifth column, they fill in the number of syllables in the word, noting that the number of vowel sounds equals the number of syllables, as each syllable has one vowel sound.

Follow the same procedure with *re-*. *Re-* means to do over or do again. Illustrations and phonetic pronunciations are aids for students' use if words are unfamiliar. They should complete the lesson and subsequent exercises.

Assessment

Students should be able to complete lessons and exercises with minimal assistance and read word lists within lessons and /or sentences following the lessons. They should be able to discuss word meanings and use the words properly in sentences. If additional work is needed, work on troublesome words with your student to ensure reading accuracy and comprehension. Make flash cards for difficult words, and have the student record those words in his notebook.

As in earlier units, spelling tests, dictation, and students' sentences all measure mastery.

Vocabulary Acquisition Strategies

Multiple Meaning Words

Multiple meaning words which are illustrated are *pry, trunk, spring*, and *tie*. Others are too numerous to list but include the following: *trace, match, fly, trial, fuel, drop, train, state, step, stick, spot, spoke, scale, skim, skin, skirt, swell, swallow, block, clip, plant, plane*, and *play*, respectively. Discuss words, their definitions, and how they are used in sentences, ensuring student comprehension.

Word Families

Lessons in "Part 2, Ending Blends", are arranged in word families such as *jump, bump*, and *lump*. Ask your students to think of additional word families, making sure they focus on the word pattern as a strategy to acquire further vocabulary. Other words in the *ump* word family include *rump, stump, clump, slump*, etc. Word families are found on every page in Part 2.

Prefixes and Antonyms

Prefixes *un-* and *re-* constitute Part 3 of Unit 8. Examples include *tie* and *untie, wrap* and *unwrap, dress* and *undress*, etc. An additional word list is as follows: *unleash, unlike, unload, unlock, unpaid, unreal, unroll, untrue, unwashed, unwell, unzip*, etc. *Un-* lends itself to a discussion of antonyms.

An additional word list for *re-* is as follows: *restock, retrain, reuse, rebuild, recast, recharge, reclaim, recoil, reconstruct, recover, regain, recoup, retrieve, recreate, reenact, reform, refresh, remake, rematch*, etc.

Unit 8: Consonant Blends

Blends are made up of 2 or 3 consonants, letters that are not the 5 vowels (a, e, i, o, u). They may **begin** a word or **end** a word or syllable.

Each letter of a blend is heard /hûrd/ or sounded.

Examples:

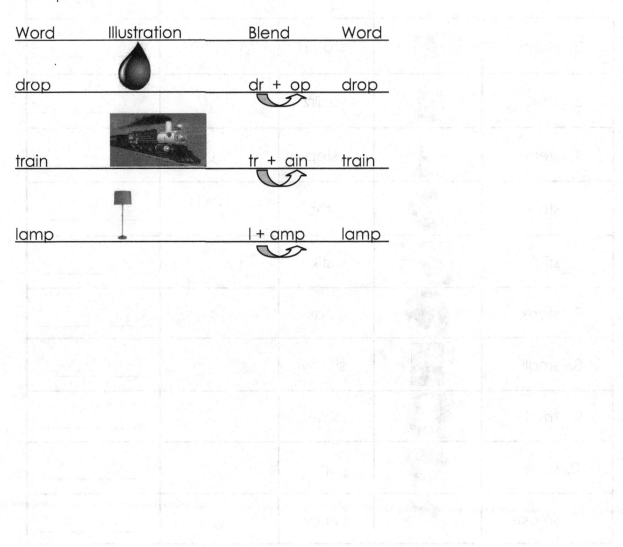

Word	Illustration	Blend	Word
drop		dr + op	drop
train		tr + ain	train
lamp		l + amp	lamp

Beginning Blends: st, sm

Word	Illustration	Sounds like	Say and trace the word.	Write the word and underline the vowel sound.
1. state		stāt	state	st<u>a</u>te
2. stamp		stămp	stamp	_____
3. stairs		stairz	stairs	_____
4. step		stěp	step	_____
5. stop		stŏp	stop	_____
6. stick		stĭk	stick	_____
7. steak		stāk	steak	_____
8. small		smawl	small	_____
9. smell		smĕl	smell	_____
10. smile		smīl	smile	_____
11. smoke		smōk	smoke	_____

Directions: Say and trace.

1. I smell smoke!

316

Beginning Blends: sl

Word	Illustration	Sounds like	Say 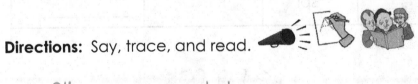 and trace the word.	Write the word and underline the vowel sound.
1. slacks		slăks	slacks	sl<u>a</u>cks
2. sled		slĕd	sled	_____
3. sleep		slēp	sleep	_____
4. sleeve		slēv	sleeve	_____
5. slip		slĭp	slip	_____
6. slice		slīs	slice	_____
7. slot		slŏt	slot	_____
8. slow		slō	slow	_____

Directions: Say, trace, and read.

1. Slip a dime in the slot.

2. Do you sleep in a sled? No, I sleep in a bed.

Beginning Blends: sp

Word	Illustration	Sounds like	Say and trace the word.	Write the word and underline the vowel sounds.
1. spell		spĕl	spell	sp<u>e</u>ll
2. spend		spĕnd	spend	_____
3. spot		spŏt	spot	_____
4. spare		spair	spare	_____
5. speak		spēk	speak	_____
6. spoke		spōk	spoke	_____
7. spoon		spo͞on	spoon	_____
8. Spain		spān	Spain	_____
9. Spanish		spăn´•ĭsh	Spanish	_____
10. spy		spī	spy	_____

Directions: (Circle,) say, trace, and read.

1. Do you speak Spanish?

2. (Yes, No) I (do, do not) speak Spanish.

Beginning Blends: s_

Directions:  Look at the pictures. (Circle) the word that matches the

picture. Say and write it on the line.

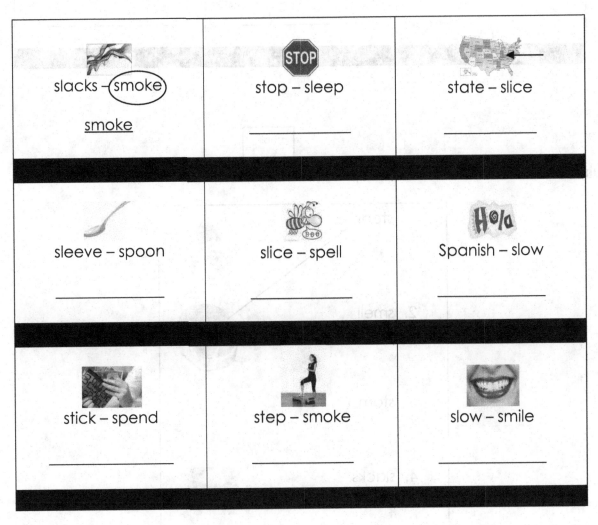

slacks – (smoke)	stop – sleep	state – slice
smoke	_____	_____
sleeve – spoon	slice – spell	Spanish – slow
_____	_____	_____
stick – spend	step – smoke	slow – smile
_____	_____	_____

Beginning Blends: s_

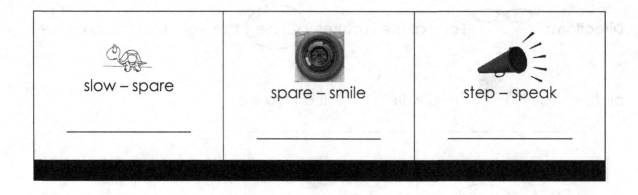

slow – spare	spare – smile	step – speak
_____	_____	_____

Directions: Match the word to its picture. [chair]

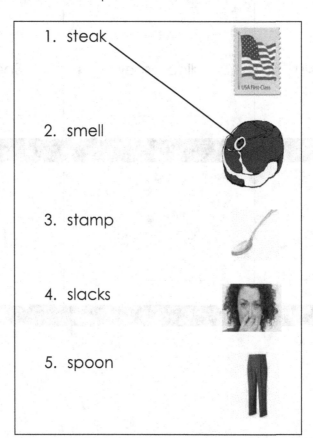

1. steak

2. smell

3. stamp

4. slacks

5. spoon

Beginning Blends: sc

Word	Illustration	Sounds like	Say  and trace the word.	Write the word and underline the vowel sound.
1. scale		skāl	scale	sc<u>a</u>le
2. scan		skăn	scan	_____
3. scare		skair	scare	_____
4. scared		skaird	scared	_____
5. scarf		skârf	scarf	_____
6. scoop		skōop	scoop	_____
7. school		skōol	school	_____

Directions: Say and trace. Read out loud.

1. If I am scared, I cry.

2. At the store, the lady puts my grapes on the scale and scans the code.

3. Scott likes school.

Beginning Blends: sk, sn

Word	Illustration	Sounds like	Say 🔊 and trace ✍ the word.	Write ✍ the word and underline the vowel sounds.
1. skate		skāt	skate	sk<u>a</u>te
2. skim		skĭm	skim	_____
3. skin		skĭn	skin	_____
4. skirt		skûrt	skirt	_____
5. ski		skē	ski	_____
6. sky		skī	sky	_____
7. snake		snāk	snake	_____
8. snack		snăk	snack	_____
9. sneak		snēk	sneak	_____
10. sneakers		snēk´•ûrz	sneakers	_____
11. snow		snō	snow	_____

Directions: Say, trace, and read.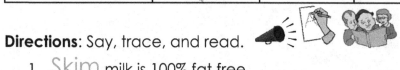

1. Skim milk is 100% fat free.
2. Did you give the snake a snack?
3. Can I wear sneakers with a skirt?
4. Can I wear sneakers to ski?

Beginning Blends: sw

Word	Illustration	Sounds like	Say and trace the word.	Write the word and underline the vowel sounds.
1. swallow		swŏl´•ō	swallow	sw<u>a</u>ll<u>o</u>w
2. swan		swŏn	swan	_____
3. sweat		swĕt	sweat	_____
4. sweater		swĕt´•ûr	sweater	_____
5. swell		swĕl	swell	_____
6. sweet		swēt	sweet	_____
7. swim		swĭm	swim	_____
8. swing		swĭng	swing	_____

Directions: Say, trace, and read.

1. Swans swim well.

2. In June, I sweat in my sweater.

Directions: Say, trace, and read.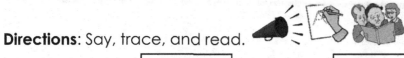

swell

swallow

Beginning Blends: sc, sk, sh, sw

Directions: Match the word to its picture.

chair

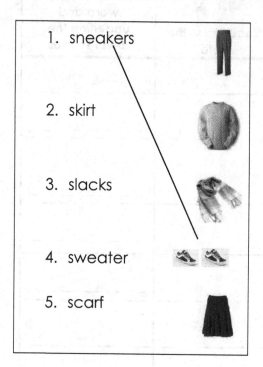

1. sneakers

2. skirt

3. slacks

4. sweater

5. scarf

Beginning Blends: sc, sk, sh, sw

Directions: Look at the picture. (Circle) the word that matches the picture. Say and write it on the line.

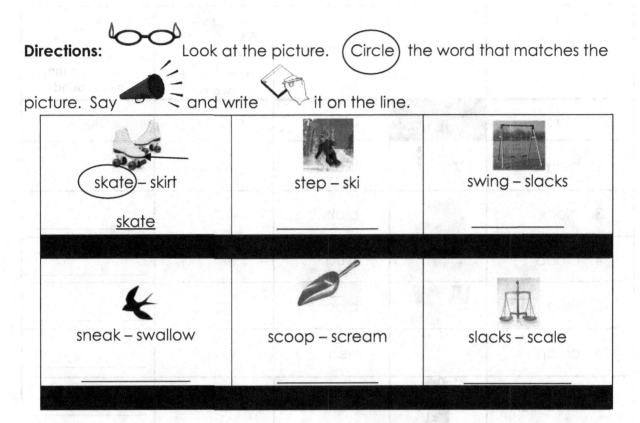

(skate)– skirt skate	step – ski _____	swing – slacks _____
sneak – swallow _____	scoop – scream _____	slacks – scale _____

Directions: Fill in, (circle) and read out loud.

1. I go to _____. (school, sky)
2. (Scan, Ski) _____ the skim milk.
3. I chew my food well and then _____ (swallow, screen).
4. A snake has hands and feet. (Yes, No)

Directions: Say, trace, and read.

1. Lick the stamp so it sticks.
2. Pick up the sticks and mow the grass, or lawn.
3. Kids like the Pick Up Sticks® game.
4. A snake has no hands or feet.

Beginning Blends: bl, cl

Word	Illustration	Sounds like	Say 📢 and trace ✍ the word.	Write ✍ the word and underline the vowel sounds.
1. black	⬛	blăk	black	bl<u>a</u>ck
2. blame		blām	blame	_____
3. block		blŏk	block	_____
4. blood		blŭd	blood	_____
5. blue		bloo̅	blue	_____
6. clean		klēn	clean	_____
7. cleanser		klĕn´•zûr	cleanser	_____
8. clip		klĭp	clip	_____
9. clock		klŏk	clock	_____
10. close		klōz	close	_____
11. close		klōs	close	_____

1. Circle and write the two (2) words that are spelled
   the same on this page: (clip, close) _____

2. Circle and write 2 color /kŭl´•ûr/ words: (clock, blue, blame, black)
   _____ _____

3. What tells time? A (block, clock) _____ tells time.

Beginning Blends: fl

Word	Illustration	Sounds like	Say  and trace the word.	Write the word and underline the vowel sounds.
1. flame		flām	flame	fl_a_me
2. flip		flĭp	flip	_____
3. floor		flôr	floor	_____
4. floss		flŏs	floss	_____
5. flour		flou´•ûr	flour	_____
6. flower		flou´•ûr	flower	_____
7. fly		flī	fly	_____

Directions: Say, trace, and read.

1. Use flour to make a cake. A cake is made with flour.

2. A bride, a groom, and flowers are /âr/ on the cake.

3. Do you floss your teeth? Yes, I floss my teeth.

Beginning Blends: gl

Word	Illustration	Sounds like	Say and trace the word.	Write the word and underline the vowel sound.
1. glass		glăs	glass	gl<u>a</u>ss
2. glad		glăd	glad	_____
3. glare		glair	glare	_____
4. glove		glŭv	glove	_____
5. glow		glō	glow	_____
6. glue		glōo	glue	_____

Directions: Say, trace, and read.

1. Glenn glues wood.
2. Glenda lost her glove.
3. I am glad to meet you.
4. This is a clean glass.
5. This glass is clean.
6. There is a glare from the sun at sunset.
7. Dad glares at me if he is mad.
8. The sun glows on a hot day.
9. I like Coke® in a clean glass.

Beginning Blends: pl

Word	Illustration	Sounds like	Say and trace the word.	Write the word and underline the vowel sounds.
1. plan		plăn	plan	pl<u>a</u>n
2. plant		plănt	plant	_____
3. plane		plān	plane	_____
4. plate		plāt	plate	_____
5. play		plā	play	_____
6. plug		plŭg	plug	_____
7. plus	+	plŭs	plus	_____
8. plastic		plăs´•tĭk	plastic	_____
9. plumber		plŭm´•ûr	plumber	_____
10. plunger		plŭnj´•ûr	plunger	_____

Directions: Say, trace, and read.

1. Pat the plumber has a plunger.
2. My kids play with toys.
3. Do not play with plugs.
4. Ten plus ten is twenty.

Beginning Blends: br

Word	Illustration	Sounds like	Say and trace the word.	Write the word and underline the vowel sound.
1. bread		brĕd	bread	br<u>ea</u>d
2. brake		brāk	brake	_____
3. break		brāk	break	_____
4. broke		brōk	broke	_____
5. brain		brān	brain	_____
6. branch		brănch	branch	_____
7. brick		brĭk	brick	_____
8. bride		brīd	bride	_____
9. bridge		brĭj	bridge	_____
10. bruise		bro͞oz	bruise	_____

Beginning Blends: cr

Word	Illustration	Sounds like	Say and trace the word.	Write the word and underline the vowel sounds.
1. crack		krăk	crack	cr<u>a</u>ck
2. cracker		krăk´•ûr	cracker	_____
3. crayon		krā´•ŏn	crayon	_____
4. (ice) cream		krēm	ice cream	_____
5. credit		krĕd´•ĭt	credit	_____
6. crew		krōo	crew	_____
7. crib		krĭb	crib	_____
8. cross		krŏs	cross	_____
9. crow		krō	crow	_____
10. crown		kroun	crown	_____
11. cry		krī	cry	_____

Beginning Blends: _r, _l

Directions: Match the word to its picture.

chair

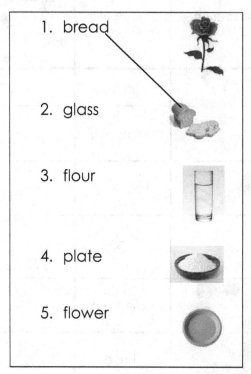

1. bread

2. glass

3. flour

4. plate

5. flower

Directions: Say, trace, (circle) and read.

1. If you drop it, it will break: (glass, stamp) or (scarf, plate).

2. Can you eat it? (cracker, crib) or (bridge, bread)

3. If you drop a glass or a plate, it will break.

4. You can eat a cracker or bread, but not a crib or bridge.

5. My house is made of brick.

6. My bruise is black and blue.

7. Cross the street.

8. Do you wear /wair/ a crown? (Yes, No), I (do, do not) wear a crown. I

   wear a (hat, crib) or a (cap, crew).

Beginning Blends: dr

Word	Illustration	Sounds like	Say 📢 and trace ✍️ the word.	Write ✍️ the word and underline the vowel sounds.
1. drain		drān	drain	dr<u>ai</u>n
2. drapes		drāps	drapes	_____
3. draw		draw	draw	_____
4. drew		dro͞o	drew	_____
5. dress		drĕs	dress	_____
6. drill		drĭl	drill	_____
7. drink		drĭnk	drink	_____
8. drank		drănk	drank	_____
9. drip		drĭp	drip	_____
10. drive		drīv	drive	_____
11. drove		drōv	drove	_____
12. drop		drŏp	drop	_____
13. dry		drī	dry	_____
14. dryer		drī′•ûr	dryer	_____

Beginning Blends: fr

Word	Illustration	Sounds like	Say and trace the word.	Write the word and underline the vowel sounds.
1. frame		frām	frame	fr*a*me
2. France		frăns	France	_____
3. French	bonjour!	frĕnch	French	_____
4. free	Free $0.00	frē	free	_____
5. freeze		frēz	freeze	_____
6. froze		frōz	froze	_____
7. frozen		frō´•zŭn	frozen	_____
8. friend		frĕnd	friend	_____
9. frog		frŏg	frog	_____
10. front		frŭnt	front	_____
11. fruit		fro͞ot	fruit	_____
12. fry		frī	fry	_____

Beginning Blends: fr, dr

Directions: Say, trace, and read.

1. I use my drill to drill holes in wood and metal /mĕt´•ŭl/.

2. The kids drew with crayons.

3. I did not (didn't) dry my dress in the dryer.

4. Do you buy /bī/ frozen foods?

5. Yes, I buy frozen French fries and frozen fruit. Frozen foods are in freezers at the front of the store. I cook food and freeze it in my freezer at home.

6. Franco frames his drawing.

7. Frida speaks French to her kids.

Beginning Blends: gr

Word	Illustration	Sounds like	Say and trace the word.	Write the word and underline the vowel sounds.
1. grade		grād	grade	gr<u>a</u>de
2. grapes		grāps	grapes	_____
3. grass		grăs	grass	_____
4. green		grēn	green	_____
5. grey		grā	grey	_____
6. grill		grĭl	grill	_____
7. grocery		grō´•sûr•ē	grocery	_____
8. ground		ground	ground	_____
9. grow		grō	grow	_____
10. grew		grōō	grew	_____

Directions: Say and trace.

1. The sky is not grey; the sun is out.

2. Grass grows fast and is green.

Beginning Blends: pr

Word	Illustration	Sounds like	Say and trace the word.	Write the word and underline the vowel sounds.
1. principal		prĭn´•sĭ•pŭl	principal	pr<u>i</u>ncip<u>a</u>l
2. pray		prā	pray	_____
3. press		prĕs	press	_____
4. price		prīs	price	_____
5. print		prĭnt	print	_____
6. prize		prīz	prize	_____
7. proud		proud	proud	_____
8. pry		prī	pry	_____
9. prune		pro͞on	prune	_____

Beginning Blends: gr, pr

Directions: Say, (circle) trace, and read.

1. Grapes are fruit. If the price is good, I buy them.

2. Frank buys /bīz/ green grapes in the grocery store. He freezes them for snacks.

3. Fred grills, broils, bakes, and fries his food.

4. Circle 2 colors /kŭl´•ûrz/: green   grey   proud

5. Green and grey are colors.

6. I am proud of my grades in math. The principal gave me a prize for my good grades.

7. Frank has /hăz/ a drill and a pry bar.

8. The grass is green in June.

Yes, I Can Read!   Unit 8

Beginning Blends: tr

Word	Illustration	Sounds like	Say and trace the word.	Write the word and underline the vowel sounds.
1. train		trān	train	tr<u>ai</u>n
2. track		trăk	track	_____
3. trade		trād	trade	_____
4. trash		trăsh	trash	_____
5. traffic (light)		trăf´•ĭk	traffic	_____
6. tree		trē	tree	_____
7. trial		trī´•ŭl	trial	_____
8. trip		trĭp	trip	_____
9. truck		trŭk	truck	_____
10. trunk		trŭnk	trunk	_____

339

Beginning Blends: tw

Word	Illustration	Sounds like	Say 🔊 and trace ✍ the word.	Write ✍ the word and underline the vowel sound.
1. twelve	**12**	twĕlv	twelve	tw<u>e</u>lve
2. twelfth	**12th**	twĕlfth	twelfth	_____
3. twenty	**20**	twĕn´•tē	twenty	_____
4. twice	**2x**	twīs	twice	_____
5. tweezers		twē´•zûrz	tweezers	_____
6. twin		twĭn	twin	_____
7. twist		twĭst	twist	_____
8. twine		twīn	twine	_____

Beginning Blends: tr, tw

Directions: Say, trace, (circle) and read.

1. Trucks get stuck in traffic /trăf´•ĭk/, but trains don't /dōn't/.

2. We took a trip on the train.

3. Fred trades cards with Bill, his twin. They are twelve.

4. I ran the mile twice. I ran two (2) miles.

Directions: Match the word to its picture.

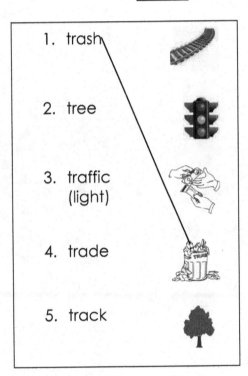

1. trash

2. tree

3. traffic
   (light)

4. trade

5. track

Beginning Blends

These are 3-letter blends that **begin** a word.

Word	Illustration	Sounds Like	Blend	Word
scream		skrēm	scr + eam	scream
stroller		strō´•lûr	str + oller	stroller
throat		thrōt	thr + oat	throat

Beginning Blends

Beginning Blends: scr

Word	Illustration	Sounds like	Say and trace the word.	Write the word and underline the vowel sounds.
1. scream		skrēm	scream	scr<u>ea</u>m
2. scratch		skrăch	scratch	_____
3. screen		skrēn	screen	_____
4. screw		skrōō	screw	_____
5. screwdriver		skrōō´•drī•vûr	screwdriver	_____
6. scrub		skrŭb	scrub	_____
7. scrub brush		skrŭb brŭsh	scrub brush	_____

Directions: Write the word and underline the vowel sounds.

2. scratch _____

5. screwdriver _____

7. scrub brush _____

Beginning Blends: spr

Word	Illustration	Sounds like	Say 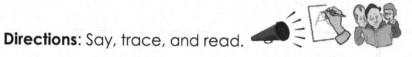 and trace the word.	Write the word and underline the vowel sounds.
1. spray		sprā	spray	spr<u>ay</u>
2. sprain		sprān	sprain	_____
3. spring		sprĭng	spring	_____
4. sprinkle		sprĭn´•kŭl	sprinkle	_____
5. sprinkler		sprĭn´•klûr	sprinkler	_____

Directions: Say, trace, and read.

1. The sprinkler sprinkles, or sprays, the shrub in front of our house.

2. Carlos screws the new screw into the screen door with his screwdriver. The screen door is in the front of the house.

3. Pat scrubs the tile floor with a cleaner and scrub brush.

4. Grass is green in the spring.

5. Do not scratch too hard; you will bleed.

6. Spray me with the hose; I am hot.

Beginning Blends: spr

Directions:  Look at the pictures. (Circle) the word that matches the picture. Say ⬤ and write ✎ it on the line.

(stroller) – spring	spray – scratch	sprain – stroller
<u>stroller</u>	_____	_____

Directions: Say and trace.

spring

spring 🌀

spring

spring

Directions: Say, trace, and read.

1. The spring in my bed broke.

2. Flowers and grass grow in spring.

3. It is springtime in May.

4. We fill our water jugs at the spring.

Beginning Blends: str

Word	Illustration	Sounds like	Say and trace the word.	Write the word and underline the vowel sounds.
1. street		strēt	street	str<u>ee</u>t
2. stream		strēm	stream	_____
3. stretch		strĕch	stretch	_____
4. straw		straw	straw	_____
5. strawberry		straw´•bair•ē	strawberry	_____
6. strainer		strā´•nûr	strainer	_____
7. straight		strāt	straight	_____
8. string		strĭng	string	_____
9. stripes		strīps	stripes	_____
10. stroller		strōl´•ûr	stroller	_____

Directions: Write the words and underline the vowel sounds.

5. strawberry _____

6. strainer _____

7. straight _____

9. stripes _____

10. stroller _____

Beginning Blends: spl, shr, squ*

Word	Illustration	Sounds like	Say ▷ and trace ✎ the word.	Write ✎ the word and underline the vowel sounds.
1. splash		splăsh	splash	spl<u>a</u>sh
2. split		splĭt	split	_____
3. shred		shrĕd	shred	_____
4. shredder		shrĕd´•ûr	shedder	_____
5. shrimp		shrĭmp	shrimp	_____
6. shrink		shrĭnk	shrink	_____
7. shrub		shrŭb	shrub	_____
8. square		skwair	square	_____
9. squeeze		skwēz	squeeze	_____
10. squash		skwŏsh	squash	_____
11. squid		skwĭd	squid	_____
12. squirrel		skwûr´•ŭl	squirrel	_____

*Q is spelled as qu, so the blend is squ and sounds like /skw/.

Beginning Blends: thr

Word	Illustration	Sounds like	Say and trace the word.	Write the word and underline the vowel sounds.
1. thrifty		thrĭf´•tē	thrifty	thr<u>i</u>ft<u>y</u>
2. thrill		thrĭl	thrill	_____
3. thread		thrĕd	thread	_____
4. three	**3**	thrē	three	_____
5. throat		thrōt	throat	_____
6. throw		thrō	throw	_____
7. threw		thro͞o	threw	_____

Directions: Say, trace, (circle) and read.

1. Squirrels eat nuts. Do you feed the squirrels? (Yes, No), I (do, do not) feed the squirrels.

2. (Squares, Squid) swim in the sea.

3. A square is a shape.

4. Squid swim in the sea.

5. Throw the ball straight.

6. Jose saves money, so he is thrifty.

7. It is a thrill for Rob to run three miles on the school track, not on the street.

Beginning Blends: Review

Directions: Look at the pictures. (Circle) the word that matches the picture. Say and write it on the line.

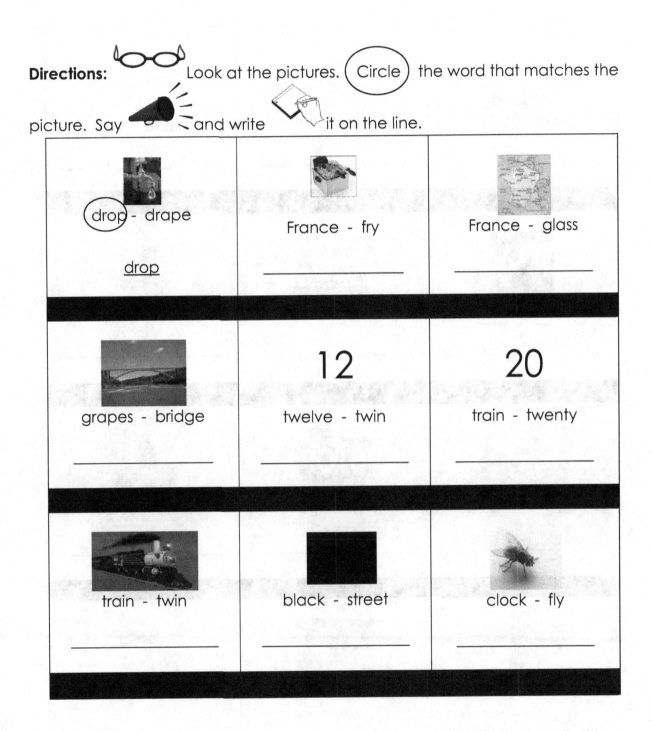

(drop) - drape	France - fry	France - glass
<u>drop</u>	_____	_____
grapes - bridge	twelve - twin	train - twenty
_____	_____	_____
train - twin	black - street	clock - fly
_____	_____	_____

Beginning Blends: Review

block - ⟨glad⟩ <u>glad</u>	plate - plane _____	plane - plot _____
slot - slip _____	smoke - scale _____	stamp - smoke _____
spot - step _____	stop - spot _____	stairs - scale _____
stop – state _____	snake – stick _____	smoke – step _____

Beginning Blends: Review

Directions: Find  and (circle) the words.

Word Find

GRAPES – DRIP – DRAPES – SLOT – SLEEP – GLASS

G	D	R	A	P	E	S
R	D	R	I	P	L	L
A	O	W	V	E	M	E
P	S	L	O	T	A	E
E	G	L	A	S	S	P
S	V	O	M	T	N	B

Directions: Say, trace, and read.

Do not splash in the stream or spray water from the stream. I will scream!

Directions: Read out loud.

Do Not Smoke
Do not smoke on the stairs.
Do not smoke on the plane.
Do not smoke on the train.
Do not smoke in the rain.
Do not smoke.

Part 2: Ending Blends

Ending Blends: st

Word	Illustration	Sounds like	Say and trace the word.	Write the word and underline the vowel sound.
1. nest		nĕst	nest	n<u>e</u>st
2. west		wĕst	west	_____
3. east		ēst	east	_____
4. waist		wāst	waist	_____
5. first		fûrst	first	_____
6. last		lăst	last	_____
7. mast		măst	mast	_____
8. wrist		rĭst	wrist	_____
9. post		pōst	post	_____
10. most		mōst	most	_____
11. ghost		gōst	ghost	_____

Ending Blends: st

Directions: Say and trace.

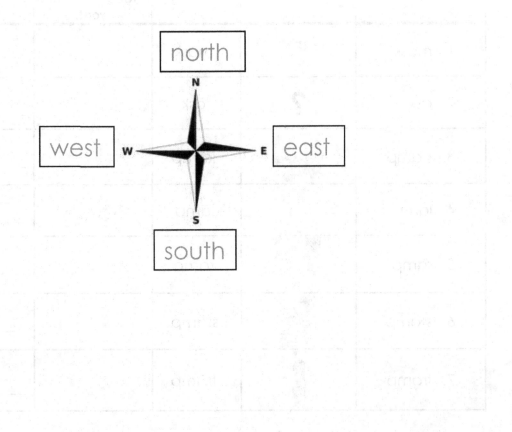

Ending Blends: sk, mp

Word	Illustration	Sounds like	Say 📣 and trace ✍ the word.	Write ✍ the word and underline the vowel sound.
1. mask		măsk	mask	m<u>a</u>sk
2. ask	?	ăsk	ask	_____
3. camp		kămp	camp	_____
4. lamp		lămp	lamp	_____
5. ramp		rămp	ramp	_____
6. stamp		stămp	stamp	_____
7. tramp		trămp	tramp	_____

Ending Blends: mp

Word	Illustration	Sounds like	Say and trace the word.	Write the word and underline the vowel sound.
1. limp		lĭmp	limp	limp
2. blimp		blĭmp	blimp	_____
3. chimp		chĭmp	chimp	_____
4. jump		jŭmp	jump	_____
5. bump		bŭmp	bump	_____
6. lump		lŭmp	lump	_____

Yes, I Can Read!   Unit 8

Ending Blends: Review

Directions: Look at the pictures. (Circle) the word that matches the picture. Say and write it on the line.

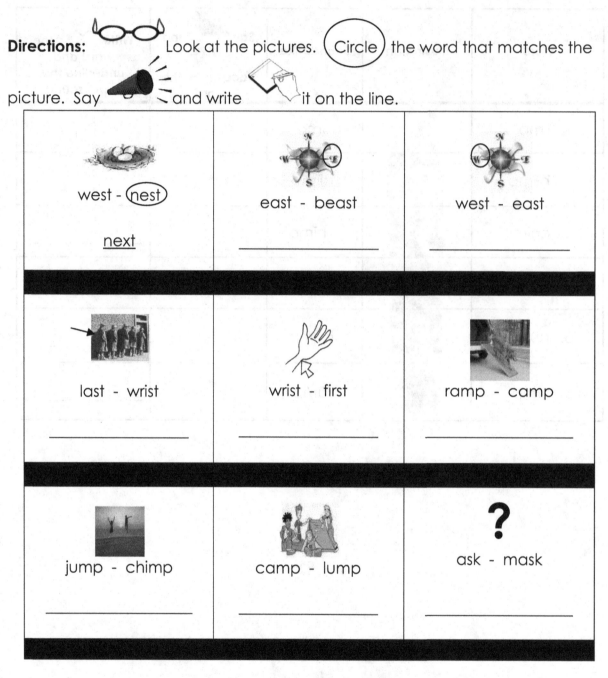

west - (nest)

next

east - beast

_____

west - east

_____

last - wrist

_____

wrist - first

_____

ramp - camp

_____

jump - chimp

_____

camp - lump

_____

ask - mask

_____

Directions: Say, trace, and read.

1. The chimp will jump off the ramp.

2. We are lost and must ask if the camp is east or west.

Ending Blends: nd

Word	Illustration	Sounds like	Say 🔊 and trace 🧦 the word.	Write ✍ the word and underline the vowel sound.
1. and	+	ănd	and	<u>a</u>nd
2. sand		sănd	sand	_____
3. band		bănd	band	_____
4. stand		stănd	stand	_____
5. end		ĕnd	end	_____
6. bend		bĕnd	bend	_____
7. mend		mĕnd	mend	_____
8. pond		pŏnd	pond	_____

Ending Blends: nd

Word	Illustration	Sounds like	Say and trace the word.	Write the word and underline the vowel sound.
1. find		fīnd	find	fïnd
2. hind		hīnd	hind	_____
3. kind		kīnd	kind	_____
4. mind		mīnd	mind	_____
5. rind		rīnd	rind	_____
6. wind		wīnd	wind	_____
7. blind		blīnd	blind	_____
8. grind		grīnd	grind	_____

Directions: Say and trace. Read out loud.

1. Do not stand in the sand.

2. Stand on land and swim in the sea.

3. The bandstand is next to the pond.

4. The pond is at the end of the street.

5. Meg will mend the pants.

6. Wind the clock on the shelf.

7. Grind the coffee beans. Peel the orange skin, or rind.

Ending Blends: ft, lt

Word	Illustration	Sounds like	Say 📢 and trace ✏️ the word.	Write ✍️ the word and underline the vowel sound.
1. raft		răft	raft	r<u>a</u>ft
2. lift		lĭft	lift	_____
3. sift		sĭft	sift	_____
4. left		lĕft	left	_____
5. melt		mĕlt	melt	_____
6. salt		sawlt	salt	_____
7. halt		hawlt	halt	_____
8. colt		kōlt	colt	_____
9. bolt		bōlt	bolt	_____
10. volt		vōlt	volt	_____

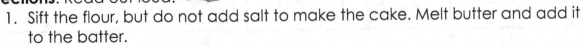

Directions: Read out loud.
  1. Sift the flour, but do not add salt to make the cake. Melt butter and add it to the batter.
  2. The raft is on the pond.

Ending Blends: ld

Word	Illustration	Sounds like	Say and trace the word.	Write the word and underline the vowel sound.
1. old		ōld	old	<u>o</u>ld
2. fold		fōld	fold	_____
3. cold		kōld	cold	_____
4. gold		gōld	gold	_____
5. mold		mōld	mold	_____
6. told		tōld	told	_____
7. hold		hōld	hold	_____
8. sold		sōld	sold	_____
9. scold		skōld	scold	_____
10. child		chīld	child	_____
11. mild		mīld	mild	_____
12. wild		wīld	wild	_____

Ending Blends: Review

Directions:  Look at the pictures. (Circle) the word that matches the picture. Say and write it on the line.

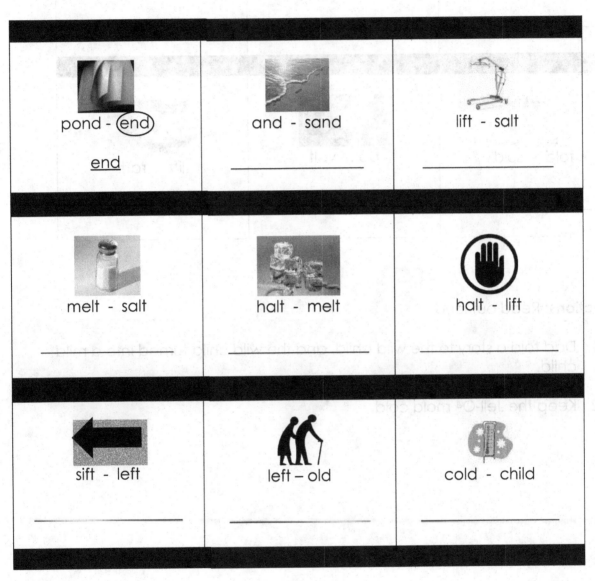

pond - (end)

end

and - sand

_____

lift - salt

_____

melt - salt

_____

halt - melt

_____

halt - lift

_____

sift - left

_____

left – old

_____

cold - child

_____

Ending Blends: Review

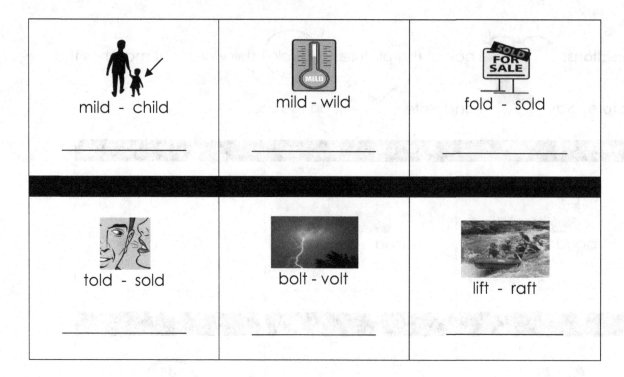

mild - child	mild - wild	fold - sold
_____	_____	_____
told - sold	bolt - volt	lift - raft
_____	_____	_____

Directions: Read out loud.

1. Dad told a story to the wild child, and the wild child turned into a mild child.

2. Keep the Jell-O® mold cold.

Ending Blends: lk

Word	Illustration	Sounds like	Say 📢 and trace ✍ the word.	Write ✍ the word and underline the vowel sound.
1. milk		mĭlk	milk ·	mi̲lk
2. silk		sĭlk	silk	_____
3. bulk		bŭlk	bulk	_____
4. sulk		sŭlk	sulk	_____

Directions: (Circle,) trace, and read out loud.

1. Dad buys skim milk in bulk.

2. Mom buys Silk® soy milk in bulk.

3. Do you sulk if you can't get your way? (Yes, No) I (do, do not) sulk if I can't get my way.

4. My dress is made of silk. It is a silk dress.

5. My tie is made of silk. It is a silk tie.

6. Can you drink milk? (Yes, No) I (can, can't) drink milk.

Ending Blends: nk

Word	Illustration	Sounds like	Say 📣 and trace ✍ the word.	Write ✍ the word and underline the vowel sound.
1. ink		ĭnk	ink	ink
2. sink		sĭnk	sink	_____
3. link		lĭnk	link	_____
4. wink		wĭnk	wink	_____
5. pink		pĭnk	pink	_____
6. drink		drĭnk	drink	_____
7. stink		stĭnk	stink	_____
8. think		thĭnk	think	_____
9. shrink		shrĭnk	shrink	_____

Ending Blends: nk

Word	Illustration	Sounds like	Say and trace the word.	Write the word and underline the vowel sound.
1. dunk		dŭnk	dunk	d<u>u</u>nk
2. bunk		bŭnk	bunk	_____
3. junk		jŭnk	junk	_____
4. skunk		skŭnk	skunk	_____
5. trunk		trŭnk	trunk	_____

Directions: Say and trace.

trunk   trunk   trunk   trunk

Directions: Read out loud.

1. If a skunk sprays a dog, the dog will blink and stink.
2. I had pink ink in my pen.
3. I think a cold drink at the sink is nice.
4. I wash my pink pants in cold water so the pants do not shrink. Then I fold them and put the pants in the trunk.
5. The twins sleep in bunk beds.

Ending Blends: nk

Word	Illustration	Sounds like	Say and trace the word.	Write the word and underline the vowel sound.
1. bank		bănk	bank	b<u>a</u>nk
2. tank		tănk	tank	_____
3. sank		sănk	sank	_____
4. blank		blănk	blank	_____
5. drank		drănk	drank	_____
6. thank		thănk	thank	_____

Directions: Say and trace. Read out loud.

1. The ice rink is cold.

2. The water in the fish tank is cold too.

3. The rock sank in the tank.

4. I will fill the gas tank in my car.

5. I will take a blank check to the bank.

Ending Blends: nk

Directions: Look at the pictures. (Circle) the word that matches the

picture. Say and write it on the line.

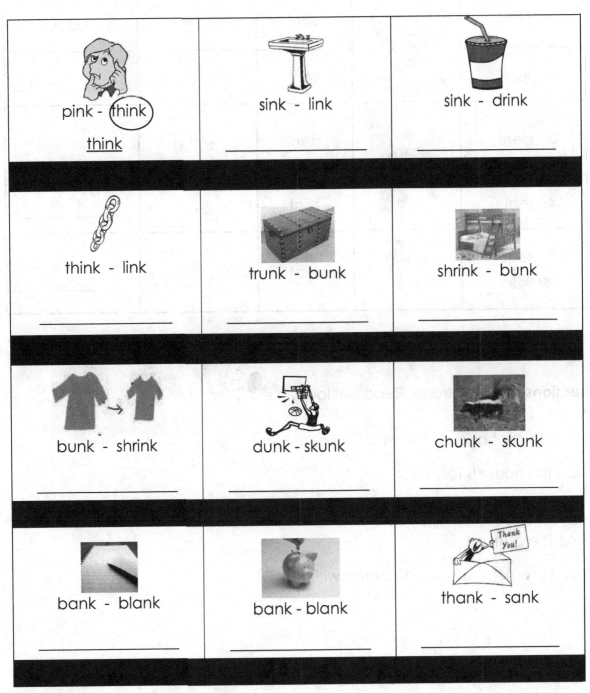

pink - (think)	sink - link	sink - drink
think		
think - link	trunk - bunk	shrink - bunk
bunk - shrink	dunk - skunk	chunk - skunk
bank - blank	bank - blank	thank - sank

Consonant Blends: nt

Word	Illustration	Sounds like	Say and trace the word.	Write the word and underline the vowel sound.
1. cent		sĕnt	cent	c<u>e</u>nt
2. tent		tĕnt	tent	_____
3. dent		dĕnt	dent	_____
4. rent		rĕnt	rent	_____
5. sent		sĕnt	sent	_____

Directions: Say and trace. Read out loud.

1. My car has a dent in it.

2. This house is for rent.

3. I sent a thank you note to my dad.

4. The gum is 1 cent.

5. I will rent a tent to camp with Brent.

Ending Blends: lt

Word	Illustration	Sounds like	Say and trace the word.	Write the word and underline the vowel sound.
1. belt		bĕlt	belt	b<u>e</u>lt
2. melt		mĕlt	melt	_____
3. felt		fĕlt	felt	_____

Directions: Read out loud.
1. I like to melt cheese on fish in the broiler.
2. The belt fits the pink pants.
3. I felt ill and was /wŭz/ pale.
4. Salt melts ice.
5. Jose felt the fuzz on his face.

Consonant Blends: lf

Word	Illustration	Sounds like	Say and trace the word.	Write the word and underline the vowel sound.
1. elf		ĕlf	elf	<u>e</u>lf
2. self		sĕlf	self	_____
3. shelf		shĕlf	shelf	_____
4. wolf		wŭlf	wolf	_____

Directions: Read out loud.
1. The elf made a shelf for himself.
2. The elf placed a wolf on his shelf.

Ending Blends: Review

Directions:  Look at the pictures. (Circle) the word that matches the picture. Say and write it on the line.

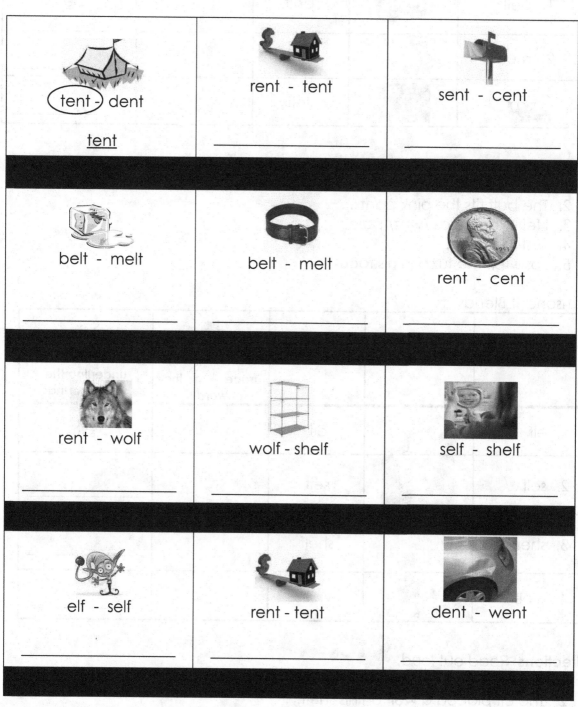

(tent) - dent	rent - tent	sent - cent
tent	_____	_____
belt - melt	belt - melt	rent - cent
_____	_____	_____
rent - wolf	wolf - shelf	self - shelf
_____	_____	_____
elf - self	rent - tent	dent - went
_____	_____	_____

Consonant Blends: sp

Word	Illustration	Sounds like	Say and trace the word.	Write the word and underline the vowel sound.
1. gasp		găsp	gasp	g<u>a</u>sp
2. grasp		grăsp	grasp	_____
3. clasp		klăsp	clasp	_____
4. crisp		krĭsp	crisp	_____

Directions: Match the word and picture.

chair

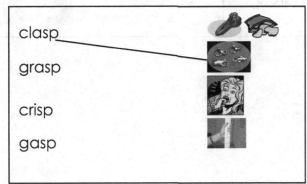

clasp

grasp

crisp

gasp

Directions: Say, trace, and read.

1. I like crisp chips.

2. Toast is crisp; crackers are crisp too.

3. Grip or grasp my hand so we can cross the street.

Part 3: Prefixes: un-

A prefix /prē´•fĭks/ is a syllable that is added to the **beginning**  of a word to change /chānj/ the meaning of the word.
Added to a word, **un** is the opposite /ŏp´•ŭ•zĭt/ of that word, or it means **not**.

Examples:

Illustration	Word	Add un	Sounds like	Illustration
	tie	untie	ŭn•tī´	
	wrap	unwrap	ŭn•răp´	
	kind	unkind	ŭn•kīnd´	
	wind	unwind	ŭn•wīnd´	
	dress	undress	ŭn•drĕs´	

Directions: Say, trace, and read.

1. Untie the rope.
2. Pop winds me up; tea lets me unwind.
3. The mean man is unkind.
4. I will unwrap my gift.

Prefixes: un-

Word	Illustration	Sounds like	Write the word and underline the vowel sounds.	# of vowel sounds = # of syllables
1. undress		ŭn•drĕs´	<u>u</u>ndr<u>e</u>ss	2
2. unfold		ŭn•fōld´	_____	_____
3. unclog		ŭn•klŏg´	_____	_____
4. unplug		ŭn•plŭg´	_____	_____
5. undo		ŭn•dū´	_____	_____

Directions: Fill in the blanks and read the sentences.

1. U_____ the lamp. (unplug, undress)

2. U_____ the drain. (unclog, unfold)

3. Jill must _____the sheets so she can make the bed.
   (unplug, unfold)

4. Mom and Dad _____ the baby so he will not get too
   hot. (undress, unfold)

5. U_____ the rope. (undo, unkind)

Directions: Read out loud.

1. Seal the jar so it will not leak. Take the jar lid off to unseal it.
2. Lock the gate to keep the dog in. Unlock the gate to let the dog out.
3. The green fruit is hard and unripe. Do not eat it if it is unripe. Eat ripe fruit.
4. Please unlock the door.
5. If the drain is clogged /klŏgd/, unclog it.

Prefixes: re-

The prefix **re** means to **do over** /ō´•vûr/ or to **do again** /ŭ•gĕn´/.

Word	Illustration	Sounds like	Write the word and underline the vowel sounds.	# of vowel sounds = # of syllables
1. rewash		rē•wŏsh´	rewash	2
2. reread		rē•rēd´	_____	_____
3. replace		rē•plās´	_____	_____
4. rewrap		rē•răp´	_____	_____
5. redo		rē•dū´	_____	_____
6. reverse		rē•vûrs´	_____	_____

Directions: Match the word and its picture.

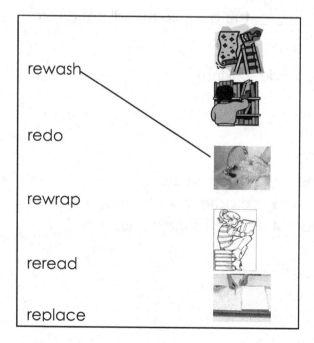

rewash

redo

rewrap

reread

replace

Directions: Say, trace, and read.

1. The car has mud on it. Rewash it.

2. Replace the book on the shelf.

3. Reheat the meat so it is hot.

4. I must stop the clock, reset it, and rewind it.

5. My kids like me to reread the same books to them.

 Congratulations!
Great job!

I, _____, Can Read!
(name)

Overview

Unit 9 is a large, varied unit on the 4th grade reading level. It contains beginning and ending digraphs, silent letters such as *b* in *lamb*, spelling rules for adding *-ing*, *-ed*, and spelling rules for forming plural and possessive word endings. It also features the *aw* sound with variant spellings as in *ball*, *walk*, and *salt*, contractions, *qu*, soft *c* and *g*, and prefixes *pre-* and *ex-*. Conjugations include to *be*, *ride*, and *sleep*.

Objectives

To learn:

1. consonant digraphs and their sounds;
2. spelling rules for adding endings ;
3. contraction definitions, usage, and spelling;
4. words beginning with *qu*;
5. words containing soft *c* and *g*;
6. definitions of *pre-* and *ex-*
7. vocabulary words contained in the lessons.

Instruction

Part 1 Beginning and ending consonant combos

Explain that a consonant combination, or "combo," is a two- or three-letter consonant combination that represents a new and different sound from its individual letters. (It is unnecessary to require students to learn the term *digraph*.) Use this digraph list as a reference, to teach digraphs and practice their sounds, and/or to acquaint students with their sound-spelling correspondence. Unit 9 lessons provide time on task for learning words containing these digraphs.

Examples

Diagraph	Sound	Examples
1. sh	sh	ship, dish
2. ch	ch	chin, church
3. ck	k	deck
4. tch	ch	match
5. th	th	thick, think
6. th	*th*	this, that
7. ph	f	phone
8. gh	f	laugh, cough
9. wh	w	whale, why
10. ng	ng	sing
11. dge	j	edge
12. zh*	zh	measure, vision, garage, azure

* *Zh* words are not included in workbook lessons because they occur more infrequently than those listed here. Additional examples include *pleasure* and *treasure*.

1. Voiceless and voiced th: Review voiceless *th* and voiced *th* until your student can pronounce both. For voiceless *th*, practice putting the tongue between the teeth and forcing air through, repeating *thick, thin, think*, etc. To make the voiced *th*, the same mouth position is used. The student should put a finger on his Adam's apple and make a sound. He should feel a vibration. He can practice saying *this, that, these, those*, etc. If, after practice, your student still cannot pronounce the difference, move on. In addition, some cultures frown on exposing the tongue in this way.

   This and *that* refer to an item close and farther way, as *these* and *those* refer to plural items close and farther away. Exercise A following the lesson targets those words. Students should read each sentence aloud, say and trace the light gray, 18-point word, and reread the entire sentence. Exercise B features the commonly confused *they're, there*, and *their*. *They're* is *they are* or *they were*. Explain that *their* is plural possessive, meaning something belong to them; *there* is at or in that place. Point out that the word *here*, which mean a place or point nearby, is in the word *there*. Both *here* and *there* indicate location.

2. Students complete each lesson by reading the word aloud across the row, saying and tracing the word in the fourth column, and writing the word and underlining its vowel sound(s) as directed in the fifth column. Next, they complete the subsequent exercises.

Part 2 Quiet combos
Discuss consonant combinations in which one or two letters are silent, or quiet, such as the silent *k* in *kn* (*knot*), silent *w* as in *wrap*, silent *gh* as in *light*, and quiet *b* as in *lamb*.
Letter (grapheme) features:
1. (p. 414) *K* is silent when followed by *n*. Other examples are *knack, knapsack, knead, knew, knob, knowledge*, and *knuckle*.
2. (p. 415) *W* is silent before *r*. Other examples include *wreath, wren, wrestle, wriggle, wring*, and *wrinkle*.
3. (p. 419) In the *mb* or *bt* combination, the *b* is usually silent. Other examples are *dumb, numb, debt*, and *subtle*.
Note: Silent h is not taught separately in *YICR* lessons, and, although it is not part of a combination, if you choose to teach it with other silent letters, examples are *hour, honest, John, honor*, and *school*. Additional silent *h* examples are listed in the Unit 12 Teacher's Guide.

Part 3: Word Endings -ing
1. Teach spelling rule #1 using information on pages 423 and 424. Review numbers 1 and 2, the completed examples, *run* and *jog*, with your students to ensure comprehension. They first double the word's ending consonant, in column 2. In column three, add *-ing*. In column four, say and write the word and underline the vowel sounds. In column five, count the number of vowel sounds, (2),

read that the number of vowel sounds equals of syllables (in a word), and write the number 2 for the number of syllables in each word.

Students should complete the lesson on pages 423 and 424. Following the lesson, students should fill in a correctly spelled -ing word from the lesson and read each sentence aloud.

2. (pp. 425-426) Because -ing words often take helping, or auxiliary words, review the conjugation of the verb to be. Review the present (current car) and past tense (antique car) symbols. Stress that present means today or now. Past means yesterday or time before. Read down the "present" tense column, top to bottom, first, second, third person singular : I am, you are, etc. , and then down the second column, past tense, in the same order.

Direct students to say, trace, and read the present tense chart from top to bottom and then the past tense column from top to bottom, following your example.

On page 426, they say, trace, and read, from top to bottom, first the verb ride and then sleep. Following the lesson, they read each sentence, trace and say the 18-point, light gray words, and then reread the sentence aloud. Repeat for the remaining three sentences.

These verb forms are included for proper usage to encourage the practice, oral and written, of including the helping (auxiliary) verb with the -ing form of the verb because many learners omit the helping verb in speech.

Spelling rules #2, #3, and #4 for adding -ing are covered on pages 427-431.
If necessary, discuss Rule #2 with your learner. In the lesson, review the completed example. Then he should, in the second column, write the word minus its e. In the third column, write the word from column two and add -ing. In the fourth column, say and write the word. Underline its two vowel sounds. He should write the number 2 in the fifth column.

Students should complete the two exercises following the lesson on page 428. If they have difficulty with the fill-in exercise, they should first read the entire sentence saying "blank" or "blanking" when they reach the blank. Next they check the choices. Using context, they fill in #1 trading; #2 closing; #3 sliding, chasing. After completing each sentence, they should reread it aloud to hear the complete sentence.

Spelling Rules #3 and #4 are on pages 429-431.
First, students should read the key words and use the "Sounds like" column for a pronunciation aid. Next, they should complete the lessons by filling in the fourth and fifth columns. There are two

vowel sounds and two syllables in words on pp. 429 and 430. In exercises on page 431 students should fill in words, trace and say words, and read completed sentences aloud.

Word Endings -*ed*

The past tense definition and three sounds when -*ed* is added are listed on p. 432: /t/ as in *helped*; /d /as in *rained*, and /ed/ as in *acted*. See Appendix C for a list of -*ed* words; also, students can read Appendix C lists for practice. They should complete the lesson and exercises on pages 432 and 433.

On pages 434-435, review spelling rules #1 and #2 for adding -*ed*, and direct students to complete the lessons.
In Exercise A, page 436, students add -*ed* to the word in parentheses following the blank. Then they read the story. Exercise B: Circle -*ed* words in the story "Baby Sal." On p. 437, they write 5 -*ed* words from the story on the lines provided in the 3 columns of -*ed* sounds. They can check their work with the words provided below.

Word endings: plurals

Three spelling rules for making nouns plural

1. Add *s*: *dog—dogs* (most common)
2. Words that end in *s, ss, x, z, ch*, or *sh* add *es*: *tax-taxes*
3. A few words change their spelling instead of adding *s* or *es*: *man-men*
   When completing the exercise, students can refer to pages 439 and 440 where the illustrated words are spelled.

Word Endings: possessives

Three spelling rules for making nouns possessive:

1. Singular nouns add an apostrophe and *s*: *dog's toy*
2. If the noun adds *s* to form its plural, as most do, just add the apostrophe after the *s*: *cats—cats' litter boxes*
3. If the noun changes its spelling to form the plural (instead of adding *s*, go back to Rule #1 and add '*s*: *women—women's jobs*

Part 4: aw sound

Students complete these lessons and exercises noting the *aw* sound spelled *all, alk*, and *alt* in featured words.

Part 5 Contractions

Direct students to the explanation and examples on page 448. Together you can read aloud the present tense forms of the verb *be*: "I am becomes I'm," etc. Read down that column. Repeat with the past and future forms, noting that they are contractions with *not*. Students should complete the exercises following the conjugation chart.

Part 6 Consonant Combos: qu /kw/

Q is always followed by *u*. At the beginning of a word, it sounds like /kw/. Additional words include *quad*, *quiz*, *squad*, *squash*, and *squid*. Sometimes *u* is silent and the *q* sounds like *k* as in *unique* or *liquor*.

Part 7: Soft c /s/ and Part 8 Soft g/j/

Shared rule: *C* and *g* before *e, i,* or *y*, have the soft sound. The soft sound of *c* is /s/ as in *ice* or *cent*; the soft sound of *g* is /j/ as in *age* or *gym*. Students complete lessons and exercises.

Part 9: Prefixes : pre-

Review the definition of a prefix and the prefix *pre-* as stated on page 457. Discuss the meanings of the six words listed and illustrated. Students write the prefix and word together as directed in the third column. They complete the exercises, looking back at the words' illustrations if necessary.

Prefixes: ex-

Define *ex-* as stated. Explain the star words, their meanings, and model their pronunciations if necessary. Students should complete the exercise and sentences on page 459 before completing the exercise and sentences on p. 460. On the last page of Unit 9, they should read the sentences aloud before and after completion. They will also trace, circle, and fill in the blanks with the correct response. Encourage students to generate their own as well as search for additional words with prefixes in the dictionary. These practices strengthen dictionary usage skills as well as vocabulary.

Assessment

As in earlier units, students should be able to read featured words in lessons and read sentences in subsequent exercises. A spelling test, dictation, or various writing assignments would also indicate mastery.

Unit 9: Consonant Combos (kōm´•bōz)
Part 1:   Beginning and ending consonant combos
Beginning sh

Word	Illustration	Sounds like	Say and trace the word.	Write the word and underline the vowel sounds.
1. ship		shĭp	ship	ship
2. shop		shŏp	shop	_____
3. shoe		sho͞o	shoe	_____
4. shell		shĕl	shell	_____
5. sheep		shēp	sheep	_____
6. short		shôrt	short	_____
7. shave		shāv	shave	_____
8. shove		shŭv	shove	_____
9. shovel		shŭv´•ŭl	shovel	_____
10. show		shō	show	_____
11. shower		shou´•ûr	shower	_____
12. shrimp		shrĭmp	shrimp	_____

Directions: Look at the pictures. (Circle) the word that matches the picture. Say and write it on the line.

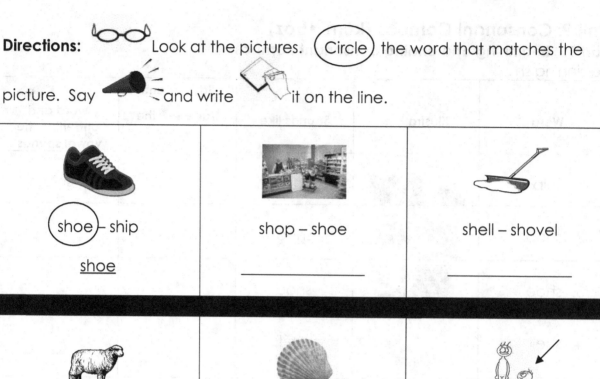

(shoe) - ship <u>shoe</u>	shop – shoe _____	shell – shovel _____

shovel – sheep _____	shell – short _____	shrimp – short _____

shrimp – shave _____	shave – ship _____	ship – shop _____

Consonant Combos: beginning sh

Directions: Say, trace, and read.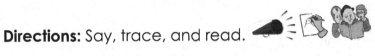

1. Shawn shaves and washes in the shower.
2. On the beach, Shelly dug with a shovel and found a shell. She saw a ship on the sea and a shrimp in the sea.

Consonant Combos: ending sh

Word	Illustration	Sounds like	Say and trace the word.	Write the word and underline the vowel sound.
1. wash		wŏsh	wash	w<u>a</u>sh
2. wish		wĭsh	wish	_____
3. dish		dĭsh	dish	_____
4. fish		fĭsh	fish	_____
5. mash		măsh	mash	_____
6. brush		brŭsh	brush	_____

Consonant Combos: ending sh

Directions:  Look at the pictures. (Circle) the word that matches the picture. Say and write it on the line.

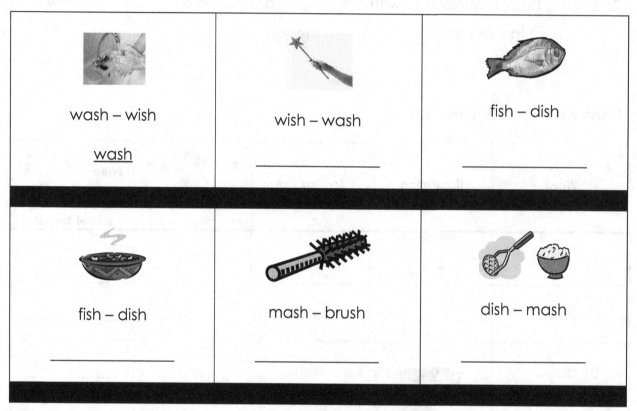

wash – wish <u>wash</u>	wish – wash _____	fish – dish _____
fish – dish _____	mash – brush _____	dish – mash _____

Directions: Say, trace, and read.

Chop the fish and mash it in a bowl. Shape the fish to make fish cakes. Fry the fish cakes in a pan. After lunch, wash the dish with soap and a dish brush.

Consonant Combos: sh

Directions: Find  and (circle) the words.

Word Find

| SHOP – WASH – SHAVE – FISH – DISH – SHE – SHOE |

A	T	R	Y	U	W	D
F	I	S	H	O	E	I
C	S	H	O	P	L	S
S	H	E	W	A	S	H
G	A	E	K	M	O	N
F	V	P	T	R	S	K
R	E	U	S	T	M	O

385

Consonant Combos: beginning ch

Word	Illustration	Sounds like	Say and trace the word.	Write the word and underline the vowel sounds.
1. chin		chĭn	chin	ch<u>i</u>n
2. chip		chĭp	chip	_____
3. chop		chŏp	chop	_____
4. chest		chĕst	chest	_____
5. child		chīld	child	_____
6. cheek		chēk	cheek	_____
7. check		chĕk	check	_____

Consonant Combos: beginning ch

Word	Illustration	Sounds like	Say and trace the word.	Write the word and underline the vowel sounds.
1. chain		chān	chain	_____
2. chair		chair	chair	_____
3. chalk		chawk	chalk	_____
4. church		chûrch	church	_____
5. cherry		chair´•ē	cherry	_____
6. chocolate		chŏk´•lŭt	chocolate	_____

Directions: Say, trace, and read.

Chuck the child ate a chocolate chip and cherry cookie.
He got chocolate on his cheek, chin, on his chest, on his chair,
and in his hair.

Consonant Combos: beginning ch

Directions:    Look at the pictures.   Circle the word that matches the

picture. Say and write it on the line.

 church – chain <u>church</u>	 chip – chain _____	 chain – chair _____
 check – cheek _____	 check – cheek _____	 chop – chin _____
 chain – chop _____	 child – cherry _____	 chest – chip _____

Consonant Combos: ending ch

Word	Illustration	Sounds like	Say and trace the word.	Write the word and underline the vowel sounds.
1. church		chûrch	church	ch<u>u</u>rch
2. wrench		rĕnch	wrench	_____
3. touch		tŭch	touch	_____
4. peach		pēch	peach	_____
5. teach		tēch	teach	_____
6. beach		bēch	beach	_____
7. bleach		blēch	bleach	_____
8. couch		kouch	couch	_____

Consonant Combos: ch

Directions: Look at the pictures. (Circle) the word that matches the picture. Say and write it on the line.

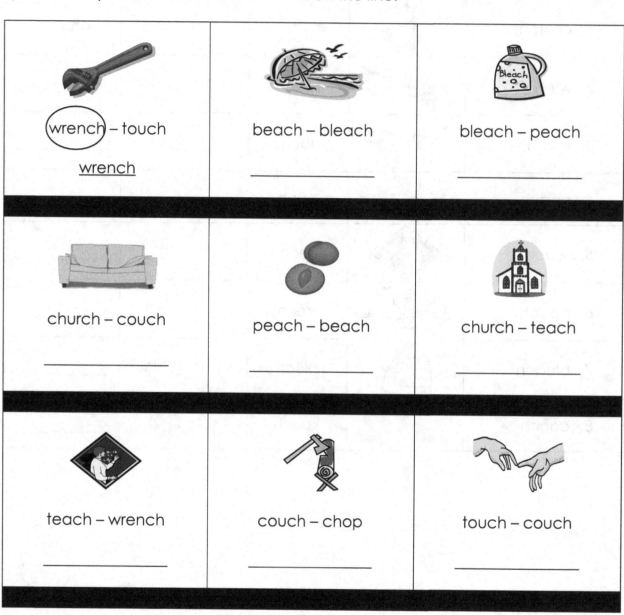

(wrench) – touch

wrench

---

beach – bleach

_____

---

bleach – peach

_____

---

church – couch

_____

---

peach – beach

_____

---

church – teach

_____

---

teach – wrench

_____

---

couch – chop

_____

---

touch – couch

_____

Consonant Combos: ch

Directions: Say, trace, and read.

Mom will wash Chuck's shirt with bleach. He can't eat a peach on the couch or the chair or a chocolate chip cookie on the couch or chair. But he can eat on the beach. Mom will teach him to be neat.

Cheech sat on the bench with the wrench. He hit his hand with the wrench and said "Ouch!"

Ch has 3 sounds:

ch as in church /**ch**ûrch/

k as in school /**sk**ōōl/

sh as in chef /**sh**ĕf/

* See **Appendix B** for a list of words with ch sounds.

Consonant Combos: ending tch

Word	Illustration	Sounds like	Say and trace the word.	Write the word and underline the vowel sound.
1. match		măch	match	m<u>a</u>tch
2. batch		băch	batch	_____
3. catch		kăch	catch	_____
4. latch		lăch	latch	_____
5. patch		păch	patch	_____
6. scratch		skrăch	scratch	_____
7. watch		wŏch	watch	_____

Directions: Say and read.

a batch of cement
Carl mixes up a batch of cement /sŭ•měnt´/.

a batch of cookies
Jill bakes a batch of cookies /kŏŏk´•ēz/.

Directions: Say and trace.

1. My socks match.

2. I lit a match.

Consonant Combos: ending tch

Word	Illustration	Sounds like	Say 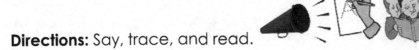and trace the word.	Write the word and underline the vowel sound.
8. itch		ĭch	itch	itch
9. ditch		dĭch	ditch	_____
10. hitch		hĭch	hitch	_____
11. pitch		pĭch	pitch	_____
12. witch		wĭch	witch	_____

Directions: Say, trace, and read.

The dog Patch was in a ditch. When he got out he felt an itch. He scratched his itch. Then Rich and Mitch hitched him to a sled, and they went for a ride.

Yes, I Can Read!   Unit 9

Consonant Combos: ending tch

Directions: Find  and (circle) the words.

Word Find

| ~~WATCH~~ – HITCH – DAD – DITCH – WITCH - CATCH |

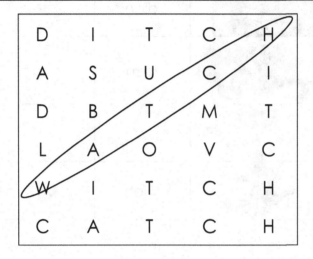

394

Consonant Combos: Review sh, ch, tch

Directions: Look at the pictures. (Circle) the word that matches the picture. Say and write it on the line.

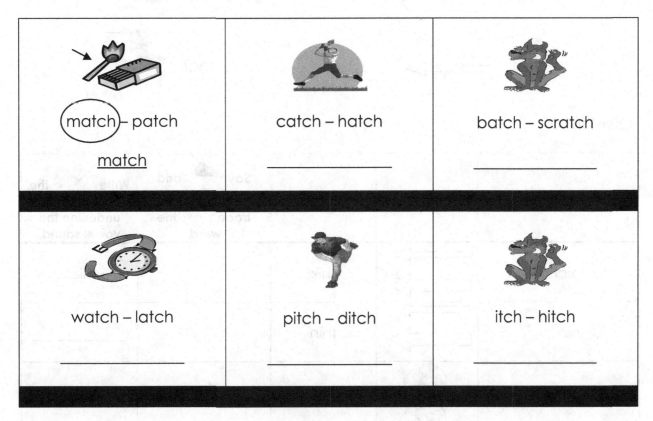

(match) – patch	catch – hatch	batch – scratch
<u>match</u>	_____	_____
watch – latch	pitch – ditch	itch – hitch
_____	_____	_____

Directions: Say, trace, and read.

1. Rich plays pitch and catch with his dad. He looks at his watch. It is 5:00. They shut the latch on the gate, and they go in the house.

2. Do not scratch an itch too much. It will bleed.

3. Watch the baby.

4. What time is it on your watch?

Consonant Combos: th, *th*

Quiet th   Voiced (voist) *th*

Examples   Examples

thick ⇒   this

thin ⇒   that

Quiet th

Word	Illustration	Sounds like	Say 📣 and trace ✍ the word.	Write ✍ the word and underline the vowel sound.
1. thick		thĭk	thick	th<u>i</u>ck
2. thin		thĭn	thin	_____
3. think		thĭnk	think	_____
4. thigh		thī	thigh	_____
5. three	3	thrē	three	_____
6. third		thûrd	third	_____

Consonant Combos: th, *th*

Voiced *th*

Word	Illustration	Sounds like	Say 📢 and trace ✍ the word.	Write ✍ the word and underline the vowel sound.
1. this		th ĭs	this	th i s
2. that		th ăt	that	_____
3. these		th ēz	these	_____
4. those		th ōz	those	_____
5. they		th ā	they	_____
6. their		thair	their	_____
7. there		thair	there	_____
8. them		th ĕm	them	_____
9. then		th ĕn	then	_____

Voiced *th*

Exercise A

Directions: Say, trace, and read.

1. This pen is Ben's.
2. That pen is Peg's.
3. Place the pen over there. Then draw with your pen.
4. These pens are Tom's.
5. Those pens are Mom's.
6. Put these pens there.
7. This pen is shorter than that pen.
8. Their pens are on the desks.

Exercise B

Star (☆) Words:
they're → means they are, they were

Word	Sounds like	Say  and trace .
they're	thair	they're
there	thair	there
their	thair	their

Directions: Say, trace, and read.

They're over there drawing with their pens at their desks.

Voiced *th*

Exercise C

Directions: Say, trace, and read.

There are three men in line. Will is the third. He is thin. These men are friends /frĕnz/. They like their hot dogs hot. They put hot mustard on their hot dogs. Then they go to the park and eat them on a bench.

Consonant Combos: ph /f/

Word	Illustration	Sounds like	Say 📢 and trace ✍ the word.	Write ✍ the word and underline the vowel sounds.
1. phone		fōn	phone	ph<u>o</u>ne
2. photo		fō´•tō	photo	_____
3. pharmacy		fârm´•ŭ•sē	pharmacy	_____
4. pheasant		fĕz´•ŭnt	pheasant	_____
5. graph		grăf	graph	_____
6. elephant		ĕl´•ŭ•fŭnt	elephant	_____

Consonant Combos: gh /f/

Word	Illustration	Sounds like	Say and trace the word.	Write the word and underline the vowel sounds.
1. laugh		lăf	laugh	laugh
2. cough		kawf	cough	_____
3. tough		tŭf	tough	_____
4. enough		ě•nŭf´	enough	_____

Directions: Say, trace, and read.

1. It is tough to laugh and cough at the same time. It is enough to laugh. You can never laugh enough.

2. Go to the pharmacy for Ralph. He has a cough.

Consonant Combos: ph, gh

Directions: Look at the pictures. Circle the word that matches the picture. Say and write it on the line.

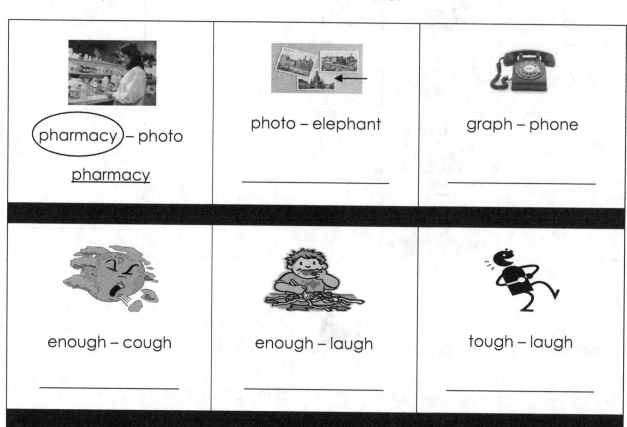

pharmacy – photo

pharmacy

photo – elephant

_____

graph – phone

_____

enough – cough

_____

enough – laugh

_____

tough – laugh

_____

Consonant Combos: ph, gh

chair

Directions: Match the word to its picture .

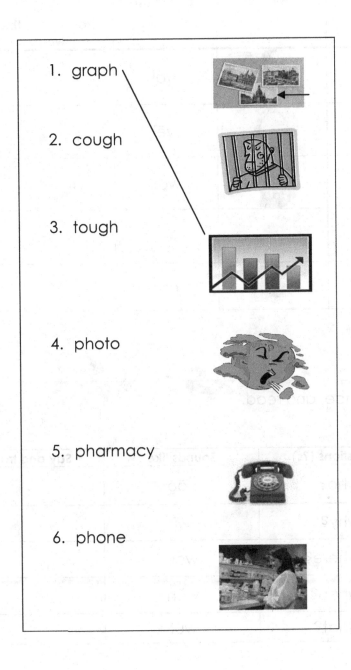

1. graph

2. cough

3. tough

4. photo

5. pharmacy

6. phone

Consonant Combos: wh

Word	Illustration	Sounds like	Say and trace the word.	Write the word and underline the vowel sound.
1. whale		wāl	whale	wh<u>a</u>le
2. wheel		wēl	wheel	_____
3. wheat		wēt	wheat	_____
4. white		wīt	white	_____
5. whole		hōl	whole	_____

Directions: Say, trace, and read.

Questions (?s)	Sounds like	Say and trace.
1. who?	hōō	who
2. why?	wī	why
3. where?	wair	where
4. when?	wĕn	when
5. what?	wŭt	what

Consonant Combos: ck

Word	Illustration	Sounds like	Say and trace the word.	Write the word and underline the vowel sound.
1. back		băk	back	b<u>a</u>ck
2. pack		păk	pack	_____
3. rack		răk	rack	_____
4. sack		săk	sack	_____
5. tack		tăk	tack	_____
6. black		blăk	black	_____
7. snack		snăk	snack	_____
8. stack		stăk	stack	_____
9. neck		něk	neck	_____
10. check		chěk	check	_____

Consonant Combos: ck

Directions: (Circle,) say, trace, and read.

1. Did you check to see if your books are in your backpack?

2. Did you get your check at the end of the week? Yes? No?

3. Did you cash your check? Yes? No? (Yes, No), I (did, did not) cash my check.

4. Write 2 parts of your body:

   a. _____ (neck, stack)

   b. _____ (tack, back)

Consonant Combos: ck

Word	Illustration	Sounds like	Say and trace the word.	Write the word and underline the vowel sound.
1. lick		lĭk	lick	lick
2. tick		tĭk	tick	_____
3. Rick		rĭk	Rick	_____
4. brick		brĭk	brick	_____
5. rock		rŏk	rock	_____
6. sock		sŏk	sock	_____
7. dock		dŏk	dock	_____
8. block		blŏk	block	_____
9. clock		klŏk	clock	_____
10. duck		dŭk	duck	_____
11. truck		trŭk	truck	_____

Consonant Combos: ck

Directions:  Look at the pictures. (Circle) the word that matches the picture. Say and write it on the line.

(back) snack _back_	lock – clock _____	truck – block _____
sack – check _____	rack – black _____	neck – brick _____
lick – sock _____	dock – brick _____	Rick – dock _____

Directions: Read out loud.

Jack put his backpack on the rack of his black truck. He had a stack of bricks in the back of his truck. He had a clock, a rock, and a box of tacks in the back of his truck. He had a snack in a sack, too.

Consonant Combos: ng

Word	Illustration	Sounds like	Say and trace the word.	Write the word and underline the vowel sound.
1. king		kĭng	king	kịng
2. ring		rĭng	ring	_____
3. sing		sĭng	sing	_____
4. wing		wĭng	wing	_____
5. sting		stĭng	sting	_____
6. spring		sprĭng	spring	_____
7. string		strĭng	string	_____

Consonant Combos: ng

Word	Illustration	Sounds like	Say and trace the word.	Write the word and underline the vowel sound.
1. song		sŏng	song	s<u>o</u>ng
2. strong		strŏng	strong	_____
3. wrong		rŏng	wrong	_____
4. hang		hăng	hang	_____
5. bang		băng	bang	_____
6. sang		săng	sang	_____

Directions: Say, trace, and read.

A ring is a thing, a wing is a thing, and a string is a thing.

Consonant Combos: ng

Directions:  Look at the pictures. (Circle) the word that matches the

picture. Say ◀◀ and write ✍ it on the line.

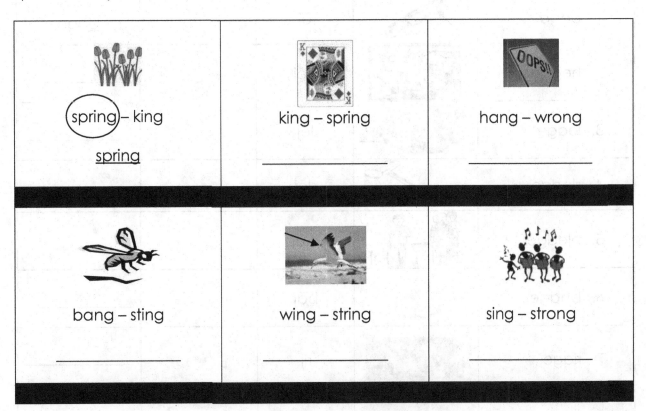

(spring)– king <u>spring</u>	king – spring _____	hang – wrong _____
bang – sting _____	wing – string _____	sing – strong _____

Directions: Say, trace, and read.

1. The door slams with a bang.
2. Sting writes and sings songs.
3. A bee sting stings. Ouch!
4. In the spring, birds sing and bees buzz.
5. My bed has strong springs.
6. I have a ring on my finger.
7. The school bell rings at three.

Yes, I Can Read! Unit 9

Consonant Combos: dge

Word	Illustration	Sounds like	Say and trace the word.	Write the word and underline the vowel sound.
1. edge		ĕj	edge	<u>e</u>dge
2. hedge		hĕj	hedge	_____
3. ledge		lĕj	ledge	_____
4. sledge		slĕj	sledge	_____
5. pledge		plĕj	pledge	_____
6. badge		băj	badge	_____
7. ridge		rĭj	ridge	_____
8. bridge		brĭj	bridge	_____

Consonant Combos: dge

Directions:  Look at the pictures. (Circle) the word that matches the picture. Say and write it on the line.

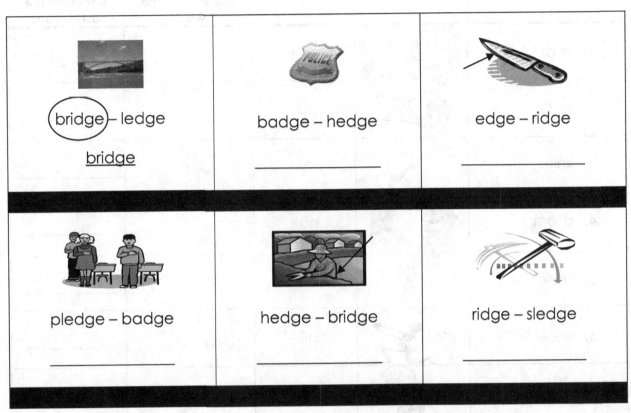

(bridge) – ledge	badge – hedge	edge – ridge
bridge	_____	_____
pledge – badge	hedge – bridge	ridge – sledge
_____	_____	_____

Directions: Say, trace, and read.

Jose used a sledge to break the rocks. He is strong. He placed them on the edge of the bridge to form a ridge.

413

Part 2: Quiet combos

Consonant Combos: quiet k (kn)

Word	Illustration	Sounds like	Say ⟍ and trace ⟍ the word.	Write ⟍ the word and underline the vowel sound.
1. knot		nŏt	knot	kn<u>o</u>t
2. knit		nĭt	knit	_____
3. knife		nīf	knife	_____
4. knock		nŏk	knock	_____
5. knee		nē	knee	_____
6. kneel		nēl	kneel	_____
7. know		nō	know	_____
8. knight		nīt	knight	_____

Consonant Combos: quiet w (wr)

Word	Illustration	Sounds like	Say and trace the word.	Write the word and underline the vowel sound.
1. wrap		răp	wrap	wr<u>a</u>p
2. wreck		rĕk	wreck	_____
3. wrench		rĕnch	wrench	_____
4. wrist		rĭst	wrist	_____
5. write		rīt	write	_____
6. wrote		rōt	wrote	_____
7. wrong		rŏng	wrong	_____

Consonant Combos: quiet gh

Word	Illustration	Sounds like	Say and trace the word.	Write the word and underline the vowel sound.
1. fight		fīt	fight	f<u>i</u>ght
2. light		līt	light	_____
3. night		nīt	night	_____
4. knight		nīt	knight	_____
5. sight		sīt	sight	_____
6. tight		tīt	tight	_____
7. right		rīt	right	_____
8. bright		brīt	bright	_____
9. eight	8	āt	eight	_____
10. sleigh		slā	sleigh	_____

Quiet Combos

Directions: Look at the pictures. (Circle) the word that matches the picture. Say and write it on the line.

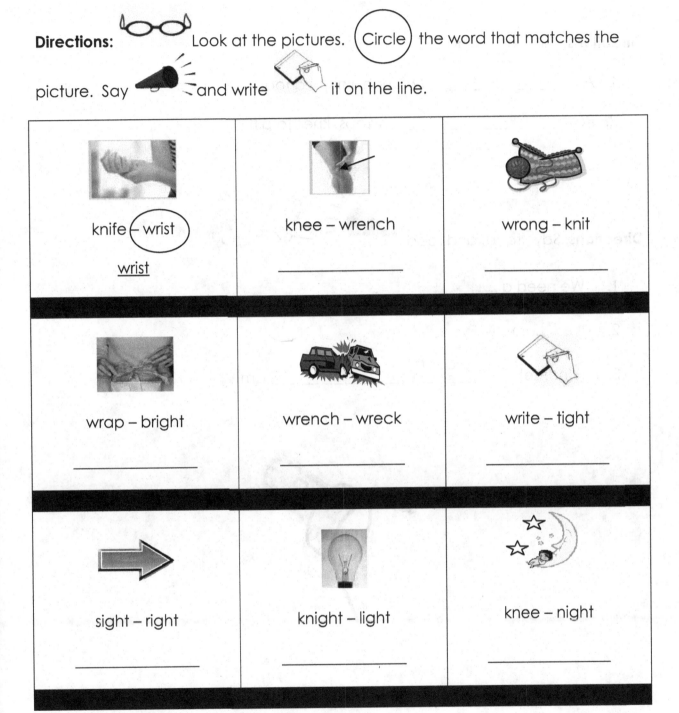

knife – (wrist) __wrist__	knee – wrench _____	wrong – knit _____
wrap – bright _____	wrench – wreck _____	write – tight _____
sight – right _____	knight – light _____	knee – night _____

Quiet combos

Directions: Fill in and read.

1. A _____(wrench, knit) is a tool.

2. Rose _____ (wraps, knee) a gift.

Directions: Say, trace, and read.

1.   We need a bright light.

2.   It is night.

3.   I, (name) _____, am bright!

Consonant Combos: quiet b

Word	Illustration	Sounds like	Say 📢 and trace ✍ the word.	Write ✍ the word and underline the vowel sound.
1. lamb		lăm	lamb	l<u>a</u>mb
2. limb		līm	limb	_____
3. comb		kōm	comb	_____
4. climb		klīm	climb	_____
5. thumb		thŭm	thumb	_____
6. doubt		dout	doubt	_____

Consonant combos: quiet l

Word	Illustration	Sounds like	Say and trace the word.	Write the word and underline the vowel sound.
1. walk		wawk	walk	w<u>a</u>lk
2. talk		tawk	talk	_____
3. chalk		chawk	chalk	_____
4. stalk		stawk	stalk	_____

Directions: Fill in the blank, say, and read out loud.

1. Write with a pen or write with _____(stalk – chalk) in class.

2. I _____ (walk – talk) with my mouth.

3. Joe likes to _____(walk – chalk), run, and climb.

Quiet Combos: Review

Directions: Find ![detective] and   circle   the words.

Word Find

SIGHT – THIGH – BRIGHT – THUMB – TIGHT

R	I	M	B	S	K	F	N
I	F	T	H	I	G	H	T
G	W	H	T	G	O	S	I
H	V	U	N	H	V	L	G
T	O	M	B	T	F	I	H
V	R	B	R	I	G	H	T

Directions: Say, trace, and read.

1. The knight gets down on his knees to find the knife and the wrench he lost by the tree. He needs a light. It is night, and the moon is not bright.

2. Take the wool from the lamb. Comb it and spin it; then knit some socks.

3. When Hugh writes, he uses the thumb, finger, and wrist of his right hand. Hugh has a bright light on his desk so he can write at night and not hurt his eyesight.

Consonant Combos: Review

Directions: Write the words on the correct lines.

chest

chest, knee, back, thigh,

wrist, finger, thumb

chin, cheek, neck

Part 3: Word Endings

Word Endings: -ing

Remember: A syllable is a word or word part that has a vowel sound. **Ing** is a syllable that is added to many /měn´•ē/ words.

The closed syllable, the 1st syllable, has a short vowel sound and ends in a consonant. (See Unit 4.)
    Example: run

 Rule #1: When you add **ing** to the end of a closed syllable, with a short vowel sound, add the ending consonant 1st, or double /dŭb´•ŭl/ the ending consonant. Then add **ing**.
    Example: run → running

Word	Add Consonant	Add -ing	Say 🔊 and write ✏ the word. Underline the vowel sounds.	# of vowel sounds = # of syllables
1. run	run + n	runn+ing	running	2
2. jog	jog+g	jogg+ing	jogging	2
3. sit				
4. hop				
5. plan				
6. win				
7. swim				
8. spot				
9. get				
10. let				
11. pet				

Word Endings: -ing

Word	Add Consonant	Add -ing	Say and write the word. Underline the vowel sounds.	# of vowel sounds = # of syllables
12. map	_____	_____	_____	_____
13. cut	_____	_____	_____	_____
14. rub	_____	_____	_____	_____
15. stop	_____	_____	_____	_____
16. drop	_____	_____	_____	_____

Directions: Use 1 of these /thēz/ ing words to fill in the blank.

1. _____ is fun.

2. _____ is nice.

3. _____ feels good.

4. I like _____.

With a closed syllable word, which has a short vowel sound and ends in a consonant, like these words, double the ending consonant when you add **ing** or other /ŭth´•ûr/ endings that begin with a vowel, such as **ed**, **er**, or **est**.

Example: plan ➞ planning, planned, planner
      Doubling /dŭb´•lēng/ the consonant keeps the vowel short.

Word Endings: -ing

When adding **ing** to a verb, you may need a helping verb that is a form of **be**.*

Examples:
      I **am** working.
      We **were** biking.

Directions: Say, trace and read.

Be

Today Present	Yesterday Past
I am	I was
you are	you were
he, she, it is	he, she, it was
we are	we were
you are	you were
they are	they were

* For a comprehensive explanation of verbs and lists of verb forms, irregular verbs, and auxiliary (helping) verbs, consult an English language arts text or English handbook.

Word Endings: -ing

Directions: Say, trace, and read.

Verb Forms

Today Present	Yesterday Past
I am riding.	I was sleeping.
You are riding.	You were sleeping.
Pat is riding.	Jo was sleeping.
We are riding.	We were sleeping.
You are riding.	You were sleeping.
They are riding.	They were sleeping.

Directions: Say, trace, and read.

1. Matt is mapping out our trip.

2. Jim is getting off work to go.

3. Rosa is dropping off the baby at her mom's.

4. I am stopping to get gas and food.

5. Bob was sleeping when I came home.

Word Endings: -ing

Rule #2
When adding **ing** to the quiet e syllable, the 2nd syllable, drop the e; then add **ing**. (See Unit 5.)
Example: bake→ baking

Word	Drop the e	Add -ing	Say and write the word. Underline the vowel sounds.	# of vowel sounds = # of syllables
1. bake	bak	bak+ing	baking	2
2. bike	_____	_____	_____	_____
3. drive	_____	_____	_____	_____
4. lose /lōōz/	_____	_____	_____	_____
5. shine	_____	_____	_____	_____
6. slide	_____	_____	_____	_____
7. write	_____	_____	_____	_____
8. use	_____	_____	_____	_____
9. close /klōz/	_____	_____	_____	_____
10. trade	_____	_____	_____	_____
11. chase	_____	_____	_____	_____
12. ride	_____	_____	_____	_____

Directions: Read.

I like riding my bike in town.

Good job!

Word Endings: -ing

Directions: Say, trace, and read.

1. Sam is baking bread.
2. The light is shining in my eyes.
3. I'm glad you are driving to work.
4. We were losing the game when Sam kicked the ball into the net; then we won /wŭn/!
5. I, (name) _____, am reading.

Directions: Fill in and read.

1. Bob is _____(trading – chasing) in his car for a used van.

2. I will be _____ (shining – closing) the store doors at 9 p.m.

3. The kids were _____(writing – sliding) on their sleds, and their dog was _____ (chasing – using) them.

Word Endings: -ing

Rule #3
If the word ends in 2 consonants, just add **ing**.
Example: roast→ roasting

Word	Add -ing	Sounds like	Say and write the word. Underline the vowel sounds.	# of vowel sounds = # of syllables
1. roast	roast+ing	rōst´•ĭng	ro̲a̲sti̲ng	2
2. toast	_____	tōst´•ĭng	_____	____
3. walk	_____	wŏk´•ĭng	_____	____
4. fish	_____	fĭsh´•ĭng	_____	____
5. camp	_____	kămp´•ĭng	_____	____
6. tent	_____	tĕnt´•ĭng	_____	____
7. spell	_____	spĕl´•ĭng	_____	____
8. limp	_____	lĭmp´•ĭng	_____	____
9. help	_____	hĕlp´•ĭng	_____	____
10. ask	_____	ăsk´•ĭng	_____	____
11. want	_____	wŏnt´•ĭng	_____	____
12. start	_____	stârt´•ĭng	_____	____

Directions: Read out loud.

Jim is limping, and Tom is helping him.

Word Endings: -ing

 Rule #4
If the word has a vowel team, or 2 vowels together, just add **ing**.

Word	Add -ing	Sounds like	Say and write the word. Underline the vowel sounds.	# of vowel sounds = # of syllables
1. eat	eat+ing	ēt´•ĭng	<u>ea</u>t<u>i</u>ng	2
2. read	_____	rēd´•ĭng	_____	___
3. speak	_____	spēk´•ĭng	_____	___
4. flow	_____	flō´•ĭng	_____	___
5. grow	_____	grō´•ĭng	_____	___
6. snow	_____	snō´•ĭng	_____	___
7. mow	_____	mō´•ĭng	_____	___
8 sleep	_____	slēp´•ĭng	_____	___
9 meet	_____	mēt´•ĭng	_____	___
10. speed	_____	spēd´•ĭng	_____	___
11. say	_____	sā´•ĭng	_____	___
12. pay	_____	pā´•ĭng	_____	___

Word Endings: -ing

Directions: Fill in the word.

| eating – sleeping – camping – fishing – helping – walking |

1. Jim, Tom, and I like to go c_____.

2. We have been /bĭn/ w_____ on the trails.

3. We go f_____ a lot.

4. We have been ea_____ the fish we catch /kăch/.

5. I am sl_____ in my own /ōn/ tent.

Directions: Say, trace, and read.

1. The stream is flowing fast.

2. Saying and speaking seem the same.

3. I am eating well and growing strong.

4. Gus is working, so he is paying the bills.

5. Pete was speeding in a school zone.

6. Reading is not so hard.

7. Lee and Ben are meeting at noon in the park.

Word Endings: -ed

The ending **ed** is added to a word to mean past tense /tĕns/, or time in the past.
When **ed** is added to a word, it may sound like:
    1. /t/ as in liked /līkt/, washed /wŏsht/, cooked /ko͝okt/
    2. /d/ as in mailed /māld/, snowed /snōd/, rained /rānd/
    3. /ĕd/ as in wanted /wŏnt´•ĕd/, started /stărt´•ĕd/, painted /pānt´•ĕd/.
When a word ends in t or d, and **ed** is added, the sound is /ĕd/, like the name
Ed.

Word	Add -ed	Sounds like	Say and write the word. Underline the vowel sounds.	# of vowel sounds = # of syllables
1. help	help+ed	hĕlpt	h<u>e</u>lped	1
2. fish		fĭsht		
3. walk		wŏkt		
4. wish		wĭsht		
5. watch		wŏcht		
6. cook		ko͝okt		
7. rain		rānd		
8. spell		spĕld		
9. act		ăkt´•ĕd		
10. lift		lĭft´•ĕd		
11. want		wŏnt´•ĕd		
12. bait		bāt´•ĕd		
13. paint		pānt´•ĕd		
14. hunt		hŭnt´•ĕd		

Word Endings: -ed

Directions: Fill in the missing word.

1. Jim _____helped_____ (worked – helped) his mom.

2. Des _____ (acted – wished) in the school play.

3. Bob _____ (acted – lifted) the box out of the truck.

4. Tom _____ (cooked – helped) lunch at home.

5. Ray _____ (punched – spelled) his time card at work.

Directions: Fill in the missing word.

1. Juan _____spelled_____ (walked – spelled) his words right on the test.

2. Kate _____ (climbed – camped) the subway steps.

3. The Smiths _____ (helped – camped) out in the tent.

4. Lynn _____ (wished – walked) 5 miles last week.

5. Sal _____ (baited – wanted) his hook and

   _____ (cooked – waited) to catch a fish.

Word Endings: -ed

Rule # 1
When adding **ed** to the end of a closed syllable, add the same ending
consonant 1st, or double the final consonant.
        Example: jog→ jogged

Word	Add consonant	Add -ed	Sounds like	Say and write the word. Underline the vowel sounds.	# of vowel sounds = # of syllables
1. hop	hop+p	hopp+ed	hŏpt	h<u>o</u>pped	1
2. drop	_____	_____	drŏpt	_____	____
3. shop	_____	_____	shŏpt	_____	____
4. stop	_____	_____	stŏpt	_____	____
5. spot	_____	_____	spŏt´•ĕd	_____	____
6. map	_____	_____	mbăpt	_____	____
7. rub	_____	_____	rŭbd	_____	____
8. skip	_____	_____	skĭpt	_____	____
9. trip	_____	_____	trĭpt	_____	____

Word Endings: -ed

Rule # 2
When adding **ed** to the quiet e syllable, 2nd syllable, take off the e; then add **ed**. (See Unit 4, Part 1, 2nd syllable.)*

Word	Drop the e	Add -ed	Sounds like	Say and write the word. Underline the vowel sound.
1. bake	bak	bak+ed	bākt	b<u>a</u>ked
2. bike	_____	_____	bīkt	_____
3. hope	_____	_____	hōpt	_____
4. lace	_____	_____	lāst	_____
5. use	_____	_____	ūzd	_____
6. close	_____	_____	klōzd	_____
7. shave	_____	_____	shāvd	_____

Review: -ed

Exercise A

Directions: Add **ed** to each word and write it in the blank. Then read the story.

Last night, we _____ (watch) the cows. They grazed and _____ (walk) through the fields. We _____ (hook) the gate so they could not get out. They _____ (stay) in the field and chased the other cows. They _____ (play) for hours. Then the farmer _____ (open) the gate. The cows _____ (march) to the barn to be _____ (milk). They _____ (act) happy as they _____ (round) the bend. Their hooves _____ (sound) loud when they hit the ground.

Exercise B

Directions: Read the story. (Circle) the **ed** words.

Baby Sal

When I found out I was going to have a baby, my husband /hŭz´•bŭnd/ and I were so pleased. We had wanted a baby. We talked about it, and I quit smoking and walked 2 miles a day so I could be fit.

When the baby was born, we named him Sal. He cried and cried, but we loved him. We changed and dressed him, and we walked him, and we rocked him. We talked to him, and he stopped crying.

When it was time for him to go to sleep, we lifted him up and placed him in his crib. He kicked his legs and rolled on his side. He started to cry, but then he went to sleep. And we loved Sal and cared for him.

Review: -ed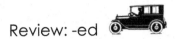

Exercise B

Directions: Using the story "Baby Sal," write 5 ed words on the lines.

/t/	/d/	/ĕd/
1. walked	1. pleased	1. wanted
2. _____	2. _____	2. _____
3. _____	3. _____	

Check your ed words with these:

/t/ = liked	/d/ = mailed	/ĕ/ = wanted
1. walked	1. pleased	1. wanted
2. talked	2. named	2. lifted
3. dressed	3. cried	3. started
4. rocked	4. loved	
5. stopped	5. changed	
6. placed	6. rolled	
7. kicked	7. cared	

* See **Appendix C** for more **ed** words.

437

Word Endings: plurals

Rule #1

Words that name people /pē´•pŭl/, places, or things, are nouns.

Many /mĕn´•ē/ nouns add **s** to mean more than 1, or plural /plur´•ŭl/.

> Examples:
> dog→ dogs
> desk→desks
> boy→ boys

Directions: Add **s** to these words to make them plural, and fill in the blanks. Then read the sentence.

1. Lace up your _____. (shoe)

2. I have 3 _____. (cat)

3. My _____(hand) are at the end of my _____(arm).

4. I stand on my 2 _____. (leg)

5. It is snowing. Put on your _____. (boot)

6. We have 2 _____ (phone) in the house.

7. We have 2 _____ .(car)

8. Birds have 2 _____ (wing). We had

   strong_____ (wind) the past

   few _____ (spring), and _____ (bird)

   needed two strong _____ (wing) to fly.

438

Word Endings: plurals

 Rule #2
If a word ends in s, ss, x, z, ch, or sh, add **es** to make it mean more than one (plural).

Directions: Say and write these words as plurals.

Word	Add es	Plural
1. box	box+es	boxes
2. fox	_____	_____
3. ax	_____	_____
4. fax	_____	_____
5. tax	_____	_____
6. mix	_____	_____

Word	Add es	Plural
1. adz	_____	_____

Word	Add es	Plural
1. glass	_____	_____
2. bus	_____	_____
3. kiss	_____	_____
4. boss	_____	_____
5. cross	_____	_____

Word Endings: plurals

Directions: Say and write these words as plurals.

Word	Add es	Plural
1. dish		
2. wish		
3. fish		
4. brush		
5. toothbrush		

Word	Add es	Plural
1. church		
2. match		
3. watch		
4. bench		
5. wrench		
6. bunch		
7. peach		
8. sandwich		

Directions: Fill in the plural of these words:

1. Jane made six box_____ of the cake mix_____.
2. Bob does tax_____for his 2 boss_____.
3. Sam washed the dish_____ and glass_____after lunch.
4. Lu has ax_____, wrench_____, and match_____ in his tool box_____.
5. Al paid his tax_____.

Word Endings: plurals

Directions: Look at the picture and write its plural.

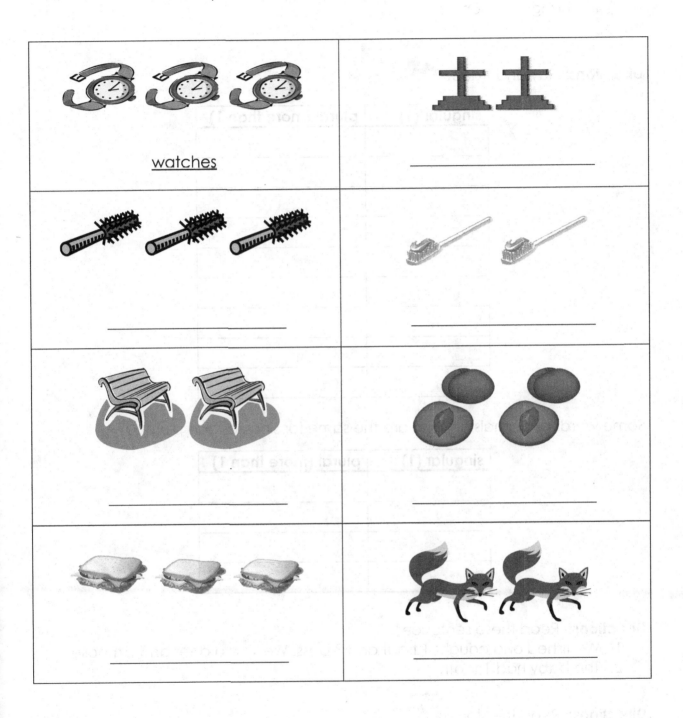

watches

_____

_____

_____

_____

_____

_____

_____

Word Endings: plurals

 Rule #3 A few nouns do not add s to form their plurals. Their spelling changes /chān´ jĕz/.

Directions: Say and trace.

singular (1)	plural (more than 1)
man	men
woman	women
child	children
foot	feet
tooth	teeth
mouse	mice
louse	lice
goose	geese
ox	oxen

Some words of animals and fish are the same for singular and plural.

singular (1)	plural (more than 1)
trout	trout
bass	bass
deer	deer
moose	moose

Directions: Read these sentences.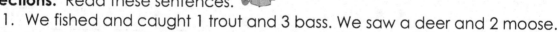
1. We fished and caught 1 trout and 3 bass. We saw a deer and 2 moose.
2. The baby had 1 tooth.

Directions: Read the story.
    The baby, Frank, has 1 tooth. Frank puts his foot in his mouth. His sister, Anna, who is a child of 3, has 20 teeth and does not put her feet in her mouth. Frank and Anna are nice children.

Word Endings: possessives

Rule #1: Singular nouns (naming words) add an ' (apostrophe /ŭ•pŏs´•trŭ•fē/) and an **s** to show ownership /ō´•nûr•shĭp/.
Example: dog's toy

Directions: Read aloud.

Word	Add 's	Possessive	Illustration
1. dog	dog's	the dog's dish	
2. boy	boy's	the boy's dog	
3. man	man's	the man's cat	
4. girl	girl's	the girl's boots	

Directions: Say, trace, and read.

1. Al's pen is on Sam's desk.

2. My cat's fur is soft.

3. Its fur is soft.

4. Your boss's smile is nice.

5. Chuck's toothbrush is on the sink.

Word Endings: possessives

Rule #2
 If the noun adds **s** as most /mōst/ do, to form its plural, just add the apostrophe (') after the s.
        Example: dog→ dogs→dogs' toys

plural (more than 1)	Add ' after the s.	Write the new word.
1. dogs	dogs'	dogs' tags
2. boys	_____	_____ books
3. girls	_____	_____ dolls
4. trees	_____	_____ branches

Rule #3
Add **'s** to the plural word that changes its spelling as in Rule #1.

Singular	Plural	Plural Possessive
1. man	men	men's hats
2. woman	_____	_____ boots
3. child	_____	_____ books

It's as easy as 1, 2, 3!

Directions: Say, trace, and read.

1. The men's hats were on the hooks in the hall.
2. Women's rights have come a long way.
3. Place the children's skates under those benches.
4. The dogs' dishes are in the hall.
5. The boys' pens are on their desks.
6. The trees' branches were waving in the breeze.

Part 4: aw sound

Combos: aw sound

Word	Illustration	Sounds like	Say and trace the word.	Write the word and underline the vowel sound.
1. all		awl	all	<u>a</u>ll
2. ball		bawl	ball	_____
3. call		kawl	call	_____
4. fall		fawl	fall	_____
5. hall		hawl	hall	_____
6. tall		tawl	tall	_____
7. wall		wawl	wall	_____
8. small		smawl	small	_____
9. stall		stawl	stall	_____
10. squall		skwawl	squall	_____

Combos: aw sound

Word	Illustration	Sounds like	Say and trace the word.	Write the word and underline the vowel sound.
1. talk		tawk	talk	t<u>a</u>lk
2. walk		wawk	walk	_____
3. chalk		chawk	chalk	_____
4. halt		hawlt	halt	_____
5. salt		sawlt	salt	_____
6. malt		mawlt	malt	_____

Combos: aw sound

Directions: Look at the pictures. (Circle) the word that matches the picture. Say and write it on the line.

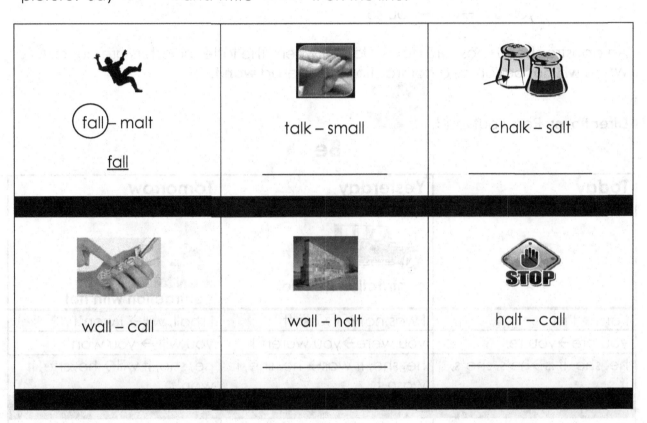

(fall) – malt

fall

talk – small

_____

chalk – salt

_____

wall – call

_____

wall – halt

_____

halt – call

_____

Directions: (Circle,) say, and write.

1. Can you make a call, walk, and talk at the same time? Yes, No I (can, cannot) make a _____, _____, and _____ at the same time.

2. Can you be fined /find/ if you drive and talk on your cell phone? Yes, No I (can, cannot) be fined if I drive and _____ on my cell phone.

Part 5 Contractions /kŭn•trăk'•shŭnz/

Contractions

A contraction /kŭn•trăk´•shŭn/ is 2 words shortened /shôrt´•ŭnd/ to make 1 word.

Example:

I am →am→I'm
you are →are→ you're

An apostrophe /ŭ•pŏs´•trŭ•fē/ is placed where the letter or letters are cut out. When **will not** becomes a contraction, it's spelled **won't**.

Directions: Read out loud.

Be

Today Present	Yesterday Past **contraction with not**	Tomorrow Future **contraction with not**
I am→ I'm	I was not→ I wasn't	I shall, will→ I won't
you are→you're	you were→you weren't	you will → you won't
he, she, it is→he's, she's, it's	he, she, it was→ he, she, it wasn't	he, she, it will→ he, she, it won't
we are→we're	we were→ we weren't	we shall, will → we won't
you are→you're	you were→ you weren't	you will → you won't
they are→they're	they were→they weren't	they will → they won't

Directions: Fill in the missing word; then read the sentence.

1. _____ (I'm, She'll) glad _____ (weren't, we're) pals.

2. _____ (I'm, We're) all going to the game.

3. _____ (Can't, Weren't) you join us?

4. Ted _____ (isn't, don't) playing in the game.

5. He _____(wasn't, won't) be back in time.

Contractions

Directions: Say, trace, and read.

1. She's the 1 girl on the team.
2. We'll all go to the game.
3. I can't do 2 things at the same time.
4. My clock doesn't work.
5. Our child won't go to bed on time.
6. It's hot in May.
7. The dogs don't sleep in the house.
8. I wasn't planning to go to the game, but I changed my mind.

Directions: Match the word to its contraction.

A.		B.	
1. they are	I'm	1. can't	are not
2. I am	won't	2. doesn't	could not
3. we are/were	they'll	3. haven't	does not
4. will not	they're	4. couldn't	cannot
5. does not	hadn't	5. wouldn't	have not
6. they will	you're	6. shouldn't	has not
7. you are	we're	7. hasn't	would not
8. had not	doesn't	8. aren't	should not

Contractions

Directions: Say, trace, and read.

1. Do you have a car? No, I don't have a car. Alex and I have a van.

2. Do you have a cat? No, I don't have a cat. Alex and I have a dog.

3. Did you walk the dog today? No, I didn't walk the dog.

4. Have you taken a ride today? No, I haven't taken a ride today.

5. I couldn't start the van.

6. Could Alex start the van? No, Alex couldn't start the van.

7. I forgot I hadn't filled the van with gas, and it wouldn't start.

8. Alex and I weren't able to take a ride.

9. Next time I won't forget to fill the van with gas; I shouldn't forget.

Congratulations! Good job!

Consonant Combos: qu /kw/

Word	Illustration	Sounds like	Say and trace the word.	Write the word and underline the vowel sound(s).
1. queen		kwēn	queen	qu<u>ee</u>n
2. quart		kwôrt	quart	_____
3. quick		kwĭk	quick	_____
4. quack		kwăk	quack	_____
5. quit		kwĭt	quit	_____
6. quill		kwĭl	quill	_____
7. quilt		kwĭlt	quilt	_____
8. quarter		kwôrt´•ûr	quarter	_____
9. quiet		kwī´•ĕt	quiet	_____

Part 6: qu

Consonant Combos: qu /kw/

Directions: Look at the pictures. (Circle) the word that matches the picture. Say and write it on the line.

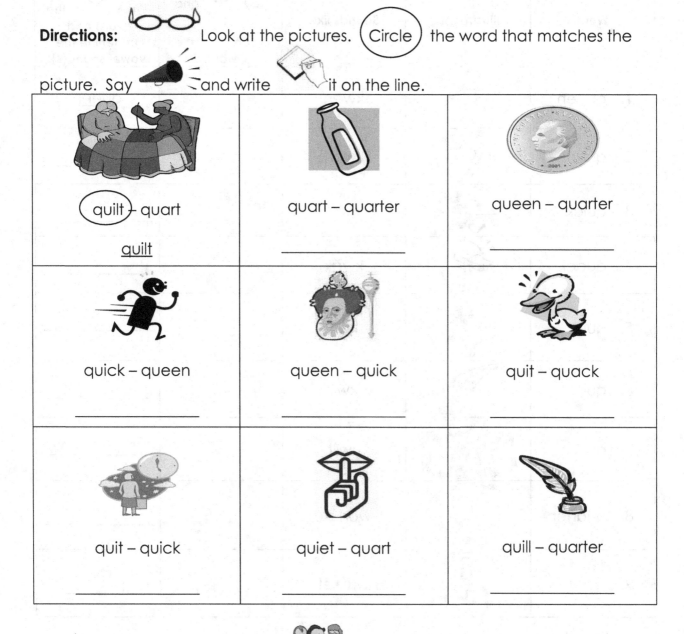

(quilt) - quart quilt	quart - quarter _____	queen - quarter _____
quick - queen _____	queen - quick _____	quit - quack _____
quit - quick _____	quiet - quart _____	quill - quarter _____

Directions: Read the story aloud.

The queen got a quart of ink and a quill. She wrote a note with the ink and quill. In it, she told the zookeeper to stop the ducks from quacking all the time, to quiet them. The zookeeper told the ducks, "I will give you a quarter to quit quacking and be quiet," or "I will tell the queen to use your feathers for a quilt." "Quick," said one duck to the other. "Be quiet."

Part 7: Soft c /s/
Soft c /s/

 Rule: When c comes before e, i, or y, it has a soft sound. The soft sound of c is /s/.

> Example:
>
> ice /īs/
> ace /ās/
> city /sĭt´•ē/
> cent /sĕnt/

C does not have its own sound. Its hard sound is /k/ as in cat, and its soft sound is /s/ as in cent.

Star (☆) Word: circle /sûr´•kŭl/

Word	Illustration	Sounds like	Say and trace the word.	Write the word and underline the vowel sounds.
1. ice		īs	ice	i̱ce
2. mice		mīs	mice	_____
3. rice		rīs	rice	_____
4. spice		spīs	spice	_____
5. face		fās	face	_____
6. race		rās	race	_____
7. brace		brās	brace	_____
8. cell		sĕl	cell	_____
9. cent		sĕnt	cent	_____

Soft c /s/

Directions:  Look at the pictures. (Circle) the word that matches the

picture. Say and write it on the line.

(ice) – cell

<u>ice</u>

spice – mice

_____

face – rice

_____

Directions: Say, trace, and read.

Ace adds spice to his rice. He makes a face at the hot rice. He

cooks in a small space, much like a cell.

Nice job!

Part 8: Soft g /j/

Soft g /j/

Rule: When g comes before e, i, or y, it has a soft sound. The sound of soft g is /j/.
Example:
giant /jī´•ŭnt/
gem /jĕm/
gym /jĭm/

Word	Illustration	Sounds like	Say and trace the word.	Write the word and underline the vowel sound.
1. age		āj	age	a̲ge
2. cage		kāj	cage	_____
3. page		pāj	page	_____
4. wage		wāj	wage	_____
5. huge		hūj	huge	_____
6. large		lârj	large	_____
7. germ		jûrm	germ	_____

Soft g /j/

Directions:  Look at the pictures. (Circle) the word that matches the picture. Say and write it on the line.

(page) – cage <u>page</u>	cage – page _____	age – wage _____
bridge – age _____	bridge – large _____	large – germ _____

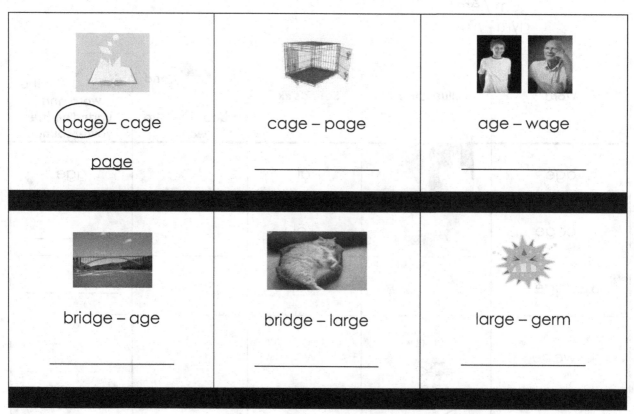

Directions: Say, trace, and read.

The aged /ā´•jĕd/ giant, Gene, was large. No, he was huge! When he sneezed, his germs went all over the page of his book. The giant crossed the bridge to go to the gym which is in the center of the city.

Part 9: Prefixes

Prefixes: pre-

A prefix /prē´•fĭks/ is a syllable that has meaning and is added to the front, or beginning of a word. The prefix **pre** means **before** /bē•fôr´/. It is an open syllable: it ends with a vowel that has a long sound. (See Unit 7 for open syllables.)

pre	word	Write the prefix and the word together.	Illustration
1. pre	school	<u>preschool</u>	
2. pre	heat	_____	
3. pre	cook	_____	
4. pre	treat	_____	
5. pre	pay	_____	
6. pre	pare	_____	

Prefixes: pre-

Directions: Say and write the word next to its picture.

1. _____

2. _____

3. _____

4. _____

5. _____

Directions: Fill in the missing word.

1. To _____ (prepay – premix) is to pay before a bill is due.

2. P_____ (Premix – Pretreat) the mess on the dress.

3. P_____ (Preheat – Preschool) the oven /ŭ´•věn/ to 350°.

4. Bea is three and goes to _____. (preschool – premix)

5. Luis is four and goes to _____. (premix – preschool)

6. P_____ (Premix – Prepare) for school or a job before it is time to go.

Yes, I Can Read!   Unit 9

Prefixes: ex-

Ex means **out**, outside, out of, or away from.

Star (☆) words:

Word	Meaning	Sounds Like
1. excess	too much	ĕks´•ĕs
2. excuse	forgive	ĕks´•kūz´
3. exhale	breathe out	ĕks´•hāl
4. express	speak or fast	ĕks •prĕs´

Word	Illustration	Sounds like	Write the word and underline the vowel sounds.	# of vowel sounds = # of syllables
1. extend		ĕks•tĕnd´	e<u>x</u>t<u>e</u>nd	2
2. expand		ĕks•pănd´	_____	___
3. exchange		ĕks•chānj´	_____	___
4. exercise		ĕks´•ûr•sīz	_____	___

Directions: Fill in the blank.

1. _____ your legs for this _____. (Extend – exercise)

2. I will _____ (exchange) my coins for your coins. Coins are change.

3. If you read a lot, you will _____ (expand) the number /nŭm´•bûr/ of words you know.

4. _____ me! (Excuse – Exit)

459

Prefixes: ex-

Word	Illustration	Sounds like	Write the word and underline the vowel sounds.	# of vowel sounds = # of syllables
5. exit		ĕgz´•ĭt	<u>exi</u>t	2
6. express		ĕks•prĕs´	_____	___
7. exam		ĕgz•ăm´	_____	___
8. exact		ĕgz•ăkt´	_____	___

Directions: Fill in the blank to finish the sentence then read out loud.

1. Look for the _____, or the way out, in case of fire. (exit)

2. Dentists _____ teeth if they must. (extract)

3. Let out your breath, or _____. (exhale)

4. Is this the local train, or an _____? (express)

5. Is this a local bus, or an _____? (express)

6. Lola will take an _____, or a test, to work for the state. (exam)

7. At K-Mart ®, Eva goes in the express lane, pays cash, and gets _____ change /chānj/. (exact)

Prefixes: ex-

Directions: Say, trace, (circle,) or fill in the missing words in the sentences.

1. How do you get to your job?

   I take the express bus, express train, drive my car, or ride my

   bike.

2. Did you take an exam to get your job?

   Yes, I did t_____   a__   e_____ .

   No, I did not t_____   a__   e_____ .

3. Pedro and Anna _____ (exercise – excuse) to stay

   healthy.

4. Eva says, "_____(Exam - Excuse /ĕks•kūz ´/*) me,"

   when she walks in front of Luis.

5. Ken was late for his job, but he had an excuse /ĕks•kūs ´/.*

6. Say or tell me what is on your mind or what you think. _____

   (Express – Exam) yourself.

* Note: Excuse ends with an /s/ sound and is a noun.

   Excuse ends with a /z/ sound and is a verb, an action word.

Congratulations!

Overview

Unit 10 focuses on r-controlled vowels in one-syllable words, then in two-syllable, compound, and star words. Part 3 focuses on words such as *chair*, *spare*, and *bear* with the /air/ sound and *hear* with the /îr/ sound. Unit 10 concludes with several prefixes and suffixes.

Objectives

Students should learn:

1. how to read r-controlled vowel words;
2. prefix and suffix meanings and be able to read and comprehend featured words with those affixes;
3. how to spell plural nouns changing *y* to *i* (*fries*) and changing *f* or *fe* to *ve* (*leaves*)and generalize to additional nouns that follow the same rules.

Instruction

Part 1: R-controlled vowels in one-syllable words

When r follows a vowel, it changes the sound of the vowel. The vowel sounds neither short nor long. This is the fifth syllable type. On the board, write the first three spellings, sounds, and words as listed below, as they share the same *ûr* sound. Then write *ar* and *or* spellings, sounds, and words. Ask for more examples of each of the five, adding and saying aloud these words. Instruct students to read them aloud with you. See pages 465-479 for more examples.

Spelling	Sound	Word
ir	ûr as in	fir
er	ûr	her
ur	ûr	turn
ar	âr	car
or	ôr	corn

Note: Other spelling variations on the r-controlled syllable included in Unit 10 are:

Spelling	Sound	Word
ar	ôr	warm
air	air	air
are	air	care
ear	air	bear
ear	îr	hear
or	ûr	worm

Read through the definition of the r-controlled syllable with your students. Correct pronunciation is important. Model and repeat words as often as necessary. Following your instruction and using the page cues, students should be able to complete the lessons and exercises. Students will most likely know most of these words and now will read them. Direct your student to note word families in most lessons or wait until he has mastered the pronunciation of the words to discuss them. Pronunciation and generalization of the r-controlled syllable are the objectives: On page 465, examples of the *ar* word family are *car, jar, far, star,* and *scar.*

Part 2: R-controlled vowels in two-syllable words includes compound words. Encourage students to discover what is unique about these words, hinting if you need to: these words contain r-controlled syllables exclusively. Students complete lessons and read the story on page 484 silently or aloud if you wish. For further practice/assessment, direct students to circle words in the story which contain one or two r-controlled syllables.

Part 3: More r-controlled vowels Point out the word *tear* on p. 488, /air/, and the same spelling on page 489, with the /îr/ (ear) sound. On page 488, use sentences #3 and #4, and on page 490, use sentence #3 to emphasize the use of context to help determine pronunciation and meaning. Students should complete lessons and exercises.

Parts 4 and 5: Prefixes and Suffixes Discuss affix meanings and words with and without those prefixes, how they reflect their prefixes, such as *sub-* meaning *below* or *under*, as in *subway,* a train running underground, and *-less* meaning *without,* as in *sleepless.* Students complete lessons and exercises. They should be able to read the featured words, explain their meanings, and use them in a sentence. Five rules for adding endings (or adding a word) to make adjective suffixes (pp. 507-514) are explained and practiced. Only delve into adjectives to the extent you wish. The emphasis is on reading and spelling these words correctly.

Parts 6 and 7: Plurals: Change *y* to *i, f* or *fe* to *ve,* and add *–es* as in *fries* and *leaves.* On p. 522, as you say the first rule, have students listen for the sing-song, rhyming nature of "Change *y* to *i* and add -es." Students can repeat it aloud. This practice should help them remember the spelling rule. Students say, trace, and read the plural nouns in the lessons and sentences that follow. They should be able to spell these plurals correctly and generalize to additional nouns that follow the same rules.

Assessment

Parts 1-4: Have students read random words in the exercises, particularly word families. They can also create their own sentences using featured words correctly.
Part 5: Students can write sentences or stories using words of your choice or theirs. Words must be used correctly in context.
Parts 6 and 7: A spelling test is a good assessment tool here.

Vocabulary Acquisition Strategies

Multiple Meaning Words

A partial list of multiple meaning words in Unit 10 includes the following: *star, dark, sharp, torn, fork, core, store, torch, for, form, short, birth, germ, serve, nerve, merge, larger, marker, partner, order, quarter, pair, fair, bear, rear, submit, incline, import,* and *embrace.* Discuss these words and their meanings and use them in sentences.

Word Families

In Parts 1-3, words are arranged in word families whenever feasible. There are many: for example, on page 469, you will find *corn, horn, torn, born,* and *thorn.* Challenge students to think of additional words in the same word family, such as *shorn.* Discuss words, use them in sentences, and be sure your students can do the same.

Homonyms (Homophones)

The following are words which sound the same but are spelled differently and have different meanings: *fur-fir; birth-berth; pair-pear-pare; fair-fare; bare-bear, stare-stair; deer-dear; hear-here; pain-pane.* Some of these words, but not all, are in Unit 10.

Dictionary Usage

The dictionary is an invaluable tool for generating more vocabulary, deepening understanding of word meanings, researching and eliciting multiple meaning words, unfamiliar words in word families, and homonyms that are not in the lesson, etc.

Unit 10: R-Controlled Vowels: 5ᵗʰ Syllable ar /âr/

Part 1 R-controlled vowels in 1-syllable words

The r-controlled vowel or syllable is the 5ᵗʰ syllable. When the vowels a, e, i, o, and u are before r, the r changes /chānj'• ĕz/the sound of the vowel. It is not long or short.

Word	Illustration	Sounds like	Say and trace the word.	Write the word and underline the vowel sound.
1. car		kâr	car	c<u>a</u>r
2. tar		târ	tar	_____
3. jar		jâr	jar	_____
4. far		fâr	far	_____
5. farm		fârm	farm	_____
6. star		stâr	star	_____
7. scar		skâr	scar	_____

R-controlled Vowels: ar /âr/

Word	Illustration	Sounds like	Say and trace the word.	Write the word and underline the vowel sound.
8. barn		bârn	barn	b<u>ar</u>n
9. yarn		yârn	yarn	_____
10. yard		yârd	yard	_____
11. card		kârd	card	_____
12. guard		gârd	guard	_____
13. dark		dârk	dark	_____
14. shark		shârk	shark	_____

R-controlled Vowels: ar /âr/

Word	Illustration	Sounds like	Say and trace the word.	Write the word and underline the vowel sound.
1. art		ârt	art	a̲rt
2. cart		kârt	cart	_____
3. tarp		târp	tarp	_____
4. sharp		shârp	sharp	_____
5. spark		spârk	spark	_____

Directions: Say, trace, and read.

The car is in the barn on Mark's farm. Mark starts the car and backs it out of the barn into the yard when it is dark and the stars are out.

R-controlled Vowels: ar /ôr/

Word	Illustration	Sounds like	Say and trace the word.	Write the word and underline the vowel sound.
1. war		wôr	war	w<u>a</u>r
2. warm		wôrm	warm	_____
3. swarm		swôrm	swarm	_____

Directions: Say, trace, and read.

1. It is a warm day in May.

2. A swarm of bees is in the tree.

3. We hope there are no more wars.

4. Make peace, and end the war.

R-controlled Vowels: or /ôr/

Word	Illustration	Sounds like	Say and trace the word.	Write the word and underline the vowel sound.
1. corn		kôrn	corn	c<u>o</u>rn
2. horn		hôrn	horn	_____
3. torn		tôrn	torn	_____
4. born		bôrn	born	_____
5. thorn		thôrn	thorn	_____
6. fork		fôrk	fork	_____
7. pork		pôrk	pork	_____

R-controlled Vowels: or /ôr/

Word	Illustration	Sounds like	Say and trace the word.	Write the word and underline the vowel sound.
8. core		kôr	core	c<u>o</u>re
9. sore		sôr	sore	_____
10. tore		tôr	tore	_____
11. store		stôr	store	_____
12. snore		snôr	snore	_____
13. shore		shôr	shore	_____
14. porch		pôrch	porch	_____
15. torch		tôrch	torch	_____
16. scorch		skôrch	scorch	_____
17. north		nôrth	north	_____

R-controlled Vowels: or /ôr/

Directions: Look at the pictures. Circle the word that matches the picture. Say and write it on the line.

thorn - (corn)	horn - corn	store - north
<u>corn</u>	_____	_____
fork - pork	fork - store	north - shore
_____	_____	_____

Directions: Fill in the missing words; then read out loud.

pork – corn – fork – snore - store

Bob can get p_____ and c_____ at the st_____. He eats

his meal with a f_____. Then he sleeps and sn_____s.

R-controlled Vowels: or /ôr/

Word	Illustration	Sounds like	Say and trace the word.	Write the word and underline the vowel sound.
1. or		ôr	or	<u>or</u>
2. for		fôr	for	_____
3. form		fôrm	form	_____
4. dorm		dôrm	dorm	_____
5. storm		stôrm	storm	_____
6. fort		fôrt	fort	_____
7. short		shôrt	short	_____
8. sport		spôrt	sport	_____
9. sword		sôrd	sword	_____

R-controlled Vowels: or / ôr/

Directions: Trace or circle the correct word. Then read and say.

1. I feel sore to the core: I ran for 3 hours/ourz/.

2. Do you play a sport? Yes/No I do/do not play a sport.

3. Do you like sports? Yes/No I do/do not like sports.

4. Sal tore his pants on a thorn.

5. Their baby was born May 1st.

6. I like to sit on my porch and look north.

R-controlled Vowels: or

Directions: Find and circle the words.

WORD FIND

~~SWORD~~ - WORD - OR - TORE - STORM - SORE - SHORT - DORM

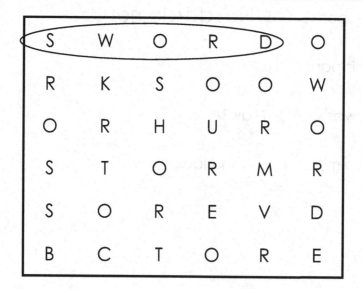

R-controlled Vowels: er, ir, ur /ûr/

Words spelled with er, ir, and ur sound like ûr.

Examples:

Word	Illustration	Sounds like
1. bird		bûrd
2. fur		fûr
3. her		hûr

Directions: Say and trace.

1. bird

2. fur

3. her

R-controlled Vowels: ir /ûr/

Word	Illustration	Sounds like	Say and trace the word.	Write the word and underline the vowel sound.
1. sir		sûr	sir	si<u>r</u>
2. fir		fûr	fir	_____
3. first		fûrst	first	_____
4. girl		gûrl	girl	_____
5. stir		stûr	stir	_____
6. dirt		dûrt	dirt	_____
7. shirt		shûrt	shirt	_____
8. skirt		skûrt	skirt	_____
9. smirk		smûrk	smirk	_____
10. third		thûrd	third	_____
11. birth		bûrth	birth	_____

R-controlled Vowels: ir /ûr/

Directions: Trace, or circle the correct word. Then read and say.

1. Dear Sir:
2. Do you have dirt on your boots?
3. (Yes/ No), I (have/do not have) d_____on my boots. They are clean.

Directions: Trace, read and say.

Their baby's birth was May first. She is a girl. She is their first girl and their third child.

Directions: Draw a line from the picture to its name.

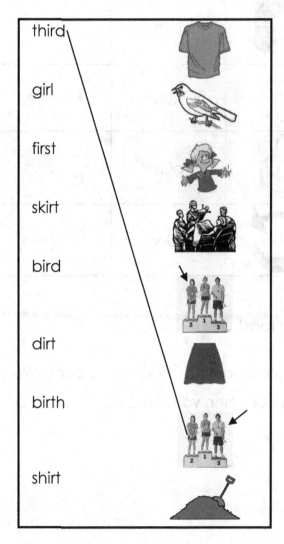

third

girl

first

skirt

bird

dirt

birth

shirt

R-controlled Vowels: ur /ûr/

Word	Illustration	Sounds like	Say and trace the word.	Write the word and underline the vowel sound.
1. fur		fûr	fur	f<u>ur</u>
2. blur		blûr	blur	_____
3. hurt		hûrt	hurt	_____
4. turn		tûrn	turn	_____
5. nurse		nûrs	nurse	_____
6. purse		pûrs	purse	_____
7. curve		kûrv	curve	_____

Directions: Say, trace, and read.

Put your purse and your fur coat in the back. We will go for a ride. Turn the wheel of the car when you are on a curve. Do not go so fast that the road is a blur.

R-controlled Vowels: er /ûr/

Word	Illustration	Sounds like	Say and trace the word.	Write the word and underline the vowel sound.
1. fern		fûrn	fern	f<u>er</u>n
2. stern		stûrn	stern	_____
3. germ		jûrm	germ	_____
4. sperm		spûrm	sperm	_____
5. serve		sûrv	serve	_____
6. nerve		nûrv	nerve	_____
7. clerk		klûrk	clerk	_____
8. merge		mûrj	merge	_____
9. berth		bûrth	berth	_____

R-controlled Vowels: er /ûr/

Directions: Read and say.

> The nurse has curls under her cap. She wears a white starched shirt and skirt. She takes orders and serves meals. She is stern with jerks if they try to flirt with her. She is the first girl in her house to be a nurse.

R-controlled Vowels: or /ûr/

Star (☆) words

Word	Illustration	Sounds like	Say and trace the word.	Write the word and underline the vowel sound.
1. world		wûrld	world	w<u>or</u>ld
2. worm		wûrm	worm	_____

Directions: Read and say.

1. We find worms in the dirt.

2. This is our world.

Part 2: R-controlled vowels in 2-syllable words

R-controlled Vowels: 2- syllable words

Word	Illustration	Sounds like	Write the word and underline the vowel sounds.	# of vowel sounds = # of syllables
1. farmer		fârm'•ûr	f<u>a</u>rm<u>e</u>r	2
2. barnyard		bârn'•yârd	_____	_____
3. larger		lârj'•ûr	_____	_____
4. marker		mârk'•ûr	_____	_____
5. partner		pârt'•nûr	_____	_____
6. order		ôr'•-dûr	_____	_____
7. border		bôrd'•ûr	_____	_____
8. dormer		dôrm'•ûr	_____	_____

481

R-controlled Vowels: 2-syllable words

Word	Illustration	Sounds like	Write the word and underline the vowel sounds.	# of vowel sounds = # of syllables
1. orchard		ôr'•-chûrd	<u>o</u>rch<u>a</u>rd	2
2. quarter		kwôrt'•ûr	_____	___
3. northern		nôr*th*'•ûrn	_____	___
4. turner		tûrn'•ûr	_____	___
5. burner		bûrn'•ûr	_____	___
6. server		sûrv'•ûr	_____	___
7. mirror		mîr'•ûr	_____	___
8. worker		wûrk'•ûr	_____	___

R-controlled Vowels: compound words

Word	Illustration	Sounds like	Write the word and underline the vowel sounds.	# of vowel sounds = # of syllables
1. sports car		spôrts kâr	sp<u>o</u>rts c<u>ar</u>	1 1
2. sport shirt		spôrt shûrt	_____ _____	___ ___
3. storm door		stôrm dôr	_____ _____	___ ___

Star (☆) words

Word	Illustration	Sounds like	Write the word and underline the vowel sounds.	# of vowel sounds = # of syllables
1. farther		fâr'•thûr	f<u>ar</u>th<u>e</u>r	2
2. further		fûr'•thûr	_____	___
3. Arthur		Âr'•thûr	_____	___

R-controlled Vowels: 2-syallable words

Word	Illustration	Sounds like	Write the word and underline the vowel sounds.	# of vowel sounds = # of syllables
1. Carlos		Kâr'•lōs	C<u>a</u>rl<u>o</u>s	2
2. Jordan		Jôr'•dŭn	_____	_____

Directions: Read the story.

Arthur the farmer put a dormer in his farmhouse. He also put one in the roof of the barn which was in the barnyard. In his backyard, near his apple orchard, Arthur had a grill. He was a good cook. He used the grill and the burner to cook large fish steaks and other food as well. He used the turner to turn the fish. When it was cooked, he was the server.

He and his partner, his wife Margo, were hard workers. On Thursdays, Arthur put on his sport shirt, and Margo and he went for a ride in their sports car. One Thursday in March, they drove farther than they had ever driven before. In fact, they ended up at the northern border of New York State.

Part 3: More r-controlled vowels

R-controlled Vowels: air /air/

Word	Illustration	Sounds like	Say and trace the word.	Write the word and underline the vowel sound.
1. air		air	air	<u>air</u>
2. pair		pair	pair	_____
3. hair		hair	hair	_____
4. fair		fair	fair	_____
5. stairs		stairz	stairs	_____
6. chair		chair	chair	_____

R-controlled Vowels: air /air/

Directions: Say, trace, and read.

1. This is a pair of pants.

2. This is a pair of socks.

3. This is a pair of boots.

4. This is a pair of gloves.

5. Use my comb and brush to comb and brush your hair.

6. I paid a fair price for my new chair.

7. I rode the rides at the fair.

8. The air is fresh outside.

9. The baby walks up 1 stair at a time.

R-controlled Vowels: are /air/

Word	Illustration	Sounds like	Say and trace the word.	Write the word and underline the vowel sound.
1. care		kair	care	c<u>a</u>re
2. bare		bair	bare	_____
3. spare		spair	spare	_____
4. stare		stair	stare	_____
5. square		skwair	square	_____

Directions: Read, circle, and say.

1. It is not nice to stare.

2. Do you have a spare tire for your car? Yes/No.

3. I have/do not have a spare tire for my car.

4. If you don't have a spare tire, you need one.

5. You are in your bare feet. Aren't your feet cold? I have a spare pair of socks and shoes for you.

R-controlled Vowels: ear /air/

Word	Illustration	Sounds like	Say and trace the word.	Write the word and underline the vowel sound.
1. bear		bair	bear	b<u>ea</u>r
2. pear		pair	pear	_____
3. tear		tair	tear	_____
4. wear		wair	wear	_____

Directions: Say, trace, or circle the correct word and read.

1. Your feet are bare. You can wear my spare pair of socks and shoes.

2. I wouldn't dare to stare at a bear eating a pear!

3. I tear my torn socks and use them for rags. Do you? Yes/No.

4. I tear/do not tear my torn socks and use them for rags.

5. Workers must wear hardhats on the job.

R-controlled Vowels: ear /îr/

Word	Illustration	Sounds like	Say and trace the word.	Write the word and underline the vowel sound.
1. ear		îr	ear	ear
2. hear		hîr	hear	_____
3. earring		îr'• ēng	earring	_____
4. year		yîr	year	_____
5. rear		rîr	rear	_____
6. tear		tîr	tear	_____
7. dear		dîr	dear	_____
8. gear		gîr	gear	_____
9. clear		klîr	clear	_____

R-controlled Vowels: ear

Directions: Fill in, and trace. Then read and say.

1. When I talk on the phone, I take off my earring so I can hear clearly.

2. What year is this? The year is _____.

3. Rosa sheds tears when she cries.

4. If you are looking for a job, you might start your letter like this: Dear Sir.

5. When Carlos parks his car, he looks in the front and the rear. When the street is clear of cars, he backs up into the parking space. Then he shifts gears into first gear and turns off the engine.

Directions: Draw a line from the picture to its name.

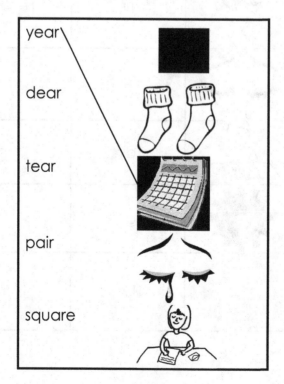

year

dear

tear

pair

square

R-controlled Vowels

Directions: Find and circle the words.

Word Find

| ~~BORDER~~ – CHAIR – MIRROR – DARE – HEAR – CLEAR – REAR - WORKER |

```
B   W   C   L   E   A   R
O   V   H   U   S   B   C
B   W   A   M   H   M   I
T   O   I   R   A   I   E
K   R   R   E   A   R   F
M   K   K   D   A   R   E
O   E   N   L   E   O   R
T   R   H   E   A   R   W
```

 **Great Job!**

Now you know the 5th syllable, the r-controlled vowels!
There is one more to go!

You can read lots of words now!

Part 4: Prefixes

Prefixes: non-

The prefix **non-** means **not**.

Added to a word, **non-** means the opposite of the word, or it means **not**.

Word	Illustration	Sounds like	Write the word and underline the vowel sounds.	# of vowel sounds = # of syllables
1. nonstick		nŏn•stĭk′	n<u>o</u>nst<u>i</u>ck	2
2. nonsmoking		nŏn•smō′•kēng	_____	____
3. nonmetal		nŏn•mĕt′•ul	_____	____
4. nonskid		nŏn•skĭd′	_____	____
5. nonstop		nŏn•stŏp′	_____	____
6. nonsense		nŏn′•sĕns	_____	____

Prefixes: non-

Directions: Fill in the missing words. Then read and say.

1. Bud talks _____ (nonskid – nonstop).

2. Pam cooks with a _____ (nonstick – nonsense) pan.

3. This is a _____ (nonsmoking – nonstop) room.

4. A rubber mat is _____ (nonsmoking – nonmetal).

5. A _____ (nonskid – nonstop) rubber mat is safe.

Directions: Say, trace and read.

1. We wipe our feet on the nonmetal, nonskid mat before we go inside.

2. Bob talks nonstop, and he talks nonsense.

Prefixes: dis-

The prefix **dis-** means **not, or reverse** /rē•vûrs'/.

Word	Illustration	Sounds like	Write the word and underline the vowel sounds.	# of vowel sounds = # of syllables
1. dis+connect		dĭs•kŭ•nĕkt'	disconnect	3
2. dis+content		dĭs•kŭn•tĕnt'	_____	_____
3. dis+close		dĭs•klōz'	_____	_____
4. dis+trust		dĭs•trŭst'	_____	_____
5. dis+card		dĭs•kârd'	_____	_____
6. dis+count		dĭs'•kownt	_____	_____
7. dis+rupt		dĭs•rŭpt'	_____	_____
8. dis+cord		dĭs'•kôrd	_____	_____

Prefixes: dis-

Directions: Fill in the missing word. Then read out loud.

1. _____(Discount – Disconnect), or unplug, the toaster when it is not in use.

2. Lola and Angel are not pals, for they _____ (disclose -distrust) each other.

3. Rosa will tell, or _____ (disclose - discord), a secret to her pal.

4. Throw away, or _____ (discontent, discard) the rest of your lunch.

5. Frank saves money when he shops for shirts on sale, or at a _____(discount-discard).

Directions: Read and say.

Did you discard part of your lunch, or did you eat all of it? I did not discard part of my lunch. I ate all of it.

Prefixes: sub-

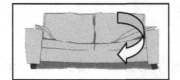

The prefix **sub-** means **below, or under**.

Word	Illustration	Sounds like	Write the word and underline the vowel sounds.	# of vowel sounds = # of syllables
1. subtract	▬	sŭb•trăkt′	s<u>u</u>btr<u>a</u>ct	2
2. subfreezing		sŭb•frēz′•ēng	_____	___
3. submarine		sŭb•mŭ•rēn′	_____	___
4. subway		sŭb′•wā	_____	___
5. submerge		sŭb•mûrj′	_____	___
6. submit		sŭb•mĭt′	_____	___
7. subfloor		sŭb′•flôr	_____	___

Prefixes: sub-

Directions: Trace or fill in the missing word. Then read out loud.

1.   The _____(subway - subtract) runs under the streets.

2.   A _____ (subway-submarine)can go under water.

3.   When a submarine is under water, it is submerged.

4.   When it is cold, or _____ (subtract-subfreezing), dress in a
       warm coat and hat.

5.   A cup of tea costs $2.00. I gave the girl $5.00. She _____
       (subtracted-subfloor) $2.00 from $5.00 and gave me $3.00.

6.   Juan submits his report on time.

Prefixes: in-, im-

The prefixes **in-** and **im-** mean **in, into** /ĭn•tōo/, **or within.**

Word	Illustration	Sounds like	Write the word and underline the vowel sounds.	# of vowel sounds = # of syllables
1. inside		ĭn•sīd'	<u>in</u>s<u>i</u>de	2
2. income		ĭn'•kŭm	_____	_____
3. infect, infection		ĭn•fĕkt' ĭn•fĕk'•shŭn	_____ _____	_____ _____
4. infest		ĭn•fĕst'	_____	_____
5. incline		ĭn'•klīn	_____	_____
6. indoors		ĭn•dôrz'	_____	_____
7. insert		ĭn•sûrt'	_____	_____

498

Prefixes: in-, im-

Word	Illustration	Sounds like	Write the word and underline the vowel sounds.	# of vowel sounds = # of syllables
8. inform		ĭn•fôrm′	_____	_____
9. inflammable		ĭn•flăm′•ŭ•bŭl	_____	_____
10. incarcerate		ĭn•kăr′•sûr•āt	_____	_____
11. impair		ĭm•pair′	_____	_____
12. import		ĭm•pôrt′	_____	_____
13. improve		ĭm•proōv′	_____	_____
14. immigrate, immigrant, immigration		ĭm′•ĭ•grāt ĭm′•ĭ•grŭnt ĭm•ĭ•grā′•shŭn	_____ _____ _____	_____ _____ _____

Prefixes: in-, im-

Directions: Look at the pictures.   Circle the word that matches the picture. Say and write it on the line.

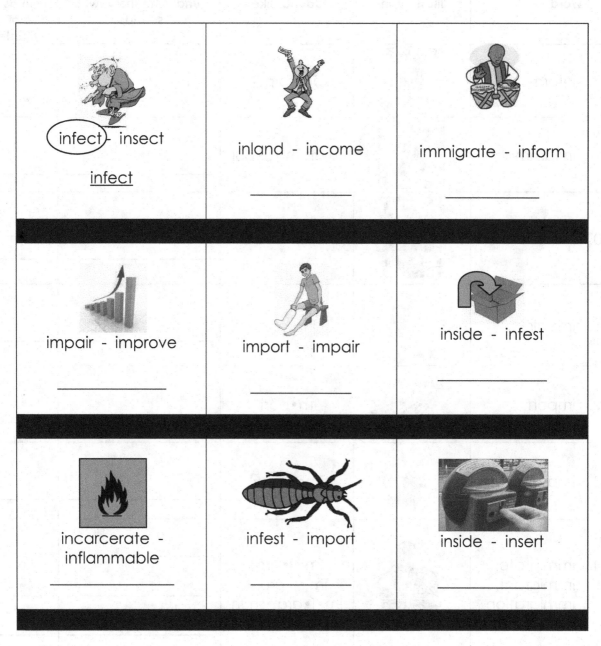

infect - insect

infect

inland - income

_____

immigrate - inform

_____

impair - improve

_____

import - impair

_____

inside - infest

_____

incarcerate - inflammable

_____

infest - import

_____

inside - insert

_____

Prefixes: in-, im-

inform - incline	inform - improve	infect - indoor
_____	_____	_____

Directions: Say, trace, circle, and read.

1. We went inside, or indoors, when it started raining.

2. A wheelchair (wēl'•chair) ramp is an incline.

3. Insert your dime in the slot.

4. Cards is an indoor game.

5. Did you immigrate to the US? (Yes, No). I (did, did not) immigrate to the US.

Prefixes: en-, em-
The prefixes **en-** and **em-** mean **put in** or **on.**

Word	Illustration	Sounds like	Write the word and underline the vowel sounds.	# of vowel sounds = # of syllables
1. enroll		ĕn•rōl′	<u>e</u>nr<u>o</u>ll	2
2. enchant		ĕn•chănt′	_____	_____
3. enter, entrance		ĕn′•tûr ĕn′•trŭns	_____ _____	_____
4. envelope		ĕn′•vĕl•ōp	_____	_____
5. energy		ĕn′•ûr•jē	_____	_____
6. engagement ring		ĕn•gāj′•mĕnt	_____	_____
7. encourage		ĕn•kûr′•ŭj	_____	_____
8. encounter		ĕn•kount′•ûr	_____	_____
9. embed		ĕm•bĕd′	_____	_____
10. embrace		ĕm•brās′	_____	_____
11. embroider		ĕm•broi′•dûr	_____	_____

Prefixes: en-, em-

Directions: Say, trace, and read.

Cal has a lot of energy. He works and goes to school.

When he enrolled in English class, he met Jen. On his job, he

works with cement. He lays, or embeds, bricks in cement.

Even when the job is hard, Cal's boss encourages him. Cal

gets his check each week in an envelope. Cal and Jen

meet, or have an encounter, each week after class. Cal

enchants Jen. After a long time, Cal gives Jen an

engagement ring. Cal and Jen plan to wed.

Prefixes: Review

Directions: Write the word that means:

1. make better   <u>improve</u>

2. burns fast   _____

3. without stopping   _____

4. not outside   _____

5. a ramp, on a slant   _____

Word Bank
~~improve~~
nonstop
indoors
incline
inflammable

Directions: Draw the line to the word that means the same:

to put in jail	disconnect
unplug	subtract
put into (as a coin)	incarcerate
to hand in	insert
take away	submit

Prefixes: Review

Directions: Look at the pictures.   Circle the word that matches the picture. Say and write it on the line.

(immigrant) incline

immigrant

income-subway

_____

disclose-discontent

_____

discount-distrust

_____

nonstick-nonsmoking

_____

nonskid-inside

_____

discard-income

_____

submit-subfloor

_____

enroll-encourage

_____

Prefixes: Review

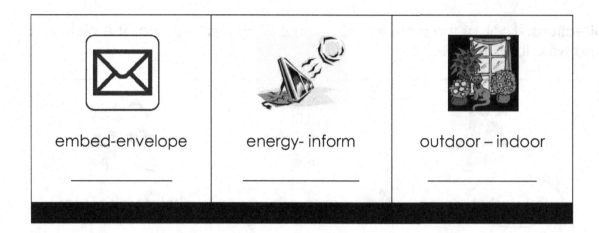

embed-envelope	energy- inform	outdoor – indoor
_____	_____	_____

Directions: Read and say.

   I wiped (wīpt) my feet on the nonskid rubber mat outside the store. Inside, there was a discount on blankets: blankets were on sale. I would (wo͝od) save $6.00. But, there were two (2) words on the tag that informed me the blankets were inflammable and flammable. They were not safe: they were unsafe. I left the store without the blankets.

Part 5: Suffixes
Adjectives and Suffixes: -er, -est
Adjectives (ăd'•jĕk•tĭvz) are words that tell more about naming words (nouns), such as **big** dog, **tall** man, **nice** boy, **fair** race, **red** hat.

In most cases, if the words are one (1) syllable, add -er to the word to compare two (2) people (pē'•pŭl) or things.

Example:

high - higher
fast - faster
old - older

Add -est to compare more than 2 people or things:

Example:

high – higher-highest
fast – faster- fastest
old – older- oldest

Word	Add-er	Add-est	Write the word and underline the vowel sounds.	# of vowel sounds= # of syllables
1. stronger	stronger	strongest	str<u>o</u>ng<u>e</u>st	2
2. long				
3. tall				
4. short				
5. high				
6. low				
7. fast				
8. slow				
9. old				
10. young /yŭng/				

Adjectives & Suffixes: -er, -est

Word	Add-er	Add-est	Write the word and underline the vowel sounds.	# of vowel sounds = # of syllables
1. smart	smarter	smartest	sm<u>ar</u>t<u>e</u>st	2
2. light				
3. tight				
4. bright				
5. dull				
6. straight /strāt/				
7. far	farther			
8. plain				
9. clean				
10. cool				
11. dark				
12. weak				

Adjectives & Suffixes: -er, -est

 Rule #1
If a word ends in a quiet, or silent e, drop the e before adding an ending that begins with a vowel.

Word	Drop-e	Add-er	Add-est	Write the word and underline the vowel sounds.	# of vowel sounds = # of syllables
1. large /lârj/	larg	larger	largest	largest	2
2. cute					
3. nice					
4. loose /lōōs/					
5. white					
6. late					

 Rule #2
If a word ends in a closed syllable, double the consonant before adding -er or -est to keep the short vowel sound.

Word	Double the final consonant	Add-er	Add -est	Write the word and underline the vowel sounds.	# of syllables
1. thin	thinn	thinner	thinnest	thinnest	2
2. fat					
3. flat					
4. hot					
5. wet					
6. sad					

Adjectives & Suffixes: -er, -est

 Rule #3
If a word ends in a **consonant and y**, change y to i and add -er or -est.

Word	Change y to i	Add-er	Add-est	Write the word and underline the vowel sounds.	# of vowel sounds = # of syllables
1. pretty /prĭt'•e/	pretti	prettier	prettiest	pr<u>e</u>t/ti/<u>e</u>st	3
2. ugly					
3. scary					
4. heavy					
5. noisy					
6. angry					
7. fancy					
8. early					
9. dry					
10. sandy					
11. windy					
12. wealthy					
13. happy					

Adjectives & Suffixes: -er, -est

Directions: Draw a line to connect the opposites /ŏp'•ŭ•zĭts/, or antonyms /ăn'•tō•nĭmz/.

Exercise A.

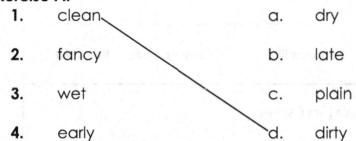

1. clean   a.   dry
2. fancy   b.   late
3. wet   c.   plain
4. early   d.   dirty
5. heavy   e.   light

Exercise B.

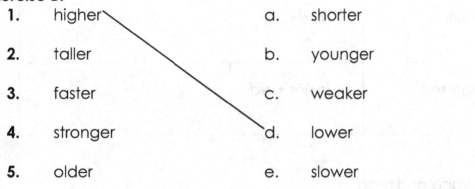

1. higher   a.   shorter
2. taller   b.   younger
3. faster   c.   weaker
4. stronger   d.   lower
5. older   e.   slower

Exercise C.

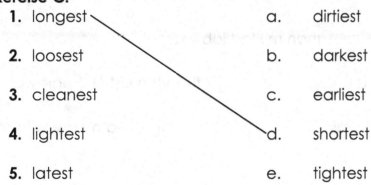

1. longest   a.   dirtiest
2. loosest   b.   darkest
3. cleanest   c.   earliest
4. lightest   d.   shortest
5. latest   e.   tightest

Adjectives: more, less

Rule #4
Adjectives that have 3 or more syllables compare 2 people or things by adding the words **more** or **less**.

Examples:

Word	Sounds like	Say and trace the word.
1. interesting	ĭn'•tûr•ĕst•ēng	interesting
2. infectious	ĭn•fĕk'•shŭs	infectious
3. difficult	dĭf'•ĭ•kŭlt	difficult
4. congested	kŭn•jĕs'•tĕd	congested

Directions: Say, trace and read.

1. My baby is more congested now than he was last night.

2. This job is less difficult than my last job was.

3. This part of the book is more difficult than the first (1st) part was.

4. When I had a cold, I was less infectious than I am now with the flu.

5. This book is more interesting than the book I had before.

Adjectives: most, least

Rule#5
Adjectives of 3 or more syllables compare 3 or more people or things by adding the words **most** or **least**.

Directions: Say, trace and read.

1. This is the most interesting book I have ever read.

2. This TV show is the least interesting show on TV. It is the worst.

3. The first (1ˢᵗ) part of this book is the least difficult, or the easiest part of the book.

4. Our zoo is the most interesting zoo I have ever visited. It is the best.

5. I have the flu, and I feel the most congested and the most infectious since I became sick, or ill.

Adjectives: most, least

Directions: Read and say.

1. Jan ran a good race, but Dan ran a better race. Dan was the best runner in the race. "You did well!" Sue said. "You are a good runner!" "I am the best runner today," said Dan. "I liked running this race. It was the most difficult and the most interesting race I have run: it had lots of hills, trees, and water."

2. Juan is the hardest worker I know, so he is the best worker. He is not the strongest; Tim is stronger. Jack is taller, and Jim is smarter, but Juan works the hardest, and he wears the whitest shirts, so the boss calls him first.

_____

Suffixes: -ful

The suffix **-ful** means **full of.**

Examples:

painful = full of pain	
truthful = full of truth	

Word	Illustration	Sounds like	Write the word and underline the vowel sounds.	# of vowel sounds = # of syllables
1. help+ful=helpful		hĕlp'•fŭl	h<u>e</u>lpf<u>u</u>l	2
2. care+ful=careful		kair'•fŭl	_____	_____
3. fear+ful=fearful		fîr'•fŭl	_____	_____
4. faith+ful=faithful		fāth'•fŭl	_____	_____

Suffixes: -ful

Directions: Fill in the missing word. Then read out loud.

faithful – painful- truthful – fearful – careful – playful - spoonful

Jill was c_____ to stay far from Smog the dog. She was afraid, or

f_____ that it might bite her if she tried to give it a sp_____of

dogfood. A bite would hurt, or be p_____. The dog, Smog, was

faith_____ to its owner (ō'•nûr) and might bite a boy or girl if he or she came

too close. The owner (ō'•nûr), Miss Brown, was tr_____ with Jill. Miss

Brown warned Jill to be c_____ not to get too close to Smog, the

dog. Smog was pl_____with her, but it wasn't with others.

Suffixes: -less

The suffix -**less** means **without**.
Added to a word, like cloud, it means without clouds, as in a sunny day, or a cloudless day.

Examples:

Word	Add-less	Write the word and underline the vowel sounds.	# of vowel sounds = # of syllables
1. cloud	cloudless	cl<u>ou</u>dl<u>e</u>ss	2
2. sleep			
3. help			
4. pain			
5. fear			
6. care			

Directions: Fill in the missing words. Then read out loud.

> cloudless – sleepless – helpless – painless – fearless

Last night, I could not sleep. I spent a sl_____ night. I went outside to look at the sky. There were no clouds, and I saw the moon and stars in the dark, cl_____ sky. My f_____ cat, who fears no one, came with me. As she ran, she fell down the steps. I just stood there and couldn't help her. I felt so h_____. It must have been a p_____ fall, for she rolled over, shook herself off, and trotted over to my side.

Suffixes: -y

The suffix **-y** shows **how something or someone feels or is**.

Examples:

Word	Add-y	Write the word and underline the vowel sound.	# of vowel sounds = # of syllables
1. sleep	sleepy	sl<u>ee</u>py	2
2. sand			
3. mess			
4. salt			
5. itch			
6. slop * (sloppy)			
7. flop *			
8. mud *			
9. run *			

 *Remember to double the last consonant before adding an ending if it is a closed syllable, the 1st syllable type.

Directions: Say, trace and read.

I wore my floppy sandals to the sandy beach and ran into the

salty sea. My nose was itchy and runny: I was getting a cold. The bay

was muddy and sloppy, so I went back to the seaside.

Suffixes: -y

Word	Add-y	Write the word and underline the vowel sounds.	# of vowel sounds = # of syllables
1. grump	grumpy	gr<u>u</u>mp<u>y</u>	2
2. sneak			
3. show			
4. cloud			
5. trick			
6. thirst			
7. luck			
8. chill			
9. ice	icy		

Directions: Fill in the missing words. Then read and say.

lucky- cloudy – icy - snowy

1.   I went for a walk on a cl _____ day.

2.   The ground was white and sn_____.

3.   I slipped on the i_____ sidewalk.

4.   But I felt I was l_____ to be outside in the fresh air.

Suffixes: -ly

Most of the time, the **-ly** ending is added to a word to make it an **adverb**, or to **tell how something /sŭm'•thēng/ is done.**

Examples:

      How did Sam walk? He walked slowly.
      How did Pam write? She wrote neatly.
      How did Ted talk? He talked slowly.

Word	Add-ly	Write the word and underline the vowel sounds.	# of vowel sounds = # of syllables
1. slow	slowly	sl<u>ow</u>ly	2
2. neat			
3. loud			
4. quick			
5. quiet			
6. careful			
7. careless			
8. bright			
9. sudden			
10. exact			
11. strange /strānj/			
12. stiff			
13. fearless			
14. fearful			

Suffixes: -ly

Directions: Circle the best words in each sentence. Then read and say.
It is all right to read quietly and not loudly.

The sun shines (brightly, tightly) on the small lake. We put on our life vests

and get into the rowboat (carefully, exactly) so it will not tip. As we row, the

boat glides over the water (brightly, quietly), without a sound. The birds are

singing (loudly, exact). (Suddenly, Brightly) in the pond next to the lake, we see

a seemingly fearless animal (stiffly, neatly) walking and feeding on plants in the

pond. Why, it is a moose! We watch it (quietly, neatly). Then, we row (slowly,

brightly) back to the other side of the lake. We have been gone (carelessly,

exactly) one (1) hour.

Part 6: Plurals: Changing y to i

 Rule: When a word ends in a consonant plus + y, change /chānj/ the y to i and add es to form the plural (more than one).

Directions: Say, trace, and read.

Word	Illustration	Change the y to i	Add –es
1. fry		fri	fries
2. fly		fli	flies

 Rule: If the word ends in a vowel plus + y, just add s.

Directions: Say, trace, and read.

Word	Illustration	Add -s
1. tray		trays
2. boy		boys
3. toy		toys

Directions: Say, trace, and read.

The boys ate fries on trays and played with their toys. Flies were on the fries and the trays, but the boys did not care. They looked at the sun's rays, and the flies took off into the sky.

Part 7: Plurals: Changing f/fe to ves

 Rule: If a word ends in **f** or **fe**, change /chānj/ the f or fe to **v** and add **-es** for the plural.

Examples:

half halv + es = halves

knife kniv + es = knives

Directions: Say, trace, and read.

Word	Illustration	Change the f/fe to v	Add –es	Sounds like
1. elf		elv	elves	ĕlvz
2. leaf		leav	leaves	lēvz
3. wife		wiv	wives	wīvz
4. wolf		wolv	wolves	wŏŏlvz

Plurals: Changing f/fe to ves

Directions: Say, trace, and read.

1. My wife and I had a shelf with a knife and a loaf of bread on it. We made 2 more shelves to hold knives, trays and loaves of bread.

2. Out in the barnyard, the hooves of the calves were full of mud. At night, wolves howled at the night skies. The roofs of the barns shone in the moon's rays.

Great Job!

You have finished Unit 10!

You can read lots of words now!

Overview
This unit is devoted exclusively to the sixth and last syllable, consonant plus *le*.

Objectives
Students learn:
1. the sixth syllable;
2. that the consonant and *le* are the last syllable in the word and that the word must have at least two syllables.
3. Students hear and underline the number of vowel sounds in each word;
4. to read the words and are able to use them in sentences.

Instruction
This is the sixth and last syllable! Consider it a "gift" because we know there are at least two syllables in the word, and the consonant plus *le* syllable ends the word. When underlining the vowel sounds in the word, underline the *l* because one hears /ŭl/. Stress that the number of vowel sounds equals the number of syllables.

(page 534) Exception to the rule: When a syllable ends in *ck* plus *le*, *le* is the last syllable in the word to preserve the *ck* blend at the end of the previous syllable. Examples are *pick le, buck le,* and *knuck le,* etc.

Note: See the Introduction for an explanation of the schwa sound.

Students complete lessons and exercises. All words have two syllables except for *mistletoe*, on page 528, which has three.

Assessment
Students should be able to read words in the lessons and sentences in the exercises.

Vocabulary Acquisition Strategies
Multiple Meaning Words
Multiple meaning words in Unit 11 include *table, cable, bubble, double, rattle, settle, wrestle, little, needle, handle, waffle, circle, cycle, puzzle, angle, pickle, buckle,* and *knuckle.*

Word Families
Word families include *able, table, cable; battle, rattle; kettle, settle; thistle, mistle, whistle; nuzzle* and *puzzle; jingle* and *single; angle, tangle; pickle, tickle; buckle* and *knuckle.*

Unit 11: Consonant + le: 6th Syllable

Congratulations! You have made it to the 6th and last syllable!
The 6th and last syllable is the consonant plus (+) le. It is at the end of a word.

Example:

Word	Sounds like	# vowel sounds = # of syllables
apple	ă´•pŭl, ăp´ŭl	2

The –le sounds like /ŭl/. The ŭ is a vowel sound. That is how a word part with a quiet e at the end can be a syllable. Underline the **l** to show the vowel sound.

Consonant + le: ble

Word	Sounds like	Say and trace the word.	Say and write the word and underline the vowel sounds.	# vowel sounds = # of syllables
1. table	tā´•bŭl	table	t<u>a</u>b<u>l</u>e	2
2. cable	kā´•bŭl	cable	_____	_____
3. able	ā´•bŭl	able	_____	_____
4. bubble	bŭ´•bŭl	bubble	_____	_____
5. double	dŭ´•bŭl	double	_____	_____
6. wobble	wŏ´•bŭl	wobble	_____	_____

Consonant + le: ple

Word	Sounds like	Say and trace the word.	Say and write the word and underline the vowel sounds.	# vowel sounds = # of syllables
1. apple	ă´•pŭl	apple	<u>a</u>pp<u>l</u>e	2
2. nipple	nĭ´•pŭl	nipple	_____	___
3. purple	pûr´•pŭl	purple	_____	___
4. people	pē´•pŭl	people	_____	___
5. simple	sĭm'•pŭl	simple	_____	___

Directions: Say, trace, fill in, circle, and read.

1. Bob threw a rock into the lake and made ripples in the water.

2. I have an apple tree and a maple tree in my backyard.

3. Mix red and blue to get _____.

4. The baby's bottle has a nipple on top.

5. Circle a food: purple   apple

6. Human beings, or persons, are (people, apple).

7. Are you able to set the table? Yes, I'm able to set the table, and I will.

8. We have cable TV at our house. Do you?   (Yes, No), I (do, don't) have cable TV at my house.

Consonant + le: tle

Word	Sounds like	Say and trace the word.	Say and write the word and underline the vowel sounds.	# vowel sounds = # of syllables
1. bottle	bŏ´•tŭl	bottle	bottle	2
2. battle	bă´•tŭl	battle	_____	_____
3. rattle	ră´•tŭl	rattle	_____	_____
4. kettle	kĕ´•tŭl	kettle	_____	_____
5. settle	sĕ´•tŭl	settle	_____	_____
6. wrestle	rĕs´•ŭl	wrestle	_____	_____
7. little	lĭ´•tŭl	little	_____	_____
8. thistle	thĭs´•ŭl	thistle	_____	_____
9. mistletoe	mĭs´•ŭl tō	mistletoe	_____	_____
10. whistle	wĭ´•sŭl	whistle	_____	_____

Consonant + le: dle

Word	Sounds like	Say and trace the word.	Say and write the word and underline the vowel sounds.	# vowel sounds = # of syllables
1. needle	nē´•dŭl	needle	n<u>ee</u>d<u>l</u>e	2
2. noodle	nū´•dŭl	noodle	_____	_____
3. handle	hăn´•dŭl	handle	_____	_____

Consonant + le: fle

Word	Sounds like	Say and trace the word.	Say and write the word and underline the vowel sounds.	# vowel sounds = # of syllables
1. waffle	wŏ´•fŭl	waffle	_____	2
2. wiffle	wĭ´•fŭl	wiffle	_____	_____
3. sniffle	snĭ´•fŭl	sniffle	_____	_____

Consonant + le: cle

Word	Sounds like	Say and trace the word.	Say and write the word and underline the vowel sounds.	# vowel sounds = # of syllables
1. circle	sŭr´•kŭl	circle	circle	2
2. cycle	sī´•kŭl	cycle	_____	_____

Consonant + le: zle

Word	Sounds like	Say and trace the word.	Say and write the word and underline the vowel sounds.	# vowel sounds = # of syllables
1. puzzle	pŭ´•zŭl	puzzle	_____	2
2. sizzle	sī´•zŭl	sizzle	_____	_____
3. nozzle	nŏz´•zŭl	nozzle	_____	_____
4. nuzzle	nŭz´•zŭl	nuzzle	_____	_____
5. muzzle	mŭz´•zŭl	muzzle	_____	_____

Consonant + le: kle

1. ankle	ăn´•kŭl	ankle	_____	2
2. wrinkle	rĭn´•kŭl	wrinkle	_____	_____

Directions: Read out loud.

1. When Joan stirs beef and noodles in the wok, they sizzle.

2. She coats the griddle with oil, turns up the heat on the stove, and when the oil sizzles, she cooks pancakes on the griddle. She always holds the handle.

Consonant + le: gle

Word	Sounds like	Say and trace the word.	Say and write the word and underline the vowel sounds.	# vowel sounds = # of syllables
1. jungle	jŭn´•gŭl	jungle	j<u>u</u>ngl<u>e</u>	2
2. jingle	jĭn´•gŭl	jingle	_____	_____
3. single	sĭn´•gŭl	single	_____	_____
4. angle	ăn´•gŭl	angle	_____	_____
5. tangle	tăn´•gŭl	tangle	_____	_____
6. Google®	gōo´•gŭl	Google	_____	_____

Consonant + le: Review

Directions: Say, trace, and read.

1. Little Hector hurt his ankle on the jungle gym.

2. Chu likes to cycle in circles on his bicycle.

3. A single shingle blew off our roof in the storm.

4. When the water boils, the kettle whistles.

5. I whistle for my horse Battle, and he trots into the barn. He nuzzles me with his muzzle, his snout, as I brush him. His mane is so tangled. Then I feed him an apple as he settles in, in his stall, for the night.

Directions: Find and circle the words.

Word Find

HANDLE – SINGLE – KETTLE – NOODLE – MIDDLE

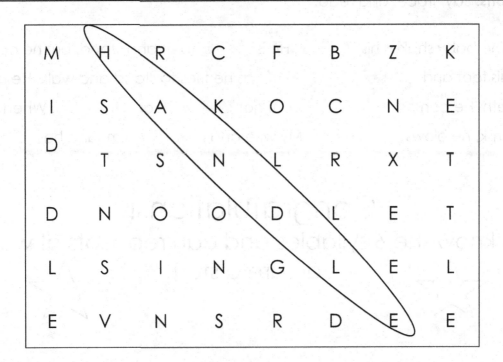

M	H	R	C	F	B	Z	K
I	S	A	K	O	C	N	E
D	T	S	N	L	R	X	T
D	N	O	O	D	L	E	T
L	S	I	N	G	L	E	L
E	V	N	S	R	D	E	E

Consonant + le: kle

When a syllable ends in **ck** and **le**, le is the last syllable in the word.
Example: tack•le

Word	Sounds like	Say and trace the word.	Say and write the word and underline the vowel sounds.	# vowel sounds = # of syllables
1. tackle	tăk´•ŭl	tackle	t<u>a</u>ck<u>le</u>	2
2. pickle	pĭk´•ŭl	pickle	_____	_____
3. tickle	tĭk´•ŭl	tickle	_____	_____
4. buckle	bŭk´•ŭl	buckle	_____	_____
5. knuckle	nŭk´•ŭl	knuckle	_____	_____

Directions: Say, trace, and read.

   The baby shakes his rattle. He is able to sit and stand, but he cannot walk. His feet and ankles wobble as he tries to stand and walk. He has five teeth. He can eat noodles but not pickles or waffles. When he drinks milk, he blows bubbles. My wife and I tickle him, and he giggles.

Congratulations!
You know the 6 syllables and can read lots of words!
You are a star!

Overview

Part 1: Syllable division and rules (pages 538-567)

The focus is on syllable division, syllabication rules, accent, and the schwa sound. For easy reference, a complete list of syllable division rules is on page 539. Syllabication practice on words illustrating the six rules is provided one rule at a time, one lesson at a time, in order. Each rule is restated (with examples) at the beginning of each of the six lessons. The Unit 12 Answer Key is located in the back of the book.

Part 2: Syllable Division: The schwa sound (pp. 568-571)

The schwa sound was first introduced in Unit 7 and is reintroduced and practiced in the context of syllabication.

Objectives

Students will comprehend:

1. accent, or stress, in a word of more than one syllable;
2. the six syllable division rules;
3. the schwa sound.
4. Students will divide words and sound them out.

Instruction

Part 1: Syllable division and rules

Review the syllabication material on page 538 on the board, illustrating the three-step method: Underline the vowel sounds, divide the word, sound it out. Review accent if necessary using the *baby* example included. Another example you can use is *palace*. Write *pal* on the board, asking students to read the word aloud. Then write *ace* on the board and ask students to read *ace* aloud. Then write *palace* on the board and explain that in a word of more than one syllable, one syllable is stressed louder or stronger than the other syllable(s) in the word. Point out the accent mark at the end of the syllable that indicates which syllable to stress. This mark is in the workbook and the dictionary, of course, but students confronted with an unfamiliar word will not have that cue, so they need to know they should play with the stress and pronunciation until they recognize the word. Again, the objective is for them to sound out the word; where the student divides the word is not an issue: His decoding is. If he still can't decode the word, he will use his knowledge of syllable types, word families, prefixes and suffixes, context, and the dictionary. If your student is starting *YICR* with Unit 12, first teach the six syllable types with the Appendix D worksheet. (See "Lesson Plan" in the Introduction) Then proceed with Unit 12.

On page 539, review the rules with your students at the board. Elicit further examples from them. The rules are logical and the material familiar; hence, the rules are easy to remember: Encourage memorization. On page 540, review the schwa sound which naturally follows any discussion of multisyllabic words and accent. In-depth explanation and practice follow in Part 2. Students should then complete the lessons that focus on Rule #1, pages 541-545. Correcting those pages will determine whether you need to do more work on dividing compound words or assign the lesson on Rule #2. You may want to repeat this procedure with each of the six rules. If students have difficulty, review the three-step method with them.

On page 562, silent *h* is present in *honorable*, #35, and *dishonorable*, in #38. If you expand on this to teach silent *h* in other words, examples include *ghost*, *heir*, *heiress*, *honest*, *honor*, *hour*, *John*, *khaki*, *rhyme*, and *school*.

<u>Part 2: Syllable Division: The schwa sound (pages 568-571)</u>
Students who started working in *YICR* in Unit 7 or who have had that instruction may be familiar with the schwa sound. If not, instruct students on the schwa sound with the information on page 568. Additional examples are *teacher*, *wagon*, and *cinnamon*, among countless others. For consistency, simplicity, and, with the decoding goal in mind, because the schwa sound is short *u*, /ŭ/, it is represented by a *u* in *YICR*. It is explained on page 568, as well as in the Introduction, that the schwa symbol is represented by (ə) in the dictionary.

Students complete the lessons with the aid of the "Sounds like" column; then they complete the subsequent exercise.

The unit review on pages 572-574 reinforces the three-step method, including tracing and reading words in context.

Assessment
Check answers for correctly underlined vowel sounds, correct number of syllables, and student's sounding out the words. Within the unit as well as the unit review, discuss word meanings to check for comprehension. Have students read sentences aloud as part of the review.

Vocabulary Acquisition Strategies
Word Lists
Once your students have mastered the six-syllable approach and have practiced syllabication in Unit 12, add a word list to their three or four other assigned materials. Graded word lists, content area lists, survival skills vocabulary, GED spelling and other appropriate spelling lists, instruction manual vocabulary, and vocational word lists are pertinent. Many content area teachers welcome this practice because struggling students often cannot read or understand basic core vocabulary they encounter in their subjects. That is one reason why it is so important to give learners a method with which they can become independent readers. Ask your student or fellow teachers if there is a word list that needs mastering. At first assign no more than ten words at a time. Direct students to try to

sound out the word, underline the vowel sounds, write the number of vowel sounds to the right of the word, divide it with slash marks, and sound it out again. Go over these words and any errors with your student, sounding out the word aloud so she can hear the vowel sounds. Tap it out with your finger and have her do the same if she cannot hear the vowel sounds. She should then repeat the process while she sits with you. Until you are confident she has mastered the method, assign no more than ten words at a time. Increase the number of words you assign as you feel she can handle them. Also, words of encouragement are real confidence boosters.

Once she has learned to decode unfamiliar words, she can use the dictionary to discover words' meanings. Discussion and writing assignments reinforce learning and usage.

Unit 12: Syllable Division

Part 1: Syllable division and rules

Underlining the vowel sounds in a word tells you how many syllables are in the word (# of vowel sounds = # of syllables). If you do not know a word, underline the vowel sounds; if you have 2 vowel sounds, divide the word 1 time (once). The same rules go for 3, 4, 5, or more vowel sounds. If you divide the word, you can sound out 1 syllable at a time to figure out the word.

> Example:
> transportation   tr<u>a</u>nsp<u>o</u>rt<u>a</u>ti<u>o</u>n   /trănz•pôr•tā´•shŭn/

Even long words are simpler when you sound out 1 syllable, or unit, at a time.

Accent /ăk´•sĕnt/
In a word of 2 or more syllables, say 1 syllable louder than the other. The accent (´) tells you which syllable to stress, or say louder.

> Example:
> baby   /bā´•bē/
>
> In baby, the ´ tells you to say /bā/ louder than /bē/.

If there is no accent mark, and you do not know the word, stress 1 syllable and sound out the word. See if you know it. If you don't know the word, stress the other syllable(s).

Most of the time, if it sounds like a word you know, you are right. Trust what you know.

Syllable Division Rules

A 1-syllable word is not divided.
   Examples: run, stop, spend

Rule #1   Compound words are divided where they were put together.
   Examples: mailbox = mail•box, playpen = play•pen, pancake = pan•cake

Rule #2   When 2 consonants are together in a word, divide between them.
   Examples: skillet = skil´•let, picnic = pic´•nic, percent = per•cent´

Rule #3   If the 1st vowel in a word is short, or if you think it is short, divide after the consonant. This is a closed syllable, the 1st syllable (Unit 4).
   Examples: upon = up•on´, cabin = cab´•in, denim = den´•im

Rule #4   If the 1st vowel in a word is long, or if you think it is long, divide after the vowel. This is an open syllable, the 4th syllable (Unit 7).
   Examples: open = o´•pen, easy = ea´•sy, beautiful = beau´•ti•ful, idea = i•de´•a

Rule #5   When a word ends in a consonant + le, divide the word so the consonant and le is the last syllable, the 6th syllable (Unit 11).
   Examples: apple = ap´•ple, table = ta´•ble, bicycle = bi´•cy•cle

Rule #6   Prefixes and suffixes: When a word has a prefix, divide the word between the prefix and the word.
   Example: prepay = pre•pay, unplug = un•plug, reread = re•read, exchange = ex•change

When a word has a suffix that has a vowel sound, divide between the suffix and the word.
   Example: helpful = help•ful, treated = treat•ed, messy = mess•y, loudly = loud•ly

Some words have both prefixes and suffixes.
   Example: employer = em•ploy•er, unyielding = un•yield•ing, repeatedly = re•peat•ed•ly

Syllable Division Rules

Accent and Schwa Sound:

In a word of 2 or more syllables, one syllable is stressed, or said louder than the other syllable(s). Relax the sound in the unstressed syllable(s), and if you hear the ŭ or ŭh sound, that is the schwa sound. In the dictionary, the stress or accent mark looks like ´ , and the schwa sound looks like ə.

Examples:

Word	Sounds Like	Schwa
alone	ŭ•lōn´	ə • lōn´
palace	păl´• ŭs	păl´• əs
telephone	tĕl´• ŭ •fōn	tĕl´• ə •fōn

Note that the schwa sound is not in the accented syllable.

Syllable Division: compound words, Rule #1

Word	Say and write the word, and underline the vowel sounds.	# of vowel sounds = # of syllables	Write, divide, and say the word.
1. backyard	b<u>a</u>cky<u>a</u>rd	2	back/yard
2. baseball	_____	____	_____
3. bedroom	_____	____	_____
4. beehive	_____	____	_____
5. breakfast	_____	____	_____
6. carpool	_____	____	_____
7. checkbook	_____	____	_____
8. cookbook	_____	____	_____
9. dashboard	_____	____	_____
10. doorknob	_____	____	_____
11. drumstick	_____	____	_____
12. flashlight	_____	____	_____

Syllable Division: compound words, Rule #1

Word	Say and write the word, and underline the vowel sounds.	# of vowel sounds = # of syllables	Write, divide, and say the word.
13. jigsaw	jigsaw	2	jig/saw
14. locksmith			
15. lunchbox			
16. mailroom			
17. passport			
18. payroll			
19. playground			
20. popcorn			
21. restroom			
22. sandbox			
23. skateboard			
24. snowboard			

Syllable Division: compound words, Rule #1

Word	Say and write the word, and underline the vowel sounds.	# of vowel sounds = # of syllables	Write, divide, and say the word.
25. teaspoon	t<u>ea</u>sp<u>oo</u>n	2	tea/spoon
26. toolbelt			
27. toothache			
28. toothbrush			
29. washroom			
30. wheelchair			
31. windshield			
32. afternoon			
33. bookkeeper			
34. employment			
35. grandparents			
36. hairdresser			

Syllable Division: compound words, Rule # 1

Word	Say and write the word, and underline the vowel sounds.	# of vowel sounds = # of syllables	Write, divide, and say the word.
37. handyman	h<u>a</u>nd<u>y</u>m<u>a</u>n	3	han/dy/man
38. housekeeper	_____	_____	_____
39. jackhammer	_____	_____	_____
40. lawnmower	_____	_____	_____
41. overpass	_____	_____	_____
42. screwdriver	_____	_____	_____
43. tablespoon	_____	_____	_____
44. motorcycle	_____	_____	_____

Syllable Division: compound words, Rule #1

Directions: Fill in, trace, circle, and read.

1. Jamal has a flashlight, screwdriver, and a toolbelt in his toolbox, but his jigsaw is in his shop at home.

2. Two parts of a car are the _____ and _____. (popcorn, windshield, dashboard, teabag)

3. _____ is a healthy snack. (Popcorn, Payroll)

4. Anna rides her wheelchair up the ramp and into school.

5. Carlos and Jake skateboard to the park to play basketball.

6. There is a beehive in the backyard near the sandbox. Be careful!

7. Ben rides in a carpool to work.

8. Lam eats breakfast at home but takes his lunchbox to work and eats his lunch there.

9. Victor locked his keys in the car and had to call a locksmith.

10. Circle the jobs, or types of employment, listed below:

    1. hairdresser   5. bookkeeper

    2. overpass   6. tunnel

    3. locksmith   7. housekeeper

    4. afternoon   8. motorcycle

Syllable Division: compound words, Rule #1

10. The part of the day from 12:00 p.m. until sunset is _____.
(sandbox, afternoon)

11. For question #10, if you circled #1, 3, 5, and 7 you were correct.
Would you like to work as one of these? (Yes, No) I (would, wouldn't) like
to work as one of these.

If yes, which one would you like to be? _____

Syllable Division: two (2) consonants together, Rule #2

When two consonants are together in a word, if they are the same or different,
divide between the 2 consonants.

    double (same) consonants:
        muffin= muf/fin
        mitten= mit/ten
        skillet= skil/let

    2 different consonants:
        basket= bas/ket
        picnic= pic/nic
        percent= per/cent

Syllable Division: 2 consonants together, Rule #2

Word	Say and write the word, and underline the vowel sounds.	# of vowel sounds = # of syllables	Write, divide, and say the word.
1. address	a<u>ddre</u>ss	2	ad/dress
2. cactus			
3. commute			
4. compute			
5. confuse			
6. dessert			
7. dispute			
8. insect			
9. helmet			
10. letter			
11. lettuce			
12. mussel			

Syllable Division: 2 consonants together, Rule # 2

Word	Say and write the word, and underline the vowel sounds.	# of vowel sounds = # of syllables	Write, divide, and say the word.
13. mustard	m<u>u</u>st<u>a</u>rd	2	mus/tard
14. napkin	_____	_____	_____
15. necktie	_____	_____	_____
16. nostril	_____	_____	_____
17. pencil	_____	_____	_____
18. percent	_____	_____	_____
19. pretzel	_____	_____	_____
20. public	_____	_____	_____
21. rabbit	_____	_____	_____
22. sandwich	_____	_____	_____

Syllable Division: 2 consonants together, Rule # 2

Directions: Say, trace, circle, and read.

1. Do you want lettuce and mustard on your sandwich? (Yes, No) I (want, do not want) lettuce and mustard on my sandwich.

2. Do you use your necktie as a napkin? No, I use my napkin as a napkin.

3. Do you compute to work? No, I commute to work.

4. Pedro wears a helmet when he rides his bike or his motorcycle.

5. The shopping mall has public restrooms, or washrooms.

6. I wrote a letter in pencil. I didn't use my computer. Then I put it in the mailbox on the corner.

7. Bugs are insects.

Syllable Division: short vowel, closed syllable, Rule #3

If the 1st vowel in a word is short, divide after the consonant. *
This is the 1st syllable, the closed syllable (Unit 4).

 Remember: A closed syllable has a short vowel and ends in a consonant.

To find out if the vowel is long or short, try the long vowel sound 1st; if the word does not sound like a word you know, try the short vowel sound.
Example: exit
Try the long vowel sound first: /ēgz´•ĭt/. It is **not** a word.
Then, try the short vowel sound: /ĕgz´•ĭt/. You know this word. It means a way out. Trust what you know.

* The consonant keeps the vowel short.

Syllable Division: short vowel, closed syllable, Rule #3

Word	Say and write the word, and underline the vowel sounds.	# of vowel sounds = # of syllables	Write, divide, and say the word.
1. cabin	c<u>a</u>b<u>i</u>n	2	cab/in
2. comic	_____	____	_____
3. credit	_____	____	_____
4. debit	_____	____	_____
5. denim	_____	____	_____
6. exit	_____	____	_____
7. finish	_____	____	_____
8. index	_____	____	_____
9. melon	_____	____	_____
10. polish	_____	____	_____
11. robin	_____	____	_____
12. solid	_____	____	_____

Syllable Division: short vowel, closed syllable, Rule #3

Word	Say and write the word, and underline the vowel sounds.	# of vowel sounds = # of syllables	Write, divide, and say the word.
13. tablet	t<u>a</u>bl<u>e</u>t	2	tab/let
14. caplet	_____	____	_____
15. toxic	_____	____	_____
16. upon	_____	____	_____
17. vomit	_____	____	_____

Directions: Fill in the missing words. Then read and say.

solid – finish – denim – comic – melon

1. Jeans are made of d_____.

2. Slice a m_____ and scoop out its seeds.

3. When I fin_____ my work, I read the c_____ strip.

4. Wood is a s_____.

Syllable Division: long vowel, open syllable, Rule #4

If the 1st vowel in a word is long, or if you think it is long, divide after the vowel. This is an open syllable, the 4th syllable. (See Unit 7)

    Examples:
        open = o/pen   /ō´•pĕn/
        radio = ra/di/o   /rā´•dē•ō/

 Remember: Underline the vowel sounds, divide the word, and sound it out.

Try the long sound 1st; if it does not sound like a word you know, try the short vowel sound.

    The open syllable, with its long vowel sound, is more common:
        music= mu/sic
        First, try /mū´•zĭk/. You know that word.

    The closed syllable, with its short vowel sound, is less common:
        cabin= cab/in
        First, try /kā´•bĭn/.   It is not a word.
        Then try /kăb´•ĭn/. Yes, it is a word!

Trust what you know! An open syllable, the 4th syllable, ends with a vowel that makes a long sound, or says its own name.

Syllable Division: long vowel, open syllable, Rule # 4

Word	Say and write the word, and underline the vowel sounds.	# of vowel sounds = # of syllables	Write, divide, and say the word.
1. baby	b<u>a</u>b<u>y</u>	2	ba/by
2. China	_____	_____	_____
3. cobra	_____	_____	_____
4. coop	_____	_____	_____
5. diet	_____	_____	_____
6. digest	_____	_____	_____
7. driver	_____	_____	_____
8. duet	_____	_____	_____
9. duplex	_____	_____	_____
10. easy	_____	_____	_____
11. erase	_____	_____	_____
12. fever	_____	_____	_____

Syllable Division: long vowel, open syllable, Rule # 4

Word	Say and write the word, and underline the vowel sounds.	# of vowel sounds = # of syllables	Write, divide, and say the word.
13. final	f<u>i</u>n<u>a</u>l	2	fi/nal
14. Friday	_____	____	_____
15. frozen	_____	____	_____
16. iron	_____	____	_____
17. ivy	_____	____	_____
18. lady	_____	____	_____
19. locate	_____	____	_____
20. movie	_____	____	_____
21. photo	_____	____	_____
22. polar	_____	____	_____
23. Polish	_____	____	_____

Syllable Division: long vowel, open syllable, Rule # 4

Word	Say and write the word, and underline the vowel sounds.	# of vowel sounds = # of syllables	Write, divide, and say the word.
24. pony	p<u>o</u>n<u>y</u>	2	po/ny
25. razor	_____	_____	_____
26. silent	_____	_____	_____
27. solo	_____	_____	_____
28. student	_____	_____	_____
29. tiny	_____	_____	_____
30. trial	_____	_____	_____
31. beautiful	_____	_____	_____
32. library	_____	_____	_____
33. librarian	_____	_____	_____
34. radio	_____	_____	_____
35. video	_____	_____	_____

Syllable Division: long vowel, open syllable, Rule # 4

Directions: Say, trace, and read.

1. Maria /mŭ•rē´•ŭ/ is the lady who lives in the duplex next door. She sings by herself, solo, or sings with her brother /brŭ´•thûr/ Pedro. When they sing together, it is a duet.

2. Amy is a student. She had a final exam last Friday, so she studied /stŭd´•ēd/ in the library where there was no radio to distract her. She studied hard, and she felt the final was easy.

Syllable Division: consonant + le, Rule # 5

If a word ends in a consonant plus (+) le, divide the word so the consonant +le is the last syllable in the word. This is the 6th syllable (Unit 11).

Example:
bottle = bot/tle

Exception: If a word ends in ck+le, leave the ck blend together and divide before the le.

Example:
pickle= pick/le
tackle= tack/le

The consonant +le is a syllable: its vowel sound is /ŭl/. Underline the l to show the vowel sound.

Example:
b<u>o</u>t/t<u>l</u>e

Syllable Division: consonant + le, Rule # 5

Word	Say and write the word, and underline the vowel sounds.	# of vowel sounds = # of syllables	Write, divide, and say the word.
1. able	a̲b̲l̲e	2	a/ble
2. angle	_____	___	_____
3. candle	_____	___	_____
4. cycle	_____	___	_____
5. double	_____	___	_____
6. drizzle	_____	___	_____
7. gargle	_____	___	_____
8. goggles	_____	___	_____
9. griddle	_____	___	_____
10. muscle	_____	___	_____
11. nozzle	_____	___	_____
12. paddle	_____	___	_____

Syllable Division: consonant + le, Rule # 5

Word	Say and write the word, and underline the vowel sounds.	# of vowel sounds = # of syllables	Write, divide, and say the word.
13. puddle	p<u>u</u>dd<u>l</u>e	2	pud/dle
14. puzzle	_____	_____	_____
15. rifle	_____	_____	_____
16. saddle	_____	_____	_____
17. shuttle	_____	_____	_____
18. single	_____	_____	_____
19. trundle	_____	_____	_____
20. Wiffle®	_____	_____	_____

Syllable Division: consonant + le, Rule # 5

Word	Say and write the word, and underline the vowel sounds.	# of vowel sounds = # of syllables	Write, divide, and say the word.
21. article	a̲rti̲c̲le	3	ar/ti/cle
22. assemble			
23. bicycle			
24. capable			
25. disabled			
26. portable			
27. possible			
28. probable			
29. rectangle			
30. syllable			
31. triangle			
32. vegetable*	ve̲ge̲ta̲ble	3	/vĕj´•tŭ•bŭl/ vege/ta/ble

* Pronunciation is 3 syllables as shown here. Dictionary syllabication is 4 syllables: veg•e•ta•ble

Syllable Division: consonant + le, Rule # 5

Word	Say and write the word, and underline the vowel sounds.	# of vowel sounds = # of syllables	Write, divide, and say the word.
33. accessible	acc<u>e</u>ssible	4	ac/ces/si/ble
34. convertible	_____	___	_____
35. honorable	_____	___	_____
36. impossible	_____	___	_____
37. improbable	_____	___	_____
38. dishonorable	_____	___	_____
39. indigestible	_____	___	_____

Directions: Say, trace, and read.

1. Pancakes are griddle cakes. They are cooked on a hot griddle.

2. Point the nozzle of the hose at the vegetables growing in the garden. Then drizzle water on the plants.

3. Pete and his son Jack do a puzzle after dinner and before bed.

4. On sunny days, Jack and Pete hit a Wiffle® ball back and forth to each other.

Syllable Division: consonant + le, Rule # 5

5. Write the word on the line. (triangle, rectangle)

_____   _____

6. Sanjay received an honorable discharge from the Navy.

7. The public library is wheelchair accessible.

8. It is improbable, but not impossible, that the rising river will flood our home.

9. Jill has a convertible stroller she can change to suit the baby's needs.

10. Omar drives his convertible with the top down on warm, sunny days.

11. Miguel, wearing safety goggles, assembled both /bōth/ the bicycle and grill he bought /bawt/.

12. The dinner Luis made was so bad that it was nearly indigestible.

13. When Bella has a sore throat, she gargles with warm salt water.

14. There is one vowel sound per syllable in each word. Underline each vowel sound so you are able to tell how many syllables are in the word. If there are 3 vowel sounds, there are 3 syllables. Underline the vowel sounds, divide the word, and sound it out.

Syllable Division: prefixes and suffixes, Rule # 6

When a word has a prefix, divide between the prefix and the word.
    Examples: **pre**pay, **un**plug, **re**read, **ex**change

When a word has a suffix that has a vowel sound, divide between the suffix and the word.
    Examples: help**ful**, loud**ly**, mess**y**, treat**ed**

Some words have both prefixes and suffixes.
    Examples: **em**ploy**er**, **un**yield**ing**, **sub**mitt**ed**

Syllable Division: prefixes and suffixes, Rule # 6

Word	Say and write the word, and underline the vowel sounds.	# of vowel sounds = # of syllables	Write, divide, and say the word.
1. distrust	d<u>i</u>str<u>u</u>st	2	dis/trust
2. faithful	_____	____	_____
3. harmless	_____	____	_____
4. homeless	_____	____	_____
5. hopeless	_____	____	_____
6. jumpy	_____	____	_____
7. likely	_____	____	_____
8. quietly	_____	____	_____

Syllable Division: prefixes and suffixes, Rule # 6

Word	Say and write the word, and underline the vowel sounds.	# of vowel sounds = # of syllables	Write, divide, and say the word.
9. successful	s<u>u</u>cc<u>e</u>ssf<u>u</u>l	3	suc/cess/ful
10. truthful	_____	___	_____
11. wasteful	_____	___	_____
12. disrupted	_____	___	_____
13. exporter	_____	___	_____
14. importer	_____	___	_____
15. infected	_____	___	_____
16. unsuccessful	_____	___	_____

Syllable Division: prefixes and suffixes, Rule # 6

Word	Say and write the word, and underline the vowel sounds.	# of vowel sounds = # of syllables	Write, divide, and say the word.
17. preheated	_____	_____	_____
18. unfaithful	_____	_____	_____
19. untruthful	_____	_____	_____
20. immigrated	_____	_____	_____
21. repeatedly	_____	_____	_____
22. uninteresting	_____	_____	_____
23. unsuccessfully	_____	_____	_____

Directions: Say, trace, and read.

1. I feel jumpy, or nervous, before job interviews.

2. Isabelle immigrated to the U.S. in 2009.

3. Yoku preheated the oven to 350°; then she put the chicken in to cook.

4. Uninteresting is another word for boring.

5. Lilly repeatedly tells her 2-year old not to throw his toys.

6. Kate was homeless for a year after she lost her job and her home.

Part 2: Syllable Division: The schwa sound

In words of two or more syllables, 1 (one) syllable is stressed or said louder than the other syllable(s) in the word. The accent /ăk´•sĕnt/ mark is at the end of the stressed syllable in the dictionary /dĭk´•shŭn•air•ē/ and looks like ´.

Relax /rē•lăks´/ the sound of the vowel in the quieter syllable(s), the unstressed syllable(s), and it sounds like /ŭ/. In the dictionary it looks like ə, a small, backwards, upside down e.

Examples:

Word	Syllables	Sounds like	Schwa Sound
button	but/ton	/bŭt´•tŭn/	bŭt´•tən
mitten	mit/ten	/mĭt´•tŭn/	mĭt´•tən
sofa	so/fa	/sō´•fŭ/	sō´•fə
butter	but/ter	/bŭt´•ûr/	bŭt´•ər
engine	en/gine	/ĕn´•jŭn/	ĕn´•jən

If you don't know how to say a word, stress 1 syllable to see if you know the word.
> Example: mitten

Try /mĭt•tĕn´/
If you don't know that word, try the stress on the other syllable.

Try /mĭt´•tŭn/

Also, if the word is in a sentence, see if the word makes sense /sĕns/ in the sentence.
> Example:
> Rose lost her mitten in the snow.

Trust what you know!

568

Syllable Division: the schwa sound

Word	Sounds like	Say and write the word, and underline the vowel sounds.	# of vowel sounds = # of syllables
1. apron	ā´•prŭn	a̲pro̲n	2
2. breakfast	brĕk´•fŭst	_____	_____
3. channel	chăn´•ŭl	_____	_____
4. lemon	lĕm´•ŭn	_____	_____
5. license	lī´•sŭns	_____	_____
6. pistol	pĭs´•tŭl	_____	_____
7. razor	rā´•zŭr	_____	_____
8. seven	sĕv´•ŭn	_____	_____
9. soda	sō´•dŭ	_____	_____
10. today	tŭ•dā´	_____	_____
11. tunnel	tŭn´•ŭl	_____	_____
12. visa	vē´•zŭ	_____	_____

Word	Sounds like	Say and write the word, and underline the vowel sounds.	# of vowel sounds = # of syllables
13. promotion	prŭ•mō´•shŭn	<u>pro</u>m<u>o</u>t<u>io</u>n	3
14. relative	rĕl´•ŭ•tĭv	_____	____
15. signature	sĭg´•nŭ•chûr	_____	____
16. telephone	tĕl´•ŭ•fōn	_____	____
17. temperature	tĕm´•pûr•ŭ•chûr tĕm´•prŭ•chûr	_____	____
18. transportation	trănz•pûr•tā´•shŭn	_____	____
19. uniform	ū´•nŭ•fôrm	_____	____
20. vertical	vûr´•tĭ•kŭl	_____	____

Syllable Division: the schwa sound

Directions: Fill in, trace, and read.

1. When you stand, you are _____ . (pencil, vertical)

2. The _____(visa, tunnel) is under the East River.

3. Many people who work in stores dress the same. They dress in

   _____ (uniforms, visa).

4. You may need a _____ (visa, total) to travel to certain
   places.

5. I use a remote control to change the _____ (channel,
   tunnel) on my TV.

6. A _____ (soda, pencil) uses lead, and a pen uses ink.

7. Angel talks on his cell phone which is _____.
   (portable, magazine)

8. Maya drives to the _____ (pharmacy, magazine)

   to get her _____ (exercise, prescription) filled.

   She reads a _____ (magazine, promotion) while
   /wil/ she waits.

9. Is an ambulance an emergency form of
   transportation? Yes, an _____ is an

   _____ form of _____ .

10. Another word for physician is doctor.

11. When you write, or sign, your name, it is your signature.

Syllable Division: Review

Word	Say and write the word, and underline the vowel sounds.	# of vowel sounds = # of syllables	Write, divide, and say the word.
1. burial	b<u>ur</u> i <u>al</u>	3	/bair´•ē•ŭl/ bur/i/al
2. cafeteria			
3. cardiology			
4. cardiologist			
5. childcare			
6. custodian			
7. dictionary			
8. identification			
9. interview			
10. kindergarten			
11. nausea			
12. necessary			

Syllable Division: Review

Word	Say and write the word, and underline the vowel sounds.	# of vowel sounds = # of syllables	Write, divide, and say the word.
13. newspaper	n<u>e</u>wsp<u>a</u>p<u>e</u>r	3	news/pa/per
14. paycheck	_____	_____	_____
15. potato	_____	_____	_____
16. rattlesnake	_____	_____	_____
17. repossess	_____	_____	_____
18. reproduce	_____	_____	_____
19. reproduction	_____	_____	_____
20. requirement	_____	_____	_____
21. salary	_____	_____	_____
22. subscription	_____	_____	_____
23. ticket	_____	_____	_____
24. tomato	_____	_____	_____

Syllable Division: Review

Directions: Say, trace, and read.

1. Do you have a subscription to the newspaper? (Yes, No) I (do, do not) have a subscription to the newspaper.

2. Juan has an interview for a job as a custodian.

3. Linda is 4 years old and is in childcare. Next year she will go to kindergarten.

4. I had to show identification at the train station to buy a ticket.

5. If Ramiro can't sound out a word or tell what it means from the sentence it's in, he looks it up in the dictionary.

 # Congratulations!
You have finished Unit 12!
You know how to sound out many words!

You are a star!

Overview

This unit focuses exclusively on the prefixes *co-*, *con-*, *com-*; *per-*, *a-*, and suffixes *-ment*, *-ness*, *-ous*, and *-able*.

Objectives

Students will:

1. learn the prefix and suffix definitions.
2. add featured words to their vocabulary.
3. demonstrate proper usage of featured words.

Instruction

Part 1: Prefixes (pages 577-584)

Discuss prefixes, their meanings, and how the words reflect those meanings, such as *co-*, *con-*, and *com-* meaning together , joint, or jointly.

Assign pp. 577-581. Students may utilize the "Sounds like" column with its phonetic pronunciation for letter sounds, number of syllables, and accent. They will write each word, underline its vowel sounds, write its number of syllables, and sound out the word. They should also learn the star words, #10-14, on page 579 and be able to use those words in sentences. Correct assigned pages. Review any words whose vowels are incorrectly underlined, number of syllables misidentified, etc. Discuss words to check pronunciation, comprehension, and usage. Note: On page 580, answers to the Word Find are vertical and horizontal except for *COMPETE* which is angled from left to right starting at the upper left-hand corner.

Follow the same procedure with the remaining prefixes.

Part 2: Suffixes (pages 585-591)

The same procedure is effective for suffixes.

Assessment

If you are confident that your student has mastered the material, he can read the last page of *Yes, I Can Read!*, congratulate himself, receive your praise, and the certificate of completion.

Vocabulary Acquisition Strategies

Dictionary Usage

Direct students to use the dictionary to find additional words that share the prefixes or suffixes featured here or ones of your choice. Particularly helpful is the etymology at the end of the entry, in brackets: A good dictionary includes word origins.

Heteronyms

There are numerous multisyllabic words which are spelled the same but are pronounced differently. Verbs are usually accented on the second syllable, while nouns and adjectives are accented on the first syllable. The following examples and the pages on which they appear illustrate heteronyms:

	Verbs		Nouns	
Page	**Word**	**Meaning**	**Word**	**Meaning**
p. 264	convert'	to transform	con'vert	one who has been converted, especially from one religion or belief to another
p. 264	conduct'	to manage or control; lead or guide	con'duct	the way a person acts
p. 265	combine'	to join or merge	com'bine	harvesting machine
p. 265	compact'	to press together	com'pact	an agreement

	Verb		Adjective	
Page	**Word**	**Meaning**	**Word**	**Meaning**
p. 268	perfect'	to bring to perfection or completion	per'fect	lacking nothing; complete

The above words are used as verbs in sentences on these pages except for *perfect*, which is used as an adjective and adverb (*perfectly*).

Multiple Meaning Words

Examples include *convert, conduct, conductor, concentrate,* and *department*.

Prefixes and Antonyms

Perfect-imperfect or *flawed, permanent-temporary, ahead-behind, afloat-submerged, nervous-calm, generous-stingy, capable-incapable, profitable-unprofitable,* and *agreeable-disagreeable* are examples of words with prefixes and their antonyms that you can elicit from your students.

Unit 13: Prefixes and Suffixes

Part 1: Prefixes

Co-, con-, and com- are prefixes that mean with or **together**, joint or jointly.

Prefixes: co-

Word	Sounds like	Write the word and underline the vowel sounds.	# of vowel sounds = # of syllables
1. copilot	kō´•pī•lŭt	c<u>o</u>p<u>i</u>l<u>o</u>t	3
2. co-chair	kō´•chair	_____	_____
3. coed	kō´•ĕd	_____	_____
4. cosign	kō´•sīn	_____	_____
5. cooperate	kō•ŏp´•ûr•āt	_____	_____

Directions: Fill in, say, and read.

1. Men and women stay in the _____ dorm.

2. Lola and Lyn co-ch_____ the PTA committee at school.

3. Mom and Dad had to cos_____ my car loan.

4. The plane has 2 pilots. One is Captain Santana. He is a

   _____.

Prefixes: con-

Word	Sounds like	Write the word and underline the vowel sounds.	# of vowel sounds = # of syllables
1. contain,	kŭn•tān´	contain	2
container	kŭn• tān´•ûr	container	3
2. contribute	kŭn•trĭb´•ūt	_____	_____
3. convert	kŭn•vûrt´	_____	_____
4. convertible	kŭn•vûr´•tĭ•bŭl	_____	_____
5. conduct,	kŭn•dŭkt´	_____	_____
conductor	kŭn• dŭk´•tûr	_____	_____
6. concentrate	kŏn´•sĕn•trāt	_____	_____

Prefixes: com-

Word	Sounds like	Write the word and underline the vowel sounds.	# of vowel sounds = # of syllables
1. combat	kŏm´•băt	c<u>o</u>mb<u>a</u>t	2
2. combine	kŭm•bīn´	_____	_____
3. commute	kŭm•mūt´	_____	_____
4. compact disc (CD)	kŏm´•păkt dĭsk	_____	_____
5. companion	kŭm•păn´•yŭn	_____	_____
6. comfort	kŭm´•fûrt	_____	_____
7. complete	kŭm•plēt´	_____	_____
8. compete	kŭm•pēt´	_____	_____
9. compass	kŭm´•pŭs	_____	_____

Star (☆) Words: Say, trace, and read.

10. compose - to make or produce /prō•dōōs´/

11. community - a group of people living in the same area; the public

12. commend - to praise

13. commerce - business /bĭz´•nŭs/

14. commence - to begin, start

Prefixes: co-, con-, com-

Directions: Find and circle the words.

Word Find

~~COMMUTE~~ – COMBINE – COED – CONVERT – COMPETE – COMPLETE

C	O	M	P	L	E	T	E	C	H	M	N	R
O	O	S	U	T	A	B	X	O	R	T	V	W
E	L	M	R	S	N	C	O	M	M	U	T	E
D	N	D	P	D	C	F	G	B	H	U	W	V
R	T	E	B	E	R	B	C	I	F	B	C	T
K	N	L	V	M	T	F	P	N	T	R	S	C
E	M	B	W	N	B	E	V	E	M	Q	V	M
R	C	O	N	V	E	R	T	F	T	B	C	F

Directions: Fill in, trace, say, and read.

1. Pete _____ (commutes, completes) 20 miles to work on the train.

2. Carlos Santana _____ (composes, comfort) and plays his music.

3. Linda and John _____ (commute, combine) their cash to buy a _____ _____. (convert, compact disc)

4. The teacher _____ (commends, commerce) her students for their good work.

5. Alex checks the _____ (compass, commend) when he hikes in the woods.

Prefixes: co-, con-, com-

6. Juan helps at the food shelf in his community.

7. What is in your community? A library, a school and a park are in my community.

8. Rosa and her family go to the library in their community.

9. Rick and Joan have a plot in their community garden.

Prefixes: per-

The prefix **per-** means **completely**, or 100% (percent)

Word	Sounds like	Write the word and underline the vowel sounds.	# of vowel sounds = # of syllables
1. perfume	pûr•fūm´	p<u>e</u>rf<u>u</u>me	2
2. perfect	pûr´•fĕkt	_____	_____
3. perform	pûr•fôrm´	_____	_____
4. perplexed	pûr•plĕkst´	_____	_____
5. permanent	pûr´•mŭ•nĕnt	_____	_____
6. perforate	pûr´•fûr•āt	_____	_____

Directions: Say, trace and read .

1. I'm perplexed; I don't understand.

2. Some perfumes have a strong smell.

3. Bo performed perfectly in the school play. He knew all his lines.

4. A tent is not permanent, but a house is.

5. Omar had a perfect score on his test; in other words, he scored 100%.

Prefixes: a-

The prefix **a-** means **on.**
　　　　Examples:
　　　　　　　　aboard - on board
　　　　　　　　above - on top of
　　　　　　　　aloud - out loud

Word	Sounds like	Write the word and underline the vowel sounds.	# of vowel sounds = # of syllables
1. aboard	ŭ•bôrd´	<u>aboa</u>rd	2
2. above	ŭ•bŭv´	_____	_____
3. afloat	ŭ•flōt´	_____	_____
4. ahead	ŭ•hĕd´	_____	_____
5. aloud	ŭ•loud´	_____	_____

Directions: Say, trace, and read.

1. Tom has a light above his desk.

2. Jose prepays his June bill in May. He pays ahead.

3. June plans her summer trip in March. She plans ahead.

Prefixes: a-

Directions: Fill in, say, and read.

1. Nina puts the book on the shelf _____(aloud, above) her head.

2. The train arrived _____ (ahead, afloat) of time; it was early.

3. When the train was ready to leave, the conductor called, "All

   _____!" (ahead, aboard)

4. The board was floating in the water. It was _____. (ahead, afloat)

5. We like to read books _____(aloud, afloat) to our baby.

6. Quit while you are _____. (above, ahead).

Part 2: Suffixes

Suffixes: -ment

A suffix is a syllable added to the end of a word to make a new word or add an ending.

> Examples:
>> appoint→ appointment
>> argue→ argument
>> jump→ jumping

If a word has a suffix with a vowel sound, divide the word where the suffix was added.

> Examples:
>> jumping= jump/ing
>> longer= long/er
>> brightest= bright/est
>> kindness= kind/ness
>> sanded= sand/ed

Suffixes: -ment

> The suffix **–ment** means a **result**, an act, or a state.

Word	Sounds like	Write the word and underline the vowel sounds.	# of vowel sounds = # of syllables
1. apartment	ŭ•pârt´•mĕnt	<u>a</u>p<u>a</u>rtm<u>e</u>nt	3
2. appointment	ŭ •point´•mĕnt	_____	_____
3. compartment	kŭm•pârt´•mĕnt	_____	_____
4. instrument	ĭn´•strŭ•mĕnt	_____	_____
5. ornament	ôr´•nŭ•mĕnt	_____	_____
6. basement	bās´•mĕnt	_____	_____

Suffixes: -ment

	Word	Sounds like	Write the word and underline the vowel sounds.	# of vowel sounds = # of syllables
7.	argument	âr´•gū•mĕnt	_____	_____
8.	department	dē•pârt´•mĕnt	_____	_____
9.	government	gŭv´•ûrn•mĕnt	_____	_____
10.	document	dŏk´•ū•mĕnt	_____	_____

Directions: Fill in, say, and read aloud.

> department – document – appointment – basement – apartment

1. Rose goes to the shoe de_____ in the

   de_____ store.

2. The De_____ of Social Services might be able to

   help you.

3. John makes an app_____ to see a

   ba_____ apa_____. It is below

   ground and has three windows. He signs a lease, or a

   doc_____, to rent it for one (1) year.

Suffixes: -ness

The suffix **–ness** is a noun ending that means **quality** or degree.
Example:
bright + ness = brightness

Word	Sounds like	Write the word and underline the vowel sounds.	# of vowel sounds = # of syllables
1. happiness	hăp´•ē•nĕs	happiness	3
2. kindness	kīnd´•nĕs	_____	_____
3. darkness	dârk´•nĕs	_____	_____
4. goodness	good´•nĕs	_____	_____
5. sadness	săd´•nĕs	_____	_____
6. preparedness	prē•pair´•ĕd•nĕs	_____	_____

Suffixes: -ous

The suffix **–ous** means **full of**.

Word	Sounds like	Write the word and underline the vowel sounds.	# of vowel sounds = # of syllables
1. nervous	nûr´•vŭs	n<u>e</u>rv<u>ou</u>s	2
2. joyous	joi´•ŭs	_____	_____
3. famous	fā´•mŭs	_____	_____
4. poisonous	poi´•zŭn•ŭs	_____	_____
5. jealous	jĕl´•ŭs	_____	_____
6. furious	fū´•rē•ŭs	_____	_____
7. generous	jĕn´•ûr•ŭs	_____	_____

Suffixes: –ment, -ness, -ous

Directions: Fill in, say, and read.

1. Ray is _____ (jealous, famous) of his baby sister,

   but Mom hugs him and calls him her helper. Ray's

   _____ (kindness, famous) shows with the baby.

2. Rattlers, or rattlesnakes, are _____ . (jealous,

   poisonous)   Cobras are _____(poisonous, generous)

   too.

3. Carl is angry, or _____. (furious, famous)

4. When Eva found out she had a dental _____

   (appointment, document), she felt _____.

   (nervous, apartment)   She went to the dentist, and he used his

   _____ (instruments, basement) to clean her

   teeth. It was not so bad! Her teeth felt clean, and the dentist gave

   her a new toothbrush. Her dentist was _____. (perform,

   generous)   How nice!

Suffixes: –ment, -ness, -ous

Directions: Find and circle the words.

Word Find

~~JOYOUS~~ – POISONOUS – FAMOUS – HAPPINESS – GOODNESS –
SADNESS – COMMUTE – BASEMENT

B	A	S	E	M	E	N	T	X	I	E	V	S
W	A	W	A	L	J	R	G	G	C	C	M	K
O	D	X	B	P	O	I	S	O	N	O	U	S
V	T	O	C	M	Y	S	A	O	G	M	B	R
S	R	U	E	N	O	M	D	D	I	M	E	B
M	M	V	F	O	U	E	N	N	O	U	S	T
F	A	M	O	U	S	K	E	E	H	T	A	G
T	N	R	G	Y	O	L	S	S	N	E	V	O
H	A	P	P	I	N	E	S	S	M	W	Z	J

Suffixes: -able

The suffix **–able** means **able to**.

Word	Sounds like	Write the word and underline the vowel sounds.	# of vowel sounds = # of syllables
1. capable	kā´•pŭ•bŭl	ca<u>pa</u>ble	3
2. washable	wŏsh´•ŭ•bŭl	_____	_____
3. profitable	prŏf´•ĭt•ŭ•bŭl	_____	_____
4. agreeable	ŭ•grē´•ŭ•bŭl	_____	_____

Directions: Fill in, say, and read.

profitable – capable – agreeable – washable

Angela sells so many dresses in her dress shop that it is

p_____: she makes money ($). Angela works hard and is

c_____, so the shop runs well. Isabel visits this dress shop a lot.

She likes Angela because Angela is easy to get along with, or is

a_____. Isabel looks at the label on her new dress to see if it is

w_____, if she can put it in the washing machine.

Congratulations!

Now you can read most words.
When you come to a new word, you can underline the
vowel sounds, divide it, and sound it out.

You are a star!

Sign your name on the certificate!
You have earned it!
Yes, I Can Read!

☆Yes, I Can Read!☆

This certifies that

_____

has been awarded this certificate for completion of

_____

_____
Instructor

_____
Date

Ea Word Lists

ea /ē/

-ea
1. pea
2. sea
3. tea

-each
1. each
2. beach
3. peach
4. impeach
5. reach
6. teach, teacher
7. bleach

-ead
1. bead
2. lead
3. read
4. knead
5. plead

-eal
1. deal
2. meal
3. real
4. seal
5. teal
6. zeal
7. steal

-eam
1. beam
2. ream
3. seam
4. team
5. dream
6. gleam
7. steam
8. stream

-ease
1. ease
2. tease
3. please
4. appease

-eat
1. eat
2. beat
3. heat
4. meat
5. neat
6. pleat
7. seat
8. treat

Others:
1. beans
2. Jean, jeans
3. leave
4. beaver
5. cleaver
6. leaf
7. leave
8. breathe
9. peace
10. reason
11. season

ea /ĕ/

-ead
1. dead
2. head
3. lead
4. read
5. ready
6. bread
7. dread
8. tread
9. thread

-eav
1. heavy
2. heaven
3. leaven

-eather
1. feather
2. Heather, heather
3. leather
4. weather

-easure
1. measure
2. pleasure
3. treasure

Others:
1. bread
2. breakfast
3. breath
4. breadth
5. health, healthy
6. stealth, stealthy

ea /ā/

1. break
2. great
3. steak

Appendix B

Three Sounds of Ch

/ch/
1. bench
2. chain
3. chair
4. chalk
5. challenge
6. champion
7. chance
8. change
9. chapel
10. charge
11. Charles
12. charm
13. chase
14. chassis
15. check
16. cheddar
17. cheek
18. cherry, cherries
19. cheese
20. chest
21. Chester
22. chicken
23. chief
24. child
25. Chile
26. chili
27. chill, chilly
28. chimney
29. chin
30. China
31. Chinese
32. chipmunk
33. chocolate
34. choice
35. choose
36. chop
37. chose
38. chosen
39. chuck
40. church
41. match
42. rich
43. such
44. watch
45. which
46. witch
47. wrench

/k/
1. ache
2. chaos
3. character
4. characteristic
5. chasm
6. chemical
7. chemistry
8. chlorine
9. chlorophyll
10. choir
11. chorus
12. Christ
13. Christian
14. Christmas
15. chrome
16. chromosomes
17. chronic
18. chronicle
19. chronological
20. chrysanthemum
21. psyche
22. psychiatry
23. psychic
24. psychology
25. schedule
26. scholastic
27. school
28. schooner
29. technical
30. technician
31. Technicolor ®
32. technique
33. technology

/sh/
1. chagrin
2. chaise
3. chandelier
4. chapeau
5. Charlene
6. Charlotte
7. chartreuse
8. chateau
9. chef
10. Chicago

Appendix C

Past Tense: -Ed

/t/

1. attacked
2. chased
3. coached
4. cooked
5. coughed
6. cracked
7. danced
8. faced
9. finished
10. fished
11. helped
12. hooked
13. jumped
14. knocked
15. laughed
16. liked
17. looked
18. mapped
19. marched
20. matched
21. mocked
22. noticed
23. packed
24. passed
25. peaked
26. peeked
27. pitched
28. practiced
29. pushed
30. reached
31. rocked
32. switched
33. taped
34. thanked
35. ticked
36. tipped
37. traced
38. tracked
39. washed
40. watched
41. wished

/ĕd/

1. acted
2. baited
3. blended
4. carted
5. excited
6. fasted
7. fitted
8. folded
9. founded
10. grounded
11. handed
12. heated
13. hunted
14. landed
15. lasted
16. lifted
17. lighted
18. listed
19. netted
20. painted
21. paraded
22. pasted
23. planted
24. pounded
25. printed
26. rested
27. rounded
28. seeded
29. selected
30. sounded
31. squirted
32. started
33. tended
34. waded
35. waited
36. wanted
37. wasted

/d/

1. aimed
2. appeared
3. armed
4. blamed
5. brewed
6. canned
7. cared
8. changed
9. climbed
10. closed
11. covered
12. cried
13. cruised
14. described
15. diseased
16. earned
17. featured
18. gazed
19. glazed
20. grazed
21. groaned
22. happened
23. leaned
24. lived
25. loved
26. mailed
27. moved
28. nailed
29. paved
30. phoned
31. piled
32. played
33. pleased
34. pulled
35. rained
36. raised
37. rolled
38. ruled
39. sailed
40. sewed
41. sneezed
42. snowed
43. spelled
44. spilled
45. spoiled
46. squeezed
47. steamed
48. supposed
49. surprised
50. tabled
51. teased
52. wheezed

Appendix D
Six Syllable Types

1. closed	2. quiet e	3. vowel team

4. open	5. r-controlled	6. consonant + le

Glossary

Accent   Stress in a word of two or more syllables, louder or stronger on one syllable: *pal' ace*.

Alphabet   Letters of the language. In English, the alphabet is composed of 26 letters and has 44 sounds that are made up of letter combinations and more than one sound for some letters. Examples: *ch, sh, th*, etc. and the *j* sound represented by *g* as in gentle, *d* as in *graduate*, or *dg* as in *judgment*.(Fox, 2005, p.15)

Analytic phonics   An approach" to teaching phonics... also known as implicit phonics. Consonants are generally not isolated but are taught within the context of a whole word." (Gunning, 2005, p. 165)

Balanced literacy program   A balance or combination of a skills-based or phonics approach and a holistic approach. (Tompkins, 2006, p.24)

Consonant   A stopped letter defined by the way the letter is formed with different parts of the mouth, including lips, tongue, teeth, and roof of the mouth. There are 21 consonants in the alphabet.

Decoding   Translating written letters into the sounds of spoken language in order to pronounce visually unfamiliar words, also referred to as "sounding out" words. (Fox, 2005, p. 229)

Digraph   A consonant digraph is a two- or three- letter consonant combination that represents a new and different sound from its single letters: *ch-chin, sh-shut, th-that, th-think*. These digraphs represent one speech sound or phoneme.

Diphthong   One sound resembling a "glide" from one sound to the other: *oi-oil, noise; oy-toy; ou-house; ow-now, cow; au-sauce; aw-saw; ay-tray, way*.

Fluency   The ability to recognize words automatically and to read with accuracy, ease, and expression.

Frustration reading level   Material that is difficult for the learner and should not be assigned for instruction or homework. Material on this level can be read to him. On an informal assessment, he reads fewer than 90% of the words correctly. (Tompkins, 2006, p. 304)

Independent reading level   Material that is easy for the learner and should be assigned for recreational, enjoyable reading that he can read without help. On an informal assessment, he reads at least 95% of the words in a passage correctly. (Tompkins, 2006, p. 304)

Instructional reading level   The level of material that should be assigned for class work, such as a basal reader. It is neither too hard nor too easy. On an informal assessment, the learner reads 90-94% of the words correctly, needs some help but not so much that he gets frustrated. (Tompkins, 2006, p. 304)

Morpheme   In language, the smallest unit of meaning, such as man. The word *hopefully* has three morphemes: *hope-ful-ly*. (Gunning, 2005, p. 255)

Onset   One or more consonant sounds that precede the vowel in a word, as *b*, *g*, and *s* in *bet*, *get*, and *set*.

Phoneme   The smallest unit of sound that distinguishes one word from another. Example: in *fat* and *cat*, *f* and *c* are phonemes. (Fox, 2005, p.230)

Phoneme-grapheme correspondence   Sound-symbol correspondence.

Phonemic awareness   "Understanding that speech is composed of a series of individual sounds" (Yopp, 1992, Dealing with Language-based Learning Disabilities in the Incarcerated Setting)

Phonics   "The study of the relationships of the letter and letter combinations in written words to the sounds they represent in spoken words. The study of phonics provides the content for developing skill in the decoding of visually unfamiliar words." (Fox, 2005, p.230)

Rime   Letters from the vowel to the end of a word, as *et* in *bet*.

Schwa   In a word of two or more syllables, the vowel sound in the unaccented or unstressed syllable(s). It sounds like *uh*, a short *u* sound. In the dictionary, it is represented by a backward, upside down, lower case *e* (ə). In the word *palace*, the second syllable *ace*, sounds like *us*: The short *u* sound is the schwa sound.

Sentence   A group of words containing a subject and verb and expresses a complete thought.

Silent letter   A letter that appears in a written word but is not heard in the spoken word: in *sign*, the *g* is silent. In *light*, the *g* and *h* are silent, in *wrap*, the *w* is silent, and in *hour*, the *h* is silent. (Fox, 2005, p. 231)

Syllable   A unit of pronunciation that has one vowel sound. Usually a syllable contains a vowel that makes a sound. A syllable may be a word or word part: *a*, and *I* are both syllables and words.

Synthetic phonics (explicit phonics)   Explicitly teaches sound-symbol correspondences before blending them to form syllables or words (part to whole approach). (Peterson, 1998)

Vowel   *A*, *e*, *i*, *o*, *u*, and sometimes *w* and *y*. A vowel is a free or fluid letter as it is formed with the breath and is not stopped by any parts of the mouth as consonants are. Vowels are classified as long, with the macron over the vowel, and short, as indicated by the breve.

Word   A syllable or syllables that have meaning, as in *man* and *in*.

Word family   Words that are spelled the same and sound the same from the vowel to the end of the word, as *et* in *bet*, *get*, and *set*. Also referred to as phonograms, rimes, sound families, word chunks, and sound chunks.

Bibliography

Aaron, J. E. (6th ed.) (2007). *Little, Brown compact handbook*. New York: Pearson Longman.

Bellafiore, J. (1981). *English language arts workbook*. New York: AMSCO School Publications, Inc.

Boggs, R.,& Dixson, R. (1991). *English step by step with pictures*. Englewood Cliffs, NJ: Prentice Hall Regents.

Chall, J. S., & Popp, H. M. (1996). *Teaching and assessing phonics: A guide for teachers*. Phonics Checklist. Cambridge: Educators Publishing Service.

Concise rules of APA style: The official pocket style guide from the American psychological Association. (2005). Washington, DC: American Psychological Association.

Costello, R. (Ed.) (1993). *The American heritage college dictionary* (3rd ed.). Boston: Houghton Mifflin.

Elwell, Murray,& Kucia. (1991). *Phonics: Level E*. Cleveland: Modern Curriculum Press.

Elwell, Murray,& Kucia. (1995). *Phonics: Level B*. Parsippany, NJ: Modern Curriculum Press.

Elwell, Murray, & Kucia. (1998a). *Phonics: Level A*. Parsippany, NJ: Modern Curriculum Press.

Elwell, Murray, & Kucia. (1998b). *Phonics: Level C*. Parsippany, NJ: Modern Curriculum Press.

Ervin, J.,Elwell, Murray, & Kucia. (1991). *Phonics: Level D*. Cleveland: Modern Curriculum Press.

Fox, B. (9th ed.) (2005). *Phonics for the teacher of reading: Programmed self-instruction*. Upper Saddle River, NJ: Pearson.

Fox, T., Johns, J., & Keller, S. (2007). *Cite it right: The source aid guide to citation, research, and avoiding plagiarism*. Osterville, MA: SourceAid, LLC.

Frey, P. (3rd ed.) (1999). *Litstart: Strategies for adult literacy and ESL tutors*. Okemos, MI: Michigan Literacy, Inc.

Fry, E. (1976). *Individual phonics criterion test of 99 phoneme grapheme correspondences: A criterion referenced test*. Highland Park, NJ: Dreier Educational Systems.

Fry, E. (1997a). *1,000 instant words: The most common words for teaching reading, writing, and spelling*. Chicago: Contemporary.

Fry, E. (1997b). *Phonics patterns: A ready reference of 321 word families*. Chicago: Contemporary.

Fry, E., Foundtoukidis, D., & Polk, J. (1985). *The new reading teacher's book of lists*. Englewood Cliffs: Prentice Hall.

Gunning, T.G. (5th ed.) (2002) *Creating literacy: Instruction for all students*. Boston: Pearson Education.

Helson, L. (1971a). *A first course in phonics reading, teacher's manual, (Rev. ed)*. Cambridge: Educators Publishing Service.

Helson, L. (1971b). A *second course in phonics reading book two, teacher's manual*. Cambridge: Educators Publishing Service.

Henney, R. (1977). Basic education: Reading. Cambridge: Cambridge Book Co.

Ives, J. P. (1973). Some clues to vowel sounds. New York University.

Keene, M. L., & Adams, K. H. (2006). *Easy access*. Boston: McGraw Hill.

Knight, J. (2001). *Starting over: A combined teaching manual and student textbook for reading, writing, spelling, vocabulary, and handwriting*. Cambridge: Educators Publishing Service, Inc.

Lunsford, A. A. (5th ed.)(2003). *The St. Martin's handbook*. Boston: Bedford/St. Martin's.

Lyon, G. R. (1998a). Why reading is not a natural process. *Educational Leadership*, 14-18.

Lyon, G. R. (1998b). *Overview of reading and literacy initiatives: Statement to committee on labor and human sources*. Washington.

Merriam Webster's Collegiate Dictionary. (10th ed). (1993). Springfield, MA: Merriam-Webster.

Microsoft Office Home and Student 2007 http://www.microsoft.com/office/

Molinsky, S. J., Bliss, B., & Saitz, H. C. (1995). *Word by word English/Spanish picture dictionary*. Prentice Hall Regents.

Moats, L. C. (1996). *Vowel spellings by mouth position*. Stern Center Handout: Elizabeth Peterson. (1998). *Phonology and structured language approaches for adult educators*. Symposium for the New York State Department of Correctional Services Adult Educators.

Monroe, M. (1964). *My second pictionary*. Glenview, Il: Scott, Foresman & Co.

Peterson, E. (1998). *Phonology and structured language approaches for adult educators*. Symposium for the New York State Department of Correctional Services Adult Educators (5th ed).

Podhajski, B. (1998). *Dealing with language-based learning disabilities in the incarcerated setting*. Symposium, Lake Placid.

Rayner, K., Foorman, B., Perfetti, C., Pesetsky, D., & Seidenberg, M. (2002, March). How should reading be taught? *Scientific American*.

Six kinds of syllables. (1996). Stern Center Handout: TIME for Teachers. Timenote 3/2, 3/12, 3/13, 3/14.

Skinner, L. & Laplount, D. T. (1993a). *Words: Writing, reading, spelling; student book 1*. Englewood Cliffs, NJ: Regents Prentice Hall.

Skinner, L. & Laplount, D. T. (1993b). *Words: Writing, reading, spelling; student book 2*. Englewood Cliffs, NJ: Regents Prentice Hall.

Skinner, L. & Laplount, D. T. (1995a). *Words: Writing, reading, spelling; student book 3*. Upper Saddle River, NJ: Cambridge Adult Education.

Skinner, L. & Laplount, D. T. (1995b). *Words: Writing, reading, spelling; student book 4*. Upper Saddle River, NJ: Cambridge Adult Education.

Stern Center. (1998). *Stern center sequence of phonological awareness, word analysis, and spelling skills: Structured language concepts*. Stern Center Handout: Stern Center TIME for Teachers.

Tompkins, G.E. (4th ed.) (2006) *Literacy for the 21st century: A balanced approach*. Upper Saddle River: Pearson Merrill Prentice Hall.

Welch, P. (1980). *Survival words*. Lakewood, CO: Jane Ward Co.

Wysocki, A. F. & Lynch, D. A. (2009). *The DK handbook*. New York: Pearson Longman.

York, B. K. (1995). *Phonics: Book D*. Austin: Steck-Vaughn Co.

Addendum

Google Search: *Images*. https://www.google.com/search. Retrieved 2010-2011.

Unit 12 Answer Key

Syllable Division: compound words, Rule #1

Word	Say and write the word, and underline the vowel sounds.	# of vowel sounds = # of syllables	Write, divide, and say the word.
1. backyard	backyard	2	back/yard
2. baseball	baseball	2	base/ball
3. bedroom	bedroom	2	bed/room
4. beehive	beehive	2	bee/hive
5. breakfast	breakfast	2	break/fast
6. carpool	carpool	2	car/pool
7. checkbook	checkbook	2	check/book
8. cookbook	cookbook	2	cook/book
9. dashboard	dashboard	2	dash/board
10. doorknob	doorknob	2	door/knob
11. drumstick	drumstick	2	drum/stick
12. flashlight	flashlight	2	flash/light

Syllable Division: compound words, Rule #1

Word	Say and write the word, and underline the vowel sounds.	# of vowel sounds = # of syllables	Write, divide, and say the word.
13. jigsaw	jigsaw	2	jig/saw
14. locksmith	locksmith	2	lock/smith
15. lunchbox	lunchbox	2	lunch/box
16. mailroom	mailroom	2	mail/room
17. passport	passport	2	pass/port
18. payroll	payroll	2	pay/roll
19. playground	playground	2	play/ground
20. popcorn	popcorn	2	pop/corn
21. restroom	restroom	2	rest/room
22. sandbox	sandbox	2	sand/box
23. skateboard	skateboard	2	skate/board
24. snowboard	snowboard	2	snow/board

Syllable Division: compound words, Rule #1

	Word	Say and write the word, and underline the vowel sounds.	# of vowel sounds = # of syllables	Write, divide, and say the word.
25.	teaspoon	teaspoon	2	tea/spoon
26.	toolbelt	toolbelt	2	tool/belt
27.	toothache	toothache	2	tooth/ache
28.	toothbrush	toothbrush	2	tooth/brush
29.	washroom	washroom	2	wash/room
30.	wheelchair	wheelchair	2	wheel/chair
31.	windshield	windshield	2	wind/shield
32.	afternoon	afternoon	3	af/ter/noon
33.	bookkeeper	bookkeeper	3	book/keep/er
34.	employment	employment	3	em/ploy/ment
35.	grandparents	grandparents	3	grand/par/ents
36.	hairdresser	hairdresser	3	hair/dress/er

Syllable Division: compound words, Rule # 1

	Word	Say and write the word, and underline the vowel sounds.	# of vowel sounds = # of syllables	Write, divide, and say the word.
37.	handyman	handyman	3	han/dy/man
38.	housekeeper	housekeeper	3	house/keep/er
39.	jackhammer	jackhammer	3	jack/ham/mer
40.	lawnmower	lawnmower	3	lawn/mow/er
41.	overpass	overpass	3	o/ver/pass
42.	screwdriver	screwdriver	3	screw/dri/ver
43.	tablespoon	tablespoon	3	ta/ble/spoon
44.	motorcycle	motorcycle	4	mo/tor/cy/cle

Syllable Division: 2 consonants together, Rule #2

Word	Say and write the word, and underline the vowel sounds.	# of vowel sounds = # of syllables	Write, divide, and say the word.
1. address	address	2	ad/dress
2. cactus	cactus	2	cac/tus
3. commute	commute	2	com/mute
4. compute	compute	2	com/pute
5. confuse	confuse	2	con/fuse
6. dessert	dessert	2	des/sert
7. dispute	dispute	2	dis/pute
8. insect	insect	2	in/sect
9. helmet	helmet	2	hel/met
10. letter	letter	2	let/ter
11. lettuce	lettuce	2	let/tuce
12. mussel	mussel	2	mus/sel

Syllable Division: 2 consonants together, Rule # 2

Word	Say and write the word, and underline the vowel sounds.	# of vowel sounds = # of syllables	Write, divide, and say the word.
13. mustard	mustard	2	mus/tard
14. napkin	napkin	2	nap/kin
15. necktie	necktie	2	neck/tie
16. nostril	nostril	2	nos/tril
17. pencil	pencil	2	pen/cil
18. percent	percent	2	per/cent
19. pretzel	pretzel	2	pret/zel
20. public	public	2	pub/lic
21. rabbit	rabbit	2	rab/bit
22. sandwich	sandwich	2	sand/wich

Syllable Division: short vowel, closed syllable, Rule #3

Word	Say and write the word, and underline the vowel sounds.	# of vowel sounds = # of syllables	Write, divide, and say the word.
1. cabin	cabin	2	cab/in
2. comic	comic	2	com/ic
3. credit	credit	2	cred/it
4. debit	debit	2	deb/it
5. denim	denim	2	den/im
6. exit	exit	2	ex/it
7. finish	finish	2	fin/Ish
8. index	index	2	in/dex
9. melon	melon	2	mel/on
10. polish	polish	2	pol/ish
11. robin	robin	2	rob/in
12. solid	solid	2	sol/id

Syllable Division: short vowel, closed syllable, Rule #3

Word	Say and write the word, and underline the vowel sounds.	# of vowel sounds = # of syllables	Write, divide, and say the word.
13. tablet	tablet	2	tab/let
14. caplet	caplet	2	cap/let
15. toxic	toxic	2	tox/ic
16. upon	upon	2	up/on
17. vomit	vomit	2	vom/it

Syllable Division: long vowel, open syllable, Rule # 4

Word	Say and write the word, and underline the vowel sounds.	# of vowel sounds = # of syllables	Write, divide, and say the word.
1. baby	baby	2	ba/by
2. China	China	2	Chi/na
3. cobra	cobra	2	co/bra
4. coop	coop	2	co/op
5. diet	diet	2	di/et
6. digest	digest	2	di/gest
7. driver	driver	2	dri/ver
8. duet	duet	2	du/et
9. duplex	duplex	2	du/plex
10. easy	easy	2	ea/sy
11. erase	erase	2	e/rase
12. fever	fever	2	fe/ver

Syllable Division: long vowel, open syllable, Rule # 4

Word	Say and write the word, and underline the vowel sounds.	# of vowel sounds = # of syllables	Write, divide, and say the word.
13. final	final	2	fi/nal
14. Friday	Friday	2	Fri/day
15. frozen	frozen	2	fro/zen
16. iron	iron	2	i/ron
17. ivy	ivy	2	i/vy
18. lady	lady	2	la/dy
19. locate	locate	2	lo/cate
20. movie	movie	2	mo/vie
21. photo	photo	2	pho/to
22. polar	polar	2	po/lar
23. Polish	Polish	2	Po/lish

Syllable Division: long vowel, open syllable, Rule # 4

Word	Say and write the word, and underline the vowel sounds.	# of vowel sounds = # of syllables	Write, divide, and say the word.
24. pony	pony	2	po/ny
25. razor	razor	2	ra/zor
26. silent	silent	2	si/lent
27. solo	solo	2	so/lo
28. student	student	2	stu/dent
29. tiny	tiny	2	ti/ny
30. trial	trial	2	tri/al
31. beautiful	beautiful	3	beau/ti/ful
32. library	library	3	li/brar/y
33. librarian	librarian	4	li/brar/i/an
34. radio	radio	3	ra/di/o
35. video	video	3	vid/e/o

Syllable Division: consonant + le, Rule # 5

Word	Say and write the word, and underline the vowel sounds.	# of vowel sounds = # of syllables	Write, divide, and say the word.
1. able	able	2	a/ble
2. angle	angle	2	an/gle
3. candle	candle	2	can/dle
4. cycle	cycle	2	cy/cle
5. double	double	2	dou/ble
6. drizzle	drizzle	2	driz/zle
7. gargle	gargle	2	gar/gle
8. goggles	goggles	2	gog/gles
9. griddle	griddle	2	grid/dle
10. muscle	muscle	2	mus/cle
11. nozzle	nozzle	2	noz/zle
12. paddle	paddle	2	pad/dle

Syllable Division: consonant + le, Rule # 5

Word	Say and write the word, and underline the vowel sounds.	# of vowel sounds = # of syllables	Write, divide, and say the word.
13. puddle	puddle	2	pud/dle
14. puzzle	puzzle	2	puz/zle
15. rifle	rifle	2	ri/fle
16. saddle	saddle	2	sad/dle
17. shuttle	shuttle	2	shut/tle
18. single	single	2	sin/gle
19. trundle	trundle	2	trun/dle
20. Wiffle®	wiffle	2	wif/fle

Syllable Division: consonant + le, Rule # 5

Word	Say and write the word, and underline the vowel sounds.	# of vowel sounds = # of syllables	Write, divide, and say the word.
21. article	article	3	ar/ti/cle
22. assemble	assemble	3	as/sem/ble
23. bicycle	bicycle	3	bi/cy/cle
24. capable	capable	3	ca/pa/ble
25. disabled	disabled	3	dis/a/bled
26. portable	portable	3	port/a/ble
27. possible	possible	3	pos/si/ble
28. probable	probable	3	prob/a/ble
29. rectangle	rectangle	3	rec/tan/gle
30. syllable	syllable	3	syl/la/ble
31. triangle	triangle	3	tri/an/gle
32. vegetable*	vegetable	3	/věj´•tŭ•bŭl/ vege/ta/ble

*Pronunciation is 3 syllables as shown here. Dictionary syllabication is 4 syllables: veg•e•ta•ble

Syllable Division: consonant + le, Rule # 5

Word	Say and write the word, and underline the vowel sounds.	# of vowel sounds = # of syllables	Write, divide, and say the word.
33. accessible	accessible	4	ac/ces/si/ble
34. convertible	convertible	4	con/ver/ti/ble
35. honorable	honorable	4	hon/or/a/ble
36. impossible	impossible	4	im/pos/si/ble
37. improbable	improbable	4	im/prob/a/ble
38. dishonorable	dishonorable	5	dis/hon/or/a/ble
39. indigestible	indigestible	5	in/di/gest/i/ble

Syllable Division: prefixes and suffixes, Rule # 6

Word	Say and write the word, and underline the vowel sounds.	# of vowel sounds = # of syllables	Write, divide, and say the word.
1. distrust	distrust	2	dis/trust
2. faithful	faithful	2	faith/ful
3. harmless	harmless	2	harm/less
4. homeless	homeless	2	home/less
5. hopeless	hopeless	2	hope/less
6. jumpy	jumpy	2	jump/y
7. likely	likely	2	like/ly
8. quietly	quietly	3	qui/et/ly

Syllable Division: prefixes and suffixes, Rule # 6

Word	Say and write the word, and underline the vowel sounds.	# of vowel sounds = # of syllables	Write, divide, and say the word.
9. successful	successful	3	suc/cess/ful
10. truthful	truthful	2	truth/ful
11. wasteful	wasteful	2	waste/ful
12. disrupted	disrupted	3	dis/rupt/ed
13. exporter	exporter	3	ex/port/er
14. importer	importer	3	im/port/er
15. infected	infected	3	in/fect/ed
16. unsuccessful	unsuccessful	4	un/suc/cess/ful

Syllable Division: prefixes and suffixes, Rule # 6

	Word	Say and write the word, and underline the vowel sounds.	# of vowel sounds = # of syllables	Write, divide, and say the word.
17.	preheated	preheated	3	pre/heat/ed
18.	unfaithful	unfaithful	3	un/faith/ful
19.	untruthful	untruthful	3	un/truth/ful
20.	immigrated	immigrated	4	im/mi/gra/ted
21.	repeatedly	repeatedly	4	re/peat/ed/ly
22.	uninteresting	uninteresting	5	un/in/ter/est/ing
23.	unsuccessfully	unsuccessfully	5	un/suc/cess/ful/ly

Syllable Division: The schwa sound

	Word	Sounds like	Say and write the word, and underline the vowel sounds.	# of vowel sounds = # of syllables
1.	apron	ā´•prŭn	apron	2
2.	breakfast	brĕk´•fŭst	breakfast	2
3.	channel	chăn´•ŭl	channel	2
4.	lemon	lĕm´•ŭn	lemon	2
5.	license	lī´•sŭns	license	2
6.	pistol	pĭs´•tŭl	pistol	2
7.	razor	rā´•zŭr	razor	2
8.	seven	sĕv´•ŭn	seven	2
9.	soda	sō´•dŭ	soda	2
10.	today	tŭ•dā´	today	2
11.	tunnel	tŭn´•ŭl	tunnel	2
12.	visa	vē´•zŭ	visa	2
13.	promotion	prŭ•mō´•shŭn	promotion	3
14.	relative	rĕl´•ŭ•tĭv	relative	3
15.	signature	sĭg´•nŭ•chûr	signature	3
16.	telephone	tĕl´•ŭ•fōn	telephone	3
17.	temperature	tĕm´•pûr•ŭ•chûr tĕm´•prŭ•chûr	temperature	4
18.	transportation	trănz•pûr•tā´•shŭn	transportation	4
19.	uniform	ū´•nŭ•fôrm	uniform	3
20.	vertical	vûr´•tĭ•kŭl	vertical	3

Syllable Division: Review

Word	Say and write the word, and underline the vowel sounds.	# of vowel sounds = # of syllables	Write, divide, and say the word.
1. burial	bur i al	3	/bair´•ē•ŭl/ bur/i/al
2. cafeteria	cafeteria	5	caf/e/ter/i/a
3. cardiology	cardiology	5	card/i/ol/o/gy
4. cardiologist	cardiologist	5	card/i/ol/o/gist
5. childcare	childcare	2	child/care
6. custodian	custodian	4	cus/to/di/an
7. dictionary	dictionary	4	dic/tion/ar/y
8. identification	identification	6	i/den/ti/fi/ca/tion
9. interview	interview	3	in/ter/view
10. kindergarten	kindergarten	4	kin/der/gar/ten
11. nausea	nausea	3	nau/se/a
12. necessary	necessary	4	nec/es/sar/y

Syllable Division: Review

Word	Say and write the word, and underline the vowel sounds.	# of vowel sounds = # of syllables	Write, divide, and say the word.
13. newspaper	newspaper	3	news/pa/per
14. paycheck	paycheck	2	pay/check
15. potato	potato	3	po/ta/to
16. rattlesnake	rattlesnake	3	rat/tle/snake
17. repossess	repossess	3	re/po/ssess
18. reproduce	reproduce	3	re/pro/duce
19. reproduction	reproduction	4	re/pro/duc/tion
20. requirement	requirement	3	re/quire/ment
21. salary	salary	3	sal/ar/y
22. subscription	subscription	3	sub/scrip/tion
23. ticket	ticket	2	tick/et
24. tomato	tomato	3	to/ma/to